PRAGMATISM AS TRANSITION

Pragmatism *as* TRANSITION

Historicity and Hope in James, Dewey, and Rorty

Colin Koopman

COLUMBIA UNIVERSITY PRESS NEW YORK

Columbia University Press
Publishers Since 1893
New York Chichester, West Sussex
Copyright © 2009 Columbia University Press
All rights reserved
Library of Congress Cataloging-in-Publication Data

Koopman, Colin.
    Pragmatism as transition: historicity and hope in James, Dewey, and Rorty /
Colin Koopman.
        p.   cm.
    Includes bibliographical references and index.
    ISBN 978-0-231-14874-0 (cloth: alk. paper) —ISBN 978-0-231-52019-5 (e-book)
    1. Pragmatism.   2. James, William, 1842–1910.   3. Dewey, John, 1859–1952.   4. Rorty,
Richard.   I. Title.

    B832.K66   2009
    144'.3—dc22
                                                                                        2009014311

CONTENTS

ACKNOWLEDGMENTS

I am grateful for the opportunity to thank the many teachers who over the course of my ongoing education have assisted me in the practical and theoretical endeavors that have led to, and are in many ways condensed in this, my first, book. Without their inspiration and edification, I would not have developed the confidence and creativity to undertake, let alone complete, a project such as this.

My first thanks are to Steve Dickerson at South Puget Sound Community College, which I attended as an eager high-school student. It was he who first convinced me to take my budding interests in philosophy seriously. Soon thereafter at The Evergreen State College, intellectual and ethical enculturation were afforded by Mark Levensky, Marianne Bailey, David Paulsen, and especially Alan Nasser. Studying for my M.A. at Leeds University, Richard Francks and Stephen French were generous with both time and advice. For their conversation and mentorship during my Ph.D. years at McMaster University, and in the time since, I remain particularly indebted to Barry Allen and Gary Brent Madison, both of whom taught me much, including how one learns well. Others who made those years rewarding also deserve thanks: Richard T. W. Arthur, Diane Enns, Elisabeth Gedge, Violetta Igneski, Jay Lampert, Brigitte Sassen, Wil Waluchow, and especially Allison Weir. A rewarding winter spent in the Bay Area as I completed a dissertation (to which I will one day return) furnished the opportunity to hang around Stanford and sit in a packed course taught by Richard

Rorty, who was enormously generous in conversation after his classes and during his office hours. After finishing my dissertation project, I came to the University of California at Santa Cruz for postdoctoral research, where David Hoy continues to offer much in the way of useful advice and constructive insight about both pragmatism and poststructuralism. Others at UCSC who have been generous with their time and are deserving of thanks include Dan Guevara, Paul Roth, and especially our yearly visitor Ian Hacking. I would also like to offer my thanks to senior colleagues at the University of California at Berkeley, whose conversations and courses have been especially insightful for me over the past few years: these include David Hollinger, Martin Jay, Hans Sluga, and most especially Paul Rabinow. I would, last, like to thank James Livingston for the inspiration yielded by his work and the provocation yielded by his frank conversation on many matters pertinent to this book.

While all of those named above have contributed in one way or another to my broader intellectual formation, this book has taken shape in the midst of exchanges with a smaller group who have generously engaged me on the issues raised herein. Two persons in particular were extraordinarily generous in reading the penultimate draft of the entire manuscript, providing me with valuable feedback throughout much of the writing process, and in general for being very good colleagues and friends. I thank John Kaag and David Rondel. I also thank two reviewers for Columbia University Press who offered comments on an earlier version. Joseph Margolis provided me with an enormously helpful review that, in measures of both length and acuity, went well beyond the expectations any author might have—his insights enabled me to see my way to crucial organizational changes and decisive shifts of argumentative load, which have led to a much transformed, and I hope much improved, result. I also thank my unnamed second reader for their helpful suggestions.

In addition, the following persons offered feedback on individual chapters, subchapters, or perhaps even subsubchapters, of the manuscript: Ryan Acton, Scott Aikin, Barry Allen, Jessica Beard, Thom Donovan, Christoph Durt, Neil Gross, Peter Hare, Larry Hickman, Charlie Hobbs, David Hoy, James Livingston, Jeremy Livingston, Gary Brent Madison, Mary Magada-Ward, Gregory Fernando Pappas, Shane Ralston, Richard Rorty, Hans Sluga, Andrew Smith, Panagiota Spyrakos, Ronald Robles Sundstrom, and Allison Weir. I thank each of you for your time and your criticisms. Though they have not seen earlier versions of much of this material, many of the ideas herein have been shaped by conversations (in person or through various wires) with Vincent Colapietro, Judith Green, and John Stuhr. As I neared the final stages of work on this project and threw myself into the beginning stages of my next, I profited enormously from conversations with Paul Rabinow and a number of students (including Gaymon Bennett, Mary Murrell, Tom Schilling, and Chris Tenove) I met through various collaborative venues in which he and these students are involved. Our conversations concerning John Dewey, Michel Foucault, critique, and inquiry were in every moment enormously generative. They also came at just the right moment. The final sections on Foucault were much improved by conversations with both Amy Allen and David Hoy. I will save other expressions of gratitude pertaining to my work on Foucault for my next book.

Among these many interlocutors, I wish to single out two for special mention. I could not possibly overstate the extraordinary generosity of professors Richard Rorty and Peter Hare in offering their comments on some of the pages that follow, despite what must have been enormous demands on their time issued from quarters certainly far more prominent than those humble ones I occupy. It is with some small sorrow that I can now bring this book into publication only after both of them have passed. Many of the ideas and arguments I have mustered in the pages to follow were written with these two philosophers in mind, anticipating their often competing concerns and hoping to impress in them some small idea that had not yet shimmered within them. I of course wrote what follows with many other imaginary readers also looking over my shoulder—and I shall not hesitate to be grateful for the opportunity to now engage them no longer in imagination alone.

I acknowledge a postdoctoral fellowship from the Social Sciences and Humanities Research Council, which I took up at the University of California at Santa Cruz. This provided me with a considerable period of time in which I was free to engage in intensive research that enabled me to complete this book and embark on other ventures, including a book on genealogy, which I plan to finish very soon.

A few chapters have been previously published, though in all instances the material included here is significantly revised. For permission to reprint some of my previously published work I make the following acknowledgments:

An earlier and quite selective version of chapter 1 appeared as "Pragmatism as a Philosophy of Hope: Emerson, James, Dewey, and Rorty," in the *Journal of Speculative Philosophy* 20, no. 2 (Summer 2006).

An earlier version of the treatment of the experience-language debates in pragmatism featured in chapters 3 and 4 appeared as "Language as a Form of Experience: Reconciling Classical Pragmatism and Neopragmatism," in the *Transactions of the Charles S. Peirce Society* 43, no. 4 (Fall 2007).

Portions of the sections on Foucault in chapter 7 are fairly significant revisions of an argument previously published as "Two Uses of Genealogy: Michel Foucault and Bernard Williams," in *Foucault's Legacy*, ed. Carlos Prado (New York: Continuum, 2009).

Parts of chapter 2, the parts that are themselves already mostly quotation, are due to appear in "Historicism in Pragmatism: Lessons in Historiography and Philosophy," in an upcoming issue of *Metaphilosophy* that should just beat this book into print.

I thank Mary Rorty for kind permission to reprint selected passages of Richard Rorty's early essay "The Philosopher as Expert." I have here cited from a manuscript version of this essay made available to me by Richard Rorty and Neil Gross in 2005. This essay has since then finally found its way into publication, in the recently reprinted edition of *Philosophy and the Mirror of Nature* by Princeton University Press.

I also thank Wendy Lochner and Christine Mortlock of Columbia University Press for their efficiency in making this project material and their faith in the project itself.

In addition to the teachers, colleagues, and organizations mentioned above, I would also like to thank friends and family who have withstood with me the times in which I devoted the work that made this into a work. I thank Tommy Thornhill for conversation and friendship that have been invaluable for this book as well as for its author. No small amount of both insight and friendship, in the crucial late stages, was generously afforded by Aaron Poser. It was many years ago that conversations with a few very close friends first inspired me to take the possibility of philosophical thought seriously: this goes back to long nights sitting around diner tables covered in wood-grain laminate sucking down endless cups of watery coffee under an oppressive fluorescent glow. This was in Olympia with Nathan, Seamus, Zied, Shane, Noel, Sunday, and sometimes with some others, including Molly and two other Nathans with whom I have since lost touch. I am not sure how to characterize that education other than to say that it was one that I have since found nowhere else. Though those times are gone, parts of them live on here, for me at least.

Last, I thank those whose love has made possible my confidence. I thank Panagiota for inspirations and understandings during the years in which I was working on this book—and for forests, for beaches, for dances. I am ever grateful for the good Dutch example steadily offered by my Beppe. I finally thank those who were first for me: my Mother and Father, whose encouragement and love inspired the sorts of selfhood requisite for the vocation I am just now learning to live up to.

Church St. and 17th St.
San Francisco, California
March 2009

PRAGMATISM AS TRANSITION

INTRODUCTION

What Pragmatism Does

This aim of this book is to describe *what pragmatism does, what it has done*, and *what it may yet do*. This does not amount to offering a definition or even a delineation of pragmatism. My intention is not to develop a determinative statement nor is it to summarize some list of supposedly essential features. Rather, I seek to loosen pragmatism up so that it can do even more work and do that work better. I want to open pragmatism out onto opportunities and potentialities yet underexplored.

What justifies this book—which may seem at first blush like yet another in a long line of books in which the author attempts to state what pragmatism is—is that the conception of pragmatism I here present is one as yet only inchoate in previous statements of pragmatism. I here present a conception of pragmatism that presses outward in decidedly new directions. My claim is not that these directions are nonexistent in the work of previous pragmatists—for were that the case, then what I here present would not be suitably dubbed pragmatism. Nor is my claim that one cannot find in the work of many other pragmatists the central themes around which my presentation of pragmatism focuses—I should hope that my work here indeed resonates well with the work of certain other writers who have been influential on the genesis of my conception of pragmatism. The particular emphasis and focus I here give pragmatism is one that has yet to fully crystallize in the work of my pragmatist predecessors. Although the writings of many previous pragmatists richly

inform the central idea around which my vision of pragmatism revolves—
transition—no pragmatist has as yet focused their own philosophical work on
this idea to the degree that I attempt here.

The vision of pragmatism that I work out in the following pages is that of
pragmatism as a philosophical mode that takes as its central concern the process of transitioning. Transitions are those temporal structures and historical
shapes in virtue of which we get from here to there. According to this transitionalist interpretation, pragmatism's most important philosophical contribution is that of redescribing the philosophical practices of thought, critique,
and inquiry such that these practices take place in time and through history.
Philosophy according to transitionalist pragmatism is best practiced as a process that takes time and is involved in history. I refer to this philosophical focus on temporality and historicity as "transitionalism" simply because other
words that suggest themselves for this role happen to be either too cumber-
some or too heavily weighed down in other philosophical debates. A list of
such synonyms might include historicism, temporalism, evolutionism, devel-
opmentalism, eventism, and processism. While each of these words can stand
for concepts that I believe more or less approximate transitionalism, they all
also stand for much else besides that need to be distinguished from transitionalism. The basic theme of transitionalism is, to put it colloquially, getting
through.

The transitionalist account of pragmatism I here develop and defend constitutes a renewed third wave of pragmatist philosophy. This third-wave pragmatism is needed both for reasons internal to the tradition of pragmatism itself and for wider philosophical reasons. Taking the internal motivations first,
the primary impetus here is a certain frustrating impasse within pragmatism
that has done much to block productive philosophical work in recent years,
and in spite of the widely celebrated resurgence of pragmatism over the same
period. The standard histories of pragmatism tell the story of pragmatism's
emergence in the late nineteenth century, decline in the mid-twentieth century, and revival in the late twentieth century as a history that culminates, at
least for the time being, in two seemingly divergent strands of thought: the
classical pragmatisms of William James, John Dewey, and Charles Santiago
Peirce, and the contemporary neopragmatisms of Richard Rorty and such of
his interlocutors as Hilary Putnam and Robert Brandom. These two lineages
of pragmatism have for the most part (notable exceptions always being the

rule) failed to engage in productive dialogue. Although Rorty claims a Deweyan legacy for his thought, contemporary pragmatist scholars of Dewey often play the role of guardian by refusing to endorse Rorty's claim to the title of pragmatist. On the other side, those swayed by Rorty too often prefer to sweep aside his claims for the importance of Dewey, focusing instead on Rorty's other philosophical inspirations, such as Wittgenstein or Heidegger. In light of these and other blocked conversations, what is most needful for pragmatism today is a renewing third wave of pragmatism that is able to integrate what is best in the two distinctive waves of pragmatist thought that have preceded it.

This sundering of pragmatism in two has played out in a wide range of philosophical debates over which there is increasing distance between Rortyans and Deweyans, or neo- and classico-. One of the most important of these concerns is the centering role played by the concept of experience in Dewey's pragmatism in contrast to the antiexperiential linguistic turn in philosophy ushered in by Rorty's pragmatism. These experience-language debates have left pragmatism torn in two. Half of us are busy expounding Deweyan, Jamesian, and Peircean epistemologies that simply do not sit well with the driving questions that have emerged over the course of the intervening "linguistic century" of philosophy. The other half of us are busy developing neopragmatist insights tailored to thoroughly linguistic philosophical projects that have risen to prominence in the hundred years since Russell used Frege to oppose James's use of Peirce. These and other schisms make it increasingly clear that pragmatism is at an impasse with itself. Other pragmatist debates, such as that concerning the priority of a distinction between public and private spheres in liberal democracy, have been raging for more than a few decades now. Many of these debates have recently begun to show signs of exhaustion. This suggests that the time is opportune for proposing a resolution.

A renewed third wave of pragmatism is thus needful today for the continued vigor of the tradition itself. But not only is such a pragmatism needed; it is also fortunately quite possible. We are finally beginning to witness the emergence of a sensibility according to which we pragmatists have something to learn from both Dewey and Rorty, both James and Putnam, both Peirce and Brandom. This sensibility runs far deeper than a look at the latest scholarly journals would suggest. Indeed, such shifts in philosophical ethos almost always outpace the entrenched organs archiving the received wisdom of former decades. Such shifts are generally most marked among younger generations of scholars. In the case of pragmatism, we are now beginning to witness the emergence of philosophers who came to Dewey and James by way of Rorty and Putnam, not the other way around. The pragmatists of this vintage do not have impressed upon them an initial motivation for prying apart classicopragmatism and neopragmatism. These newer pragmatists find in both lineages common themes, which they put to productive use in their own philosophical projects. This book offers a way of bringing these common themes into focus so that the next generation of pragmatists, but also those in prior generations who have sensibly resisted the quick separation of Dewey and Rorty by their peers, can confidently and cogently draw on a pragmatism that extends from the nineteenth century to the twenty-first.

These impasses, frustrations, and exhaustions now plaguing pragmatism are by no means pragmatism's alone. As such, a third-wave pragmatism should prove useful not only for the tradition itself but also for contemporary philosophy and the broader intellectual currents in which it swims. Widespread interest in issues dealing with experience and language are still at the center of epistemology, and widespread anxiety over public versus private fuels growing bodies of work in political theory and ethics. Other disciplines and subfields draw generously upon, and make their own important contributions to, this work. It is thus clear that it is not just within pragmatism that there is an increasing sense that some of these impasses result from problems having been falsely posed. It is not unreasonable to hope that a resolution of these problems in pragmatism might yet lead to a broader resolution rippling throughout other currents of philosophy. I here propose a possible way toward the resolution of some of these impasses in pragmatist terms. The hope is that this may help us more adequately address the core problems, arguments, and insights that have led us to some of the broadest philosophical crossroads we find ourselves at today.

The vista of transitionalism here explicated helps us gain a better understanding of themes common across the tradition of pragmatism. The hope is that this better understanding will better equip us to deploy these pragmatist themes with increased confidence. The transitionalist sensibility of historicity and temporality provides a lens for bringing into focus that which unites classicopragmatists and neopragmatists across a range of philosophical topics. Transitionalism also helps us understand how pragmatism has always been an

engaged form of philosophical practice in which philosophy is best understood as meliorist cultural criticism. The project of cultural melioration is one
of pragmatism's best contributions to modern philosophy. The theme of transitionalism helps us see that every major version of pragmatism is concerned,
primarily, with the ways in which philosophy can help us improve those situations in which we already find ourselves. Whether this theme is read through
work on epistemological, ethical, or political conceptions, these are deep affinities that unite otherwise diverse strands of pragmatist thought. These affinities, I argue, are no small matter, and they do much to establish pragmatism
as a distinctive philosophical tradition that has much to offer to other traditions that have failed to take transitions seriously. If pragmatists today fail to
cultivate the meliorating potential of transitions, then we shall lose what is best
in pragmatism and we shall lose much of what is good in philosophy too.

This further explains not only why transitionalism has something to offer to
pragmatism but also why pragmatism has yet something to offer to philosophy.
One way of developing this thought is to consider what role pragmatism might
play in the future of philosophy. My wager is that the day of philosophy as system is over. The coming century is likely to see philosophy taken up not for the
sake of explanations of everything but rather for the purpose of contributing
thought to our most critical moments. Philosophy in these conditions will be
at its best as a means of orienting and adjusting our practices of critique and
inquiry. For these purposes, the now-classic image of philosophies as clashing
systems will come to seem increasingly antiquated. Philosophers will not im-
pose upon the traditions and figures from which they draw a requirement that
individual schools and singular thinkers be able to do everything we should
want from a philosophy. We will rather turn to pluralities of philosophical
thought in order to draw from them concepts, arguments, and other tools that
may prove useful for the critical inquiries we will regard as our primary vocation. In these conditions, pragmatists will freely avail themselves of resources
offered up by their nonpragmatist colleagues, including not only philosophers
inquiring in the context of other problems but also historians, anthropologists, policy analysts, and engineers.

From the perspective of this future philosophy, the history of twentieth-
century philosophy will likely come to be seen as playing out the final moves of
an exasperated game of philosophy as system. Much of twentieth-century philosophy is indeed already recognizable in these terms. Consider the longtime

mutual incomprehension between so-called Analytic and Continental philosophy. I doubt that the familiar labels of Analytic and Continental philosophy refer any longer to anything as coherent as traditions or schools, but there is no doubt that the latter decades of twentieth-century philosophy were largely animated by trivial hostilities between those who took, say, Quine or Carnap seriously and those who preferred to read, say, Derrida or Heidegger. Now that these turf wars have finally begun to cool off, in recent years philosophy once again finds itself looking for ways of mediating among seemingly disparate approaches to critique and inquiry. One way in which pragmatists can offer their services as mediators in the midst of this metaphilosophical change of heart is to emphasize ways in which pragmatist philosophy can contribute to and draw nourishment from some of the best work by the leading lights of other philosophical traditions.

This is why I am particularly eager in what follows to point out some of the ways in which pragmatist thought can benefit from an engagement with and at the same time inform the work of a diverse crew of philosophers. I engage at some length with work by Bernard Williams, Stanley Cavell, Pierre Bourdieu, and especially Michel Foucault. I also discuss, though not in any extraordinary detail, other important contemporary thinkers including Amartya Sen, Michael Walzer, Paul Rabinow, Axel Honneth, and Iris Marion Young. I aim for a capacious pragmatism. Although none of these figures is a conventional philosopher on any tradition's reckoning, Williams and Foucault at least are taken often enough as representatives of so-called Analytic and Continental philosophy, respectively, at least by those on the other side of the yawn. Showing that pragmatism has much in common with representatives of diverse philosophical traditions helps us position pragmatism as potentially mediating certain unnecessarily prohibitive philosophical divides.

As a way of offering a fuller impression of how I understand transitionalism to function both within pragmatism and within philosophy more generally, I conclude this introduction with a brief summary of the major themes of each of the chapters that follow. Taken on the whole, the aim of these chapters is to show just how much is to be gained in theory and practice by reconstructing pragmatism as transitionalism.

I begin in chapter 1 by laying out a vision of pragmatism as a project of cultural critical philosophy. I explicate the central concepts of this vision: transitionalism, meliorism, historicity, and temporality. Transitionalism is characterized in terms of passing through time and history from one situation to the next. Meliorism is characterized in terms of rendering these transitions into reconstructions, or processes of improvement, progress, and growth. Focusing pragmatism through both of these lenses leads to my conception of pragmatism as engaged cultural criticism. For the pragmatist, the work of philosophy takes place in time and through history such that philosophical melioration is best understood in terms of reconstructing the cultural presents in which we find ourselves. I show how this leads to a redescription of the pragmatist canon such that the core of the tradition is best represented by usual suspects such as William James and John Dewey but also by previously neglected thinkers including Ralph Waldo Emerson and Richard Rorty. It is above all in Emerson, James, Dewey, and Rorty that we find evinced that practice of philosophy as transitional and meliorative cultural criticism that I take as the best part of the tradition.

In chapters 2 and 3, I move on to efforts more erudite in ambition. These chapters lay out competing interpretations of the intellectual history of pragmatism. On the one hand, I am eager to show that my favored transitionalist themes are characteristic of every major pragmatist thinker. On the other hand, I am also keen to point out that all of these pragmatists have taken some other theme to be more at the heart of pragmatism.

The aim in chapter 2 is to feature the richness of transitional themes as they have surfaced in the writings of the great pantheon of pragmatists. I consider first the classical pragmatisms of James and Dewey and then two streams of midcentury pragmatism as these lead to the present. One stream was navigated by thinkers inflecting pragmatism with positivism, leading from Willard Van Orman Quine and Wilfrid Sellars to Richard Rorty and Robert Brandom. A second stream was explored in midcentury by many of Dewey's own students, carried forward by John Herman Randall and John McDermott, and culminates for the moment in contemporary classicopragmatism as represented by Joseph Margolis, Larry Hickman, and John Stuhr. This chapter is largely an effort in quotation. By quoting previous pragmatisms in such a way as to feature points of resonance across a diverse array of pragmatists from classico- to neo- and back again, I intend to seed the idea that there is much to be gained by emphasizing the deep continuities that run throughout these waters. Transitionalist themes of historicity and temporality play such a unifying purpose.

In chapter 3, I contrast my proposal for a third-wave transitional pragmatism with other items of conceptual emphasis that have tended to remain at the fore over the history of the first two waves of pragmatism. This chapter offers a review of those contentious debates over language and experience that continue to divide adherents of Jamesian and Deweyan classicopragmatism from advocates of Rortyan pragmatism. I am concerned to point out certain deficiencies that result from placing too much stress on experience or language rather than on the processes of transitioning in which both experience and language ought to be situated. But I am also keen to point out that there is something right in both approaches. James and Dewey were correct that a transitionalist philosophy like pragmatism must take experience seriously. But Rorty was correct to see that if we take experience too seriously we risk turning it into a foundation for knowledge, morality, or politics. This motivates a requirement for a third version of pragmatism that could blend classicopragmatist insights about experience with neopragmatist caution about foundationalism, representationalism, and givenism. I conclude this chapter by briefly considering two other recent attempts to lay out a path for a third-wave pragmatism: one of these I take as deeply misguided and the other I take as broadly inspirational.

In chapters 4, 5, and 6, I explicate transitionalism by showing how it provides the best way of bringing into focus the distinctive advantages of pragmatist contributions to epistemology, ethical theory, and political philosophy. The point of these chapters is not to show that pragmatism definitively resolves the crucial philosophical difficulties featured in these areas (for that would take at least three additional volumes). Rather, the point is to discern the specific orientation offered by pragmatism's intervention in these debates such that we can begin to recognize why a transitionalist interpretation better focuses the distinctive advantages of pragmatism's contribution than do the usual metaphors offered for these purposes. My aim is to show that the familiar pragmatist themes of experimentalism, pluralism, humanism, contextualism, fallibilism, and democratic liberalism yield their best philosophical advantages when inflected by the core pragmatist commitment to transitionalism.

Chapter 4 lays out a version of pragmatist epistemology that stresses the idea of knowledge as an evolving and developing practical process. I explicate the pragmatist theory of knowing as one in which knowledge is a process whereby past projections lead to future eventualities. Affirming this view requires some amount of metaphilosophical reconsideration of what sort of work we might expect from philosophical theories of truth and knowledge. But if these metaphilosophical shifts and their attendant philosophical reconceptualizations of knowledge can be accepted, then a transitionalist pragmatist epistemology can offer an improved conception of the relation between experience and language, which has proven so vexing for previous pragmatists. To make some of the points urged in this chapter, I explicate pragmatism in conversation with the work of the philosopher-sociologist Pierre Bourdieu.

Chapter 5 works toward a reinterpretation of pragmatist ethics. I argue that pragmatist transitionalism enabled James and Dewey to develop a new approach to ethical inquiry in which they suggested a way for integrating the crucially important concerns developed by the two great modern moral traditions of deontology and utilitarianism. In elaborating the idea of a pragmatist transitionalism about ethics, I also connect my conception of pragmatism to the moral philosophy of Stanley Cavell, whose Emersonian moral perfectionism shares much more with the pragmatisms of James and Dewey than is commonly recognized, even by Cavell himself.

Chapter 6 shows how pragmatist transitionalism can make a valuable contribution to political theory. A transitionalist conception of political theory finally enables philosophy to overcome the failings of the prevailing modes of utopian, dystopian, and conservative political criticism. In the place of these dominant modes, a transitionalist and meliorist political philosophy urges as its central idea that the situations in which we find ourselves already contain the resources requisite for improving those situations. After explicating this view in a diverse set of pragmatists including Randolph Bourne, Walter Lippmann, James, Dewey, and Rorty, I turn to another contemporary melioristic political philosopher not usually associated with pragmatism, namely Bernard Williams. I conclude this chapter by outlining the advantages of a transitionalist version of pragmatist democratic theory vis-à-vis other contemporary pragmatist approaches to democracy, including language-centric deliberativism and experience-centric communitarianism. This foray into democratic theory enables me to explicate connections between pragmatism and the critical theoretic work of Iris Marion Young and Axel Honneth.

Finally, in chapter 7 I turn to showing how pragmatism in a transitionalist key can equip us with models for critique and inquiry in a way that will prove crucial for future philosophical work no longer confined by the old paradigm of philosophies as systems. The first step in this argument is recognizing that a pragmatism that takes transitions seriously is also a pragmatism for which philosophy and history must come together. Of course, pragmatists must not involve themselves in just any form of history. Rather, they must work with the sorts of histories that result from a distinctively pragmatist historiography. I show how pragmatism can benefit from involving itself with another tradition of thought that is also simultaneously philosophical and historical, namely genealogy, and especially as developed by Michel Foucault. My conclusion is that pragmatist transitionalism paves the way for a new hybrid model of critique and inquiry, which I call genealogical pragmatism. As I envision this hybrid philosophy, genealogy supplies the problematizations that then motivate the work of reconstructive problem solving supplied by pragmatism. This sort of collaboration with genealogy enables me to show how pragmatists can finally offer convincing responses to two criticisms that have been persistently pressed against pragmatism for well over a century now: namely, the related criticisms that, first, pragmatism is Panglossian in downplaying the place of the tragic in our lives, and, second, that it is Promethean in overemphasizing the prowess of instrumental means-end rationality. In pressing pragmatism beyond a position in which it is susceptible to these long-running criticisms, I propose a philosophical-historical genealogical pragmatism that offers ample opportunities for developing effective critical inquiries into the actual situations in which we find ourselves today. This helps us see how pragmatism can best engage the practical realities wherein critique and inquiry make their greatest difference.

One

TRANSITIONALISM, MELIORISM,

AND CULTURAL CRITICISM

Bringing Transitionalism Into Focus

A working summary of the idea of transitionalism will be useful at the outset, although it must be stressed that it is the primary goal of this book to illustrate in lush detail what pragmatist transitionalism has already done and can yet do in the future. Any summary offered in anticipation of what follows can only be provisional.

Transitionalism can be described as a philosophical temperament that focuses ideas, concepts, and things in terms of the way in which they are both part of and constitutive of transitional processes. Transitional processes are those temporal and historical media in virtue of which we work through a situation from old to new, past to future, prior to posterior. A transitionalist account of truth would focus on truth as a dynamic process with temporal duration rather than as a static quality that holds either momentarily or eternally. A transitionalist account of ethics would focus on ethical processes whereby we improve our living rather than on the supposed correctness of some isolable act extracted from the transitional relations that define its contexts. Such accounts, in short, would emphasize that the true and the good themselves admit of temporal duration. One way of thinking about transitionalism would be to urge that instead of talking about certain practices as true or good, we should instead talk about them as truer and better. Instead of focusing on epistemic or moral rightness, we should instead focus on epistemic or moral melioration, improvement, development, and growth.

Transitionalism as I here develop and deploy it gathers together a number of philosophically complex concepts, including temporality, historicity, evolution, development, process, and event. The concept of transitions, which I find central to pragmatism, serves as a focal point for making sense of this complex bundle. In some ways, transitionalism can be usefully thought of as a lens that brings into focus a fairly wide network of interrelated concepts and themes central to the pragmatist tradition. It might also be usefully thought of as a figure that establishes a connected coherence among a diverse array of elements.

Transitionalism, both the idea and the word, is an improvisation on an immensely generative insight offered by William James: "Life is in the transitions" (1904b, 212). I offer transitionalism for the purposes of providing a generous canopy under which a wide range of pragmatists and thinkers from other traditions can gather. It might thus be inadvisable to pick out any single pragmatist as guiding my vision, lest this lead to subtle exclusions of those to whom I wish to extend an invitation. But at the same time, it is immensely helpful to pick out a name that reaches back into the very tradition of which I am attempting a revision. If I must begin by following somebody's lead, then, I think it best to follow James's. In the pages that follow, I turn to James more than any other single thinker to make my points, though I certainly turn to plenty of others in addition (most notably Ralph Waldo Emerson, John Dewey, and Richard Rorty). Although my following James could indeed lead to the subtle sorts of exclusions that I wish to avoid, I believe that it will minimize the inevitable cliquishness if only for the reason that James is clearly the most intellectually and morally generous pragmatist in the tradition. It is that generosity which I wish to invoke in borrowing from James the title for the conception of pragmatism here offered. It is through such generosity that a renewing wave of pragmatism may yet prove capacious enough to gather philosophical work from across the entire tradition and from other traditions besides.

A more problematic way to court subtle exclusions at the outset would be to offer up a rigorous definition or logical account of transitionality at the fore. This way of proceeding would be quite distant from the spirit of transitionalism itself. It will nonetheless be helpful to begin by more carefully specifying the concept of transitionality. Doing so requires that I explicate without going all the way to logical or formal stipulating.

Transitionality, in the sense in which it is central for pragmatism, needs to be distinguished from mere change. Transitionality suggests temporally mediated development, whereas change suggests temporally mediated difference. The difference between development and difference, however, makes all the difference for transitionality.

The best way in which to state this difference is in terms of a distinction between purposive activity and undirected change. Transitionality connotes purposiveness and directedness such that change can be regarded as something more than just random or dumb difference. A conception of transitionality as purposive already places transitionality at the center of pragmatism, insofar as pragmatism follows Kant in conceiving of thought as a thoroughly purposive and directive activity. Mind for the pragmatist is act, effort, and deed. It is this active dimension that distinguishes transitionality from passive change. The way in which a boulder rolls down a mountain and the way in which a hummingbird and a human being strive toward the glory of the sun are two very different ways of transitioning. They are not entirely different, and there is much that these two processes share. But it is crucial to note that there are differences, the most important of which is the difference between development and mere difference. The boulder does not develop itself in rolling down the hill. But the hummingbird and the human being do, for better or for worse.

For better or for worse? Isn't that the crucial thing? Of course it is. Everything within the vast spaces of the human heart and head, and perhaps also in the hummingbird's, depends on whether or not our purposive transitions result in definite improvements or in definite degenerations. It is crucial to the pragmatist way of thinking that we not specify in advance the particular pattern or shape that will determine whether or not any given transition amounts to melioration or decline. We cannot say in advance what success will amount to. This is unsurprising, because it means that the emergence of new futures is not fully determined by the structures of old pasts. The past constrains but does not determine the future. For the new to be truly new, it must be able to develop out of the old without merely rehearsing the old. This suggests that the difference that purposiveness introduces between difference and development cannot be strictly delimited in advance. While purposiveness, in the pragmatist way of thinking, connotes thought, intelligence, meaning, and rationality, it does not connote intellectualism, the view that rationality must conform to some pattern, method, or logic which precedes it. The very value of rationality, the pragmatist insists, is that it can introduce new differences where they did not formerly inhabit old structures. Thought must always respect the constraints of the situations in which it finds itself, but the difference between thoughtful transition and the dumb changes undergone by inert matter is that between a thought that develops a situation according to its constraints and a change that finds itself wholly determined by the past preceding it.

That purposive activity cannot be wholly determined in advance suggests that transitions are a kind of neutral field within which both progress and decay are possible. This is indeed the case. The fact of transitionality, the fact that we are thoughtful beings, does not mean that things will always get better, that improvement will always ensue, or that rationality is the destiny of humanity or of the universe. Whether or not purposive activity achieves progress or depletes itself is something that can only be worked out in the context of actual transitions themselves. There are no universal rules of rationality that we can specify in advance. We can work with the epistemic, ethical, and political resources already available to us within a given situation, but there is no point in insisting that these resources are the sure route to success in every context, in every time, and in every place. In this sense, purposive transitionality and the temporal structure of practice are neutral fields out of which we can with effort develop forms of epistemic and ethical success. Recognizing that our possibilities are constrained only by the historical and temporal contingencies that shape them, however severe those constraints might be, enables us to focus on how we might work toward our futures and then actually achieve them on the basis of the resources already available to us within the situations in which we find ourselves. It is characteristic of the four pragmatists I take as the best exemplars of the tradition (namely Emerson, James, Dewey, and Rorty) that they continuously worked to leverage their transitionalist sensibility into a meliorist hope with which they sought to turn the transitions toward which they found themselves flowing into processes of betterment.

Before turning to the ways in which the meliorism of my four leading pragmatists describes the proper focal range for pragmatist transitionalism, allow me to roll out a little bit further the two ideas at the core of transitionalism: temporality and historicity. Transitionality connotes purposive change in light of the shifting circumstances of temporal and historical context. But what are temporality and historicity? I shall often use these two concepts more or less interchangeably. This is justified insofar as in many contexts these two concepts do function in more or less the same way. Nevertheless, there are occasions when it is helpful to distinguish temporality and historicity, and so I would like to offer a brief explication of my different use of these concepts. Distinguishing them in this way also enables me to better explicate how I take these concepts to function.

I understand temporality and historicity as implying one another in the sense that they are two aspects of the same underlying phenomenon of transitionality, development, or purposive change. Temporality refers to the form of transitionality itself. Historicity refers to the determinate contents through which transitions occur. It follows that historicity needs temporality as its form and temporality needs historicity as its content. While temporality is the general form that transitionality assumes, such form must always manifest in particular historical contents. And while historicity refers to the determinate content of transitionality, these contents must always be informed by the general structure of temporality. Take experience. Temporality refers to the flowing-ness of experience. Historicity refers to the actual ways in which experience flows. Temporality indicates *that* it flows, and historicity indicates *how* it flows. That I have an experience of something being *before* something else that is *after* it refers to the temporality of experience. But the particular way in which *this* thing is before *that* other thing that is after it invokes the historicity of experience. Temporality captures the structural relations of transitions, and historicity captures the actual situated occurring of transitions. Transitions always take place through the form of temporality as expressed in the historicity of particular contents. Given this account of the relation between temporality and historicity, we can say that transitionalism focuses on knowledge, ethics, politics, and critique as temporally structured and historically situated.

This clarifies the often puzzling relationship between temporality and historicity. But there remains another puzzling pair of relationships between temporality and time on the one hand and historicity and history on the other. It is not my aim here to resolve longstanding philosophical questions concerning these matters, but a few words are nonetheless in order. If temporality refers to a particular form of practice and historicity refers to the particular content of practices that accord with that form, we might say at first blush that this implies that practice takes place in time and through history. This is true enough. Historicity invokes the historical content that invests every practice, while temporality invokes the temporal form that every practice so invested takes on. My arguments in later chapters thus concern the way in which pragmatism enables us to focus on the thoroughgoing historicity and temporality of epistemic, ethical, and political practice. But as it turns out, this is to say something quite more than is revealed by the first-blush impression that our practices take place in history and time. For we can go further than this and say that the content of our practices is irreducibly historical and that their form is irreducibly temporal. We can say, in short, that historicity and temporality invest all of our practices with the form of real flowing time and the contents of actual flowing history. Our practices are not merely located in time and in history but are also themselves constituted in their entirety by practical content that is itself historical and temporal. Our practices not only flow through time and history but are also made up of material that is irreducibly historical and temporal. This is related to why I prefer "transitionalism" to "transitionism"—the latter states the fact of flow while the former invokes the process of flowing in action. Best, of course, would be "transitioningism," but that word is too ugly to want to invent.

Bringing Meliorism Into Focus

Transitionalism inflects our practical and theoretical activity with an interrelated family of notions including historicity, history, time, and temporality. When philosophy itself is interpreted through the lens of these transitionalist notions, it turns out that philosophy is best understood as a theory and practice of hopeful cultural criticism. One name that pragmatists have used to refer to such a conception of philosophical practice is meliorism. The central idea of meliorism is that a philosophically robust conception of hope can function as a guide for critique and inquiry. As put forth here, this melioristic conception of philosophy as hopeful cultural criticism is meant to be extensive enough to function usefully across epistemic, ethical, and political contexts. The function of philosophy on this melioristic view is to engage in the long labor of reconstructing and reorienting the epistemic, ethical, and political realities in which we find ourselves flowing.

This melioristic conception of philosophical hope helps focus the transitionalism that is at the heart of pragmatism. Although transitionalism is the centermost conception for the pragmatist way of thinking, the conception of meliorism helps clarify the specific value of the transitionalist perspective. I noted above that transitionalism easily appears neutral with respect to development or decay. Meliorism, by contrast, clearly connotes something valuable at the same time as it connotes something effective and workable. If transitionalism connotes merely purposive change, then meliorism connotes purposive change for the better. These two outlooks are obviously complementary: meliorism standing for the attitude of improvement, progress, and betterment at the heart of pragmatist cultural critique and transitionalism for the temporal and historical perspective within which this melioristic cultural critique is situated. Pragmatism, which is best focused in terms of this transitional perspective, is commonly summarized as offering a conception of inquiry in which human thought and action is an affair of traveling from hypotheses to their outcomes, or from conceptions to their effects, as Peirce originally put it. Those travelings in which our conceptions successfully lead us to their objects are meliorative. Whether or not our travelings are successful or not is something that must always be worked out in practice. The only general thing that the pragmatist is willing to say about them is that travelings are successful where they offer a resolution of the problems we face in practice.

Pragmatism offers a technical term for such resolutions: reconstruction. Meliorism is successful transitionalism. *Meliorist transitionalism is a philosophical practice of reconstruction.* This is as summary a statement of pragmatism as I can muster. But such compact and glistening summaries, I hasten to remind, are often less illuminating than the grey and meticulous volumes meant to explicate them.

The characteristic attitude of the pragmatist is hope. The pragmatist engaged in reconstruction is at bottom a meliorist transitionalist. Hope expresses the faith that we can make a better future. Such faith posits its intended outcome before it has arrived. In doing so, it helps us work toward realizing that outcome. That the faith of hope braces our energies and efforts constitutes the difference between that attitude and the more passive optimisms and pessimisms that insist that our destiny shall arrive, be it for better or for worse. There is, of course, no way of guaranteeing the realization of the objects of our hopes before their emergence, but there is in almost every instance plenty we can do to assist them. Melioristic hope thus suggests a philosophical practice that is both fully situated amid the transitions in which we find ourselves and rightly confident that we can, through our effort, see these transitions through to better futures. Meliorism is a transitionalism that is confident, energetic, and generous toward our prospects.

When philosophy invests itself in transitionalist themes of historicity and temporality, it is best practiced as a melioristic project of reconstructing the cultural problems that we find ourselves facing in the present. Philosophy, according to the distinctively pragmatist methodology of reconstruction, is thus best understood as a practice of cultural criticism. This practice involves working toward the resolution of our most pressing cultural problems. Explicating this conception of pragmatism as a philosophy of cultural hope adds nuance and detail to the more general conception of pragmatist transitionalism that is my main concern in this book. The remainder of this chapter is focused on the crucial but too often neglected topic of what philosophy as a practice of cultural criticism might involve. On the basis of the paradigm offered in this chapter, later chapters can then explicate more detailed cases of what pragmatist reconstruction involves for core philosophical topics including knowledge, ethics, and politics.

Truth in Hope

In recent years, there has been an increasing surge of interest in pragmatism's melioristic perspective, as attested by an increasing number of books and articles calling attention to the role that hope plays in the pragmatist way of thinking.[1] But despite this increase of interest in pragmatist meliorism and the widespread acknowledgment that meliorism is somehow central to pragmatism, it remains to be spelled out exactly how meliorism contributes to pragmatism. I understand pragmatism, and find it at its best, as a philosophical way of taking hope seriously. Pragmatism, on this view, develops the philosophical resources of hope. One implication is that traditional philosophical categories look different when seen pragmatically, where they are inflected with, and interpreted through, hopefulness. It is thus that traditional philosophical concepts are widely understood to be severely reconstructed by pragmatism. Yet the motivations for, and philosophical significance of, these reconstructions remain obscure so long as the meliorism at the heart of pragmatism goes unexplained.

One way of looking at hopefulness, which in its more philosophically robust moments can be called *meliorism*, is as a combination of *pluralism* and *humanism*, two central themes in the pragmatist vision. Pluralism is the thesis that the realities we inhabit are many. As William James put it, "the world we live in exists diffuse and distributed" (1907, 126). There is no one way that things are. The world is dynamic and shifting. Pluralism takes contingency seriously by applying it to reality itself. The result is that things could always be different than they happen to be. The world is thus a pluriverse, not a universe. A corollary of pluralism, humanism is the thesis that we humans make definitive contributions to this pluriverse. Again in James's words, the idea is that "the world stands really malleable, waiting to receive its final touches at our hands. . . . Man *engenders* truths upon it" (1907, 123). What reality is depends on our contributions, interests, and purposes. Meliorism, holding together pluralism with humanism, is the thesis that we are capable of creating better worlds and selves. If pluralism is the thesis that better futures are possible and humanism the thesis that possibilities are often enough decided by human energies, then meliorism combines the two in asserting that better futures are made real by our effort. Meliorism, then, is best seen as humanism and pluralism combined and in confident mood.

James conceptualized meliorism as follows: "Meliorism treats salvation as neither necessary [as would optimism] nor impossible [as would pessimism]. It treats it as a possibility." Melioristic hope offers a genuine alternative to the familiar pessimistic and optimistic moods that are almost universally proffered in modern philosophy. These moods share a common assumption that progress and decline are inevitable. Meliorism, on the other hand, focuses on what *we* can do to hasten our progress and mitigate our decline. Pragmatic meliorism thus posits possibilities for which we are "live champions and pledges." These possibilities, said James, are "such a mixture of things as will in the fullness of time give us a chance, a gap that we can spring into." This leads us to the crucial question of meliorism: "Does our act then *create* the world's salvation so far as it makes room for itself, so far as it leaps into the gap?" James sees no reason why not: "Why may [our acts] not be the actual turning-places and growing-places which they seem to be, of the world, why not the workshop of being where we catch fact in the making, so that nowhere may the world grow in any other kind of way than this?" (James 1907, 137, 138). Pragmatist meliorism, James here makes evident, is the view that our energies and efforts can make a definite contribution to the realities we inhabit. Our acts can change the world for the better—and indeed the improvement of the world may itself require our work for its sustenance. It is only with our acts, uncertain and hopeful, that the possibilities of improvement may be actualized. It is in this sense that James wrote that "the pragmatism . . . I defend has to fall back on a certain ultimate hardihood, a certain willingness to live without assurances or guarantees" (1906, 124). Meliorism is the name for that hardihood and willingness—that uncertain hope.

One way of further explicating the pragmatist conception of meliorism is to consider the way in which pragmatism reconstructs traditional philosophical conceptions. This would involve showing not only how pragmatism transforms the philosophical content of our lives but also how pragmatism expresses a commitment to philosophy as a practice of reconstructing the situations in which we find ourselves. For the timeless philosophical idol of contemplation, pragmatism substitutes a transitional philosophical practice of reconstruction. I begin by considering James's reconstruction of truth for ameliorative purposes before using his work as a platform for looking backward to Emerson and forward to Dewey and Rorty.

"*The* Truth: what a perfect idol of the rationalistic mind!" (James 1907, 115). James's reconstruction of truth radically broke from the debilitating assumption that possession of the truth places us in harmony with the way the world itself really is. This assumption renders us impotent because it authorizes an optimism regarding truth's emancipating power—but this optimism is easily reversed by those pessimistic about our qualification for possession of truth. The common assumption of optimists and pessimists alike is that freedom is truth's consequence. This thesis renders superfluous any effort in experimentation. But pragmatism refocuses attention on the possibilities of our efforts in holding that the truth does not make us free.

James's conception of truth, which he described in transitionalist terms as something that "*happens* to an idea," can be appreciated in terms of the meliorism internal to that conception. What specifically happens to an idea when it "*becomes* true, is *made* true" is that the idea successfully leads us from one part of the temporal and historical field of experience to another part of that field that we find improved—"the truth of a state of mind means the function of *a leading that is worth while*." James was clear that the transitions that the pragmatist refers to in terms of truth are precisely those transitions that meliorate or improve the situations in which we find ourselves. It is in this sense that James situated truth as a good, or, as he put it, "truth is *one species of good*" (1907, 97, 98, 42). In this sense, the *what* of truth and the *why* of truth are not dichotomous for the pragmatist. This is why James was not only interested in a logical conception of truth but was instead committed to a broader inquiry into how truth functions and what truth means in our lives. James's pragmatism thus co-locates truth as simultaneously epistemological and axiological. He offers a specification of truth, a concept of obvious epistemological significance, in terms that specify truth as a species of improvement, a concept of obvious axiological significance. This suggests that he takes neither epistemology nor axiology as prior to the other. Rather, his pragmatism indicates that epistemology and axiology enhance one another and can be made sense of only insofar as they are regarded as interactive. This deep-running philosophical rejection of the classic dichotomy between facts and values is essential to the pragmatist vision of knowledge, ethics, and politics as reconstructive enterprises.

A crucial aspect of James's meliorism involves thinking of truth in terms of processes though which we *free ourselves* so as to break away from the classical assumption that the truth *makes us* free. James abandoned the most problematic tendencies of the philosophic tradition that we should want him to, most notably the idea that truth is the name of a power that we ought to hook ourselves into. Truth is nothing we can rely on, for it is not the name of a power extrinsic to human action. Truth is human action in potent phase. Truth names our power, our success, our accomplishment—contrast this to a concept of truth as an external force bestowing its blessings upon us. It is notable that commentators have generally failed to realize the most important implications of this view. As an example of this unfortunate misinterpretation of pragmatist truth, I take a passage from an otherwise invaluable book on the subject where Harvey Cormier explicates James's conception as follows: "the *value* of truth lies in its power to make the world and our human lives in it better" (2001, 28). This claim is representative of a quite typical misinterpretation of the pragmatist approach to truth that is deeply rooted in the very philosophical tradition that pragmatism works its way out of. My alternative view is that truth for James is not powerful in itself but is rather a name for our being powerful. Any supposed effectiveness commonly attributed to truth is really our effectiveness. This is what it means to take a melioristic perspective on truth. Meliorism focuses on improvements that are due to our energies and efforts. Truth, understood melioristically, is an improvement resulting from our work. Richard Poirier sounds the crucial element in this pragmatist meliorism: "James, like Emerson, foregoes any supports for the self that are extrinsic to its own workings" (1987, 196). The innovation of pragmatism is the inscription of truth within the circle of human work. This reverses the old philosophical picture of the success of our work as an effect of truth. Here is how Herman Melville put this quintessentially pragmatist point in one of his grand inaugural works of American literature: "it is not for man to follow the trail of truth too far, since by doing so he entirely loses the directing compass of his mind" (1852, 231). I have long had the hunch that one can mine Melville for nearly all the riches of pragmatism. But this would, of course, be another project.

Emerson, if not also Melville, was long a preoccupation of James's. As a young student in Europe, James looked forward to a time "when Emerson's philosophy will be in our bones" (James, in Matthiessen 1947, 432). Nearly thirty years later, at a 1903 Emerson Centenary, James sounded the quintessential pragmatist themes of pluralism and humanism: "The world is still new and untried. In seeing freshly, and not in hearing of what others saw, shall a man find what truth is" (1903b, 455). The good that James and Emerson recognize as truth is the good of innovation. Truth renews traditions and thus neither insipidly repeats nor impudently abandons them. Truth, James would write a few years later in *Pragmatism*, is "a go-between, a smoother-over of transitions. It marries old opinion to new fact so as ever to show a minimum of jolt, a maximum of continuity" (1907, 35). This central idea of pragmatist transitionalism holds that melioration consists in simultaneously accepting and criticizing our inherited traditions. Melioration occurs at the confluence of old and new.

At the heart of pragmatist philosophy is a resolute hopefulness in the abilities of human effort to create better future realities. James finds this too in Emerson. It is not a cheap optimism, an "indiscriminate hurrahing for the Universe," but rather a firm belief that "the point of any pen can be an epitome of reality." This democratic meliorism James named "Emerson's revelation," lauding it as "the headspring of all his outpourings" (1903b, 455). And while it may seem an embellishment to describe Emersonian tendencies as deeply democratic, I take courage for this thought in the precedent set by pragmatism's most respected visionary of democracy. Dewey hoped, also in 1903, that "the coming century may well make evident what is just now dawning, that Emerson is not only a philosopher, but that he is the Philosopher of Democracy... when democracy has articulated itself, it will have no difficulty in finding itself already proposed in Emerson" (1903b, MW3.190–3.191). Dewey further noted of Emerson that "he finds truth in the highway, in the untaught endeavor, the unexpected idea" (1903b, MW3.189). In this view Dewey found a melioristic conception of truth consistent with his own.

Dewey wrote of truth: "The adverb 'truly' is more fundamental than either the adjective, true, or the noun, truth. An adverb expresses a way, a mode of acting." Truth, for Dewey, looks forward to consequences and thus anticipates a meliorism that "arouses confidence and a reasonable hopefulness." Dewey thought of truth in this way because he understood truth as performing a "reconstruction" (1920, 156/MW12.182). Truth, in Dewey's lingo, names a form of success in which we reconstruct problematic situations into ones that are more secure. In thinking of truth as an achievement in this way, Dewey agreed with James that "verification and truth completely coincide." The crux of the view is that the truth can for us have no practical meaning until the beliefs that *may* be true lead us to the realities of which they *are* true. Following James, belief for Dewey is "hypothetical until the course of action indicated has been tried." This is because "the event or issue of such action *is* the truth or falsity of the judgment" (1915a, 346/MW8.21). Truth for the pragmatist is thus thoroughly reconstructive. It names our working well in the situations in which we find ourselves by instituting changes in those situations on the basis of the resources furnished within them. It is thus that Dewey conceived of truth in terms that are decidedly melioristic. A melioristic philosophy of growth as "the only moral end" (Dewey 1920, 177/MW12.181) is emphasized throughout Dewey's pragmatism, in his work on truth and science as much as in his work on ethics and democracy.

These are all Emersonian echoes. Emerson held that truth, like life, is a transitional sort of thing: "Life only avails, not the having lived. Power ceases in the instant of repose; it resides in the moment of transition from a past to a new state, in the shooting of the gulf, in the darting to an aim" (1841, 144). A world completed yesterday cannot be infused with value today. Only if the world is in the making can our acts make a difference. These and other anticipations of pragmatism are evident throughout Emerson's work. I shall consider the pluralism, humanism, and meliorism in just one essay, "Self-Reliance."

Here is Emerson's pluralism in that essay: "If you are true, but not in the same truth with me, cleave to your companions; I will seek my own. I do this not selfishly, but humbly and truly. It is alike your interest, and mine, and all men's, however long we have dwelt in lies, to live in truth." Emerson does not refute those who counter his own truth—truth is plural, there is room in it enough for all, only we must hold fast to ourselves, else we cease to live in truth. Self-reliance also connotes humanism because it involves a recentering of the soul around the self's successful creations and away from the powers supposedly possessed by independent truth. Emerson's humanism is thus this: "You take the way from man, not to man." This pluralism and humanism balance on the melioristic invocation of confidence and hope that are at the heart of Emerson's melioristic faith in our own energies: "To believe your own thought, to believe that what is true for you in your private heart is true for all men—that is genius" (1841, 146, 143, 132).

Unfortunately, Emerson's melioristic vision of what he once called in his journals "the infinitude of the private man" (April 7, 1840, in Emerson 1960, 7.342) is regarded by too many of his readers as expressing an elitist and egoistic individualism. Countering this influential misinterpretation, I agree with those who read Emersonian personality as an accomplishment not of isolation but of better worlds between persons.[2] For Emerson, as for James and Dewey, the democratic contribution is thoroughly *personal*.[3] This means that it is simultaneously *individual* and *social* just insofar as all persons find themselves simultaneously individuating from and associating with other persons: "It is easy in the world to live after the world's opinion; it is easy in solitude to live after our own; but the great man is he who in the midst of the crowd keeps with perfect sweetness the independence of solitude" (Emerson 1841, 136). The kind of ethical commitment consonant with this vision of democracy is exemplified in Emerson's famously puzzling remark on charity: "Then again, do not tell me, as a good man did to-day, of my obligation to put all poor men in good situations. Are they my poor? I tell thee, thou foolish philanthropist, that I grudge the dollar, the dime, the cent I give to such men as do not belong to me and to whom I do not belong" (1841, 135). Emerson's ethical commitment is to other persons as they are in their actuality, *my* poor, not to other persons in the abstract according to idealized principles, *the* poor. So it is that democratic melioration occurs between persons, not between persons and principles.

Emerson wrote of personality as "art": "The difference between persons is not in wisdom but in art" (1844, 267). Art is Emerson's name for acts of renewal: creation in relation to tradition, living new ways by breathing life into old ways. His essay "Art" meditates on this line with which it opens: "Because the soul is progressive, it never quite repeats itself, but in every act attempts the production of a new and fairer whole" (1844, 274). The old is made new: mere repetition is no novelty. Art for Emerson best captures that transitional combination of recurrence and variance. It is the production of a new whole that is new only in relation to what precedes it. Emerson's "art" is a counterpart to James's "truth"—both flow fastest at the confluence of old and new. Art and truth are in this way understood by pragmatists as transitional reconstructions. Truth is like art in that it makes no provisions for us. The provision is our doing, our art, our hope. Truth and art are the effectiveness of human effort, not powers that inform it from some great glory beyond.

Writing on Dewey's essay on Emerson quoted above, Rorty re-sounds the quintessential pragmatist theme of hopefulness: "For Dewey, Emerson's talent for criterionless hope was the essence of his value to his country" (1989b, 120). Rorty's own pragmatism similarly evinces a "willingness to substitute imagination for certainty, and curiosity for pride" (1994a, 88). Rorty offers neither bland optimistic reassurance nor pessimistic suspicion but a unique hopefulness that we can create better selves and worlds without "prophecy and claims to knowledge" but only with a "generous hope" which "sustain[s] itself without such reassurances" (1998e, 209).

Few commentators stress the centrality of hope in Rorty's philosophical outlook, and even fewer engage with it as a philosophical concept worthy of attention in its own right.[4] Yet what is most abidingly valuable in Rorty's intellectual career are not his by now familiar rails against essentialism, universalism, representationalism, givenism, and foundationalism. Important as these criticisms remain and as much as I draw from them in what follows, there is clearly something of more enduring worth in Rorty's work than his having launched the latest salvo against the increasingly insolvent cottage industries that continue to define the entire scope of the intellectual agenda of more than just a few professional philosophers. This something of greater worth emerges when we read Rorty as he recommends we read others: "we should skip lightly past the predictions, and concentrate on the expressions of hope" (1998e, 205).

Read in this way, we can begin to discern in Rorty's pragmatism an expression of the hope that we can make the difference between a world sustained by our values and a world to which our values are irrelevant. Rorty thus places pragmatism in the service of meliorism's enabling mood. Describing Dewey more or less as a figure for himself, Rorty writes that "Dewey urges that the quest for certainty be replaced with the demand for imagination— that philosophy should stop trying to provide reassurance and instead encourage what Emerson called 'self-reliance.'" The melioristic view Rorty finds central to the pragmatist tradition is the view that "one should stop worrying about whether what one believes is well grounded and start worrying about whether one has been imaginative enough to think up interesting alternatives to one's present beliefs." The same point was again put by Rorty in a somewhat different way when he wrote that "substituting hope for knowledge, substituting the idea that the ability to be citizens of the full-fledged democracy which is yet to come, rather than the ability to grasp truth, is what is important about being human" (1994a, 34; 2000a, 3). In these and other passages, Rorty gives expression to the hope that we can make the difference between a world cultivated by our values and one to which our values are irrelevant. It is basic to the vision of pragmatism I am calling melioristic that human values and interests are understood to occupy the center of our pluriverse.

Concerning truth, Rorty followed Emerson, James, and Dewey in disclaiming traditional identifications of truth with emancipation: "'Truth' is not the name of a power that eventually wins through" (1994c, 226). Like the earlier pragmatists, Rorty reversed traditional formulas of truth's liberating power in claiming that "if you take care of freedom, truth will take care of itself" (1989b, 118). Barry Allen makes this point in a passage that qualifies him as a pragmatist under Rorty's influence: "Truth has no power of its own, no utopian potential, no affinity for good, and will not make us free" (1993, 182). It is an old faith that the truth emancipates us—it is the new pragmatist hope that we emancipate ourselves. The crucial contrast is between a philosophy that preaches obedience to a greater glory that may yet subsume us and a philosophy that provokes the courage and confidence of our humble human hopes. Antialethism was for Rorty but a species of a more crucial antiauthoritarianism.[5]

Rorty always held that we do not stand in need of a theory of truth if we can get an adequate theory of justification.[6] "True," for James, was a name for the satisfaction of felt cravings and doubts. For Rorty, this satisfaction was better glossed as "justified," but the project of redefinition remains the same. Despite superficial differences, the common upshot of both views is that there simply is no craving for truth itself taken apart from any human interest. Rorty's idea that hope may suitably *replace* truth rather than *reconstruct* it, as other pragmatists have claimed, may indeed be terminologically troubling, but more important is the broader resonance of his view with the earlier pragmatist rejection of any attempt to puff up truth as some superhuman power commanding our allegiance. Rorty was in good pragmatist fashion when he railed (as he frequently did) against any concept crediting a "nonhuman authority to whom we owe some sort of respect" (1998d, 150). Rorty's redescription of truth under the auspices of justification is best seen as his way of attempting to credit the more meliorist hope that we may improve our living by our own lights.

I can now sum up my discussion with the suggestion that there is a common pragmatist meliorism running from Emerson through James and Dewey to Rorty according to which truth is sustained by our effort and energy. These pragmatists all reverse the old philosophical pretence that the truth sustains us. Their view is that the truth will not set us free—our humble human efforts, not supreme inhuman energies, are the only forces of freedom. These pragmatists all reject the worship of truth and refuse to offer up prayers of obedience to this most hollow and august philosophical idol. They use pragmatism to refocus philosophy on the differences we humans might make. Hope is the mood in which they expect that we can make the requisite differences. This is the mood of meliorism.

Pragmatism as Cultural Criticism

In melioristic transitionalism, it falls on us to better the flows in which we find ourselves. It follows from this that a primary task of philosophy ought to be to participate in this betterment. A philosophy that insists on the irreducible transitionality of our lives, that is, ought to see its primary task in terms of contributing to the ameliorative improvement of these transitions in their evolution. This implies a conception of philosophy that is close to the most pressing cultural issues of its day.

The point I wish to stress is that melioristic cultural critique remains the best legacy of pragmatism for contemporary philosophy. According to this view, the work of philosophy should steer clear of the ponderous and the profound. Philosophy should not dive to the depths—it should travel widely with intensity and flair. We philosophers should see our commission as that of articulating, problematizing, and reconstructing the plural publics and cultures in which we find ourselves. According to this view, the best work in philosophy is public thought or cultural critique. This vision of philosophy has been most ably developed in our tradition by the American pragmatists, although there is no reason to think or hope that we pragmatists might have exclusive license here.

I could draw on all four of my pragmatists to make this point. Emerson, James, Dewey, and Rorty were all leading intellectual voices of their years. Each of them occupied that once prominent but now relegated role of the public intellectual or, to use terms I much prefer, public thinker or philosopher of culture. It is undeniable that Emerson is best read as an American cultural critic in this sense—he is perhaps the paradigm of our concept of an American public intellectual. And though they have been read otherwise, it is quite difficult to make sense of much of what James and Dewey did and wrote without regarding them as cultural critics after an Emersonian example—thus I follow others in asserting that James and Dewey are best read as cultural critics in this Emersonian sense. Rorty too is best read in this light—though this has not been recognized nearly so well.[7]

Rather than drawing on all of my pragmatists to illustrate my point, however, I shall focus only on Rorty. The reason I do so is because there remains an ongoing difficulty among Rorty's audience, particularly philosophers, concerning how to best understand his work. Philosophers are too often exasperated and baffled, rather than challenged and edified, by Rorty. This kind of resistance on the part of philosophy to Rorty also occurs, though less severely, in the case of James and Dewey, and it is perhaps even more pronounced in the case of Emerson. Explicating just how it is that Rorty's philosophy should be understood can assist philosophers in coming to terms with the project of pragmatism as a whole insofar as this project is in its best instances an effort in cultural criticism. The idea is that the ensuing discussion of Rorty as cultural critic will stand as somewhat representative of the cultural-critical impulse of pragmatism on the whole.

I understand Rorty's work as operating in three spaces or domains. He writes histories of philosophy, metaphilosophy, and what I will call cultural philosophy, by which I just mean cultural criticism. Corresponding to these three spaces, Rorty can be read as a historian-anthropologist of philosophy, as a metaphilosopher who also draws upon the history and sociology of philosophy, or as a cultural philosopher who often expounds upon the historical and contemporary relevance of philosophy. I understand these spaces not so much as hierarchically higher or lower than one another but rather as extensively broader or narrower than one another.

Rorty as a historian of philosophy is exemplified by *Philosophy and the Mirror of Nature*. In this book, Rorty was not so much striking out in his own direction as he was weaving together various strands in twentieth-century philosophy that had been left dangling. The story he told went as follows: the criticisms of the tradition of modern philosophy authored by Dewey, Heidegger, and Wittgenstein finally demonstrated the obsolescence of the great problems devised by Descartes, Locke, and Kant. What Rorty helped us see were the intellectual conditions within which the great modern philosophers had formed the research program of the last two hundred years of philosophy. By the middle decades of the twentieth century, these conditions had clearly expired. Two other underannounced heroes of Rorty's book, Quine and Sellars, showed the need for fully breaking from the leading assumptions and dichotomies of high-modern philosophy. Rorty drew together these rather diverse strands of argumentation and showed how they all converge on a single undeniable point: philosophy in the form of foundationalist epistemology and metaphysics no longer had anything of intellectual value to offer to the rest of culture. The familiar old problems simply no longer itched anybody except philosophers.

This controversial argument led Rorty to turn his sights to the important metaphilosophical implications of the conclusions he had reached. These implications concerned the fate of professional philosophy in a culture that no longer took the profession's proclaimed problems very seriously. Rorty had convinced himself that the tradition had exhausted its own relevance to wider problems. But if the research agenda of philosophy is seen as having outlived its usefulness, then the inevitable next question is "What is a philosopher to do?" This aspect of Rorty's work is exemplified in such early essays as "Philosophy in

America Today" and "Method, Social Science, and Social Hope" as well as some of his most important later work, including the central portions of the book that is the most quintessentially Rortyan text (by both my accounting and Rorty's), namely *Contingency, Irony, and Solidarity.* In all of these pieces, Rorty's claim was that philosophers should enjoy the freedom to keep on doing what they have always done but that they should no longer think of their activities in their remote academic corners as the intellectual and moral center of the universe. Philosophy has its own history and its own set of problems, but we have no better reason for thinking that solving these problems will save humanity than we do for thinking that writing a really good poem or making a really good film will do the trick. In light of this rather gloomy metaphilosophical conclusion, Rorty began the long project of retooling his thought by means of refashioning himself into a more capacious humanist intellectual. The implicit assumption of this retooling was that philosophy could reestablish itself only by moving its province to a more theoretically interdisciplinary and practically engaged effort.

In his contributions to this wider metaphilosophical space, Rorty's thought was always plagued by a tension that many of his readers, especially philosophers, have found entirely frustrating. On the one hand, there are Rorty's gloomy predictions about the fate of professional philosophy as an isolated and insulated form of highbrow kibitzing. Most philosophers have been guarded about Rorty's predictions, and rightly so, even if in many cases this guardedness was purchased with the valuable instrument of denial. On the other hand, however, there is Rorty's own intellectual practice of ranging well outside of the familiar disciplinary matrices in order to critically engage his culture and its potentialities in generous terms. This tension is one of the longest-running divisions at the core of Rorty's relationship to philosophy—it persisted until his very last writings and it can be traced back as far as the early sixties to an unpublished essay entitled "The Philosopher as Expert."[8]

This early essay nicely frames some of the most persistent tensions in Rorty's metaphilosophy, and it is worth considering here even if Rorty never saw it through to publication. In this short piece, Rorty attempted to explain to himself how the academic philosophy establishment in which he was finding himself increasingly ensconced in the early 1960s might find a way of legitimating itself in the face of the rude questions that skeptics so often pose to established academics. This attempted explanation led him to two thoughts that are not easy to reconcile. On the one hand, Rorty admits in the essay that "professional philosophers do, by and large, talk only to each other," such that they invite the skeptical question about whether or not we could ever know if "the whole profession" is "on the fix." Rorty admits that there is no easy way of answering this skeptic. He entertains the possibility that perhaps it is for the best that only philosophers are entitled to pass judgments on philosophy. If this breeds disciplinary insularity, then so be it. Rorty concludes not only that "professional philosophers in America are doing, by and large, about what they should be" but also that "they receive about the right amount of attention," which is, of course, very little. This seems to be an admission that philosophy ought to model itself on other specialized disciplines such as science or art. If this means that philosophy might, like science, descend into arcane technicalities that only scientists understand, then so be it. Or if this means that philosophy might, like art, retreat into private enclaves increasingly separated from the most pressing problems of the day, then so be it. In short, we find in this essay an early statement of a view that Rorty would later become quite well known for: the view that philosophy is best understood as a private pursuit with its own processes of self-certification and self-legitimation that need not concern themselves with the wider public good. However, there is another side to Rorty's metaphilosophy already evidenced in this early essay but never quite foregrounded enough in his subsequent metaphilosophical musings. On this other hand, Rorty explicitly claims in his early essay that the models of science and art are "equally misleading and unfruitful" for coming to grips with philosophy's prospects in the present. He suggests instead that "philosophy's product can only be *dialogue*," in anticipation of his later Gadamerian brief in *Philosophy and the Mirror of Nature* on behalf of philosophy as the conversation of culture. He even suggests that philosophy's only responsibility is to the "*continuance*" of its dialogue or conversation. Now even though this dialogue that is philosophy is self-legitimating, it is inevitably articulated in terms drawn from the culture in which it is suffused. In its mode of rigorous questioning, philosophy constantly finds itself dealing with cultural crises that arise in other disciplines, other practices—in short, other arenas of its culture. Rorty concludes the essay by asserting that "although philosophy is formally autonomous, it is not materially self-sufficient." This clever little formulation concisely captures the tension that would from that point on haunt Rorty's metaphilosophy. For according to this formulation, philosophy is both an isolated academic enclave and a practice of thought that must draw its nourishment from the cultural contexts that afford philosophy its initial invitations.

Rorty would never convincingly resolve this metaphilosophical tension. But this does not mean that there is not to be found in his work a distinctive contribution to contemporary thought that takes place in that wider space of cultural criticism that manages to encompass both the history of philosophy and metaphilosophy. Although Rorty is better known among philosophers for his downbeat portrayals of the profession, it is undeniable that his work also at times features a more upbeat tone of hopeful cultural criticism, for which he is perhaps better known among those more accustomed to other disciplines. It is my view that Rorty's thought is at its most quintessentially pragmatist wherever he breaks out of the narrower spaces he often occupied in order to stake out a position on a wider intellectual plane, where he lets himself play the role of the cultural philosopher. When occupying this space, Rorty saw what he did as less continuous with Ludwig Wittgenstein and Martin Heidegger and as more continuous with the work of thinkers like John Stuart Mill (the parts that most philosophers do not bother to read), Matthew Arnold, Thomas Carlyle and, more recently, Isaiah Berlin and Irving Howe. The best models of this sort of engaged public criticism for Rorty's money were always William James and John Dewey. Like James and Dewey before him, Rorty's work in this wider cultural-critical space is certainly involved in the history of philosophy and metaphilosophy, but it is also an attempt to offer up a more capacious vision of what our liberal democratic culture is up to around here just now. This aspect of Rorty's work is best exemplified in his later work, especially the latter chapters of *Contingency, Irony, and Solidarity*, in essays such as "Trotsky and the Wild Orchids" and "Postmodernist Bourgeois Liberalism," and in editorials and reviews for *The New York Times*, *The London Review of Books*, *The Nation*, and *Dissent*. This side of Rorty is best illustrated in his self-definition as a "moralist of knowledge" and a "cultural critic" (1995b, 225n11 and 1989, 81) and in the title he chose for his final volume of collected papers, *Philosophy as Cultural Politics*. Neil Gross, in his valuable sociological-historical portrait of Rorty, illuminatingly refers to Rorty's work as increasingly informed by a "self-concept" of "leftist American patriot" (2008, 320).[9] The important thing about being a leftist patriot, for Rorty, was a dedication to the American democratic experiment and the hopeful meliorism implied therein. This dedication was most fully expressed in Rorty's own contributions to the American project in the form of his cultural-critical coups. I will return below to the distinctively American context that has for more than a century now played host to the cultural-critical philosophy of the pragmatists.

So how does all this help us interpret Rorty? Most contemporary philosophers tend to read Rorty as little more than a brilliant historian of philosophy who also happens to offer up a provocative set of metaphilosophical challenges. According to this familiar reading, Rorty was busy hawking a pragmatism that never aspired to, in William James's pregnant phrase, "the most completely *impressive* way" (1907, 25) of practicing philosophy. Against the grain of this common misreading, I urge that we should read Rorty as having the characteristically pragmatist ambition to impressiveness. Seeing his work as primarily and increasingly an effort in cultural philosophy enables us to engage with him on that most important level. Seen through this lens, Rorty's criticisms of philosophy will no longer appear as metaphilosophical betrayals, because they will be recognized as thoughtful suggestions for what contemporary liberal democratic culture ought to try if it wants to become even more liberal and more democratic.

Today, there remain only a dwindling handful of public intellectuals among us hanging around a few increasingly remote corners of our increasingly remote academic establishments. The great age of the public intellectual has passed. Gone are the legion of scholars who aspire to adjacency and connectedness when they enter graduate programs—of this small lot remaining, only a few harbor these grandiose ambitions after they pass through the dangerous professionalizing trials of dissertation defense, academic publication, and the higher-education job market. What caused the great decline in our public thought? I cannot here venture an answer to this enormously difficult question. The story and its possible causes have been recited before by others who have broached these thorny topics in impressive detail.[10] I have nothing to add to existing accounts. I simply wish to invoke the important role played by public thought in bygone years so as to indicate the capaciousness of what was once uncontroversially accepted as a cultural-critical conception of pragmatism. That philosophers today might even conceive of denying that James and Dewey were in the first place public thinkers and only in the second place professional academics is but a mark of the distance of today's academic pragmatism from yesteryear's engaged pragmatism. Pragmatism as I am presenting it developed as an impressive contribution to a wider tradition of public thought or cultural criticism in America. Indeed, the American variant of this tradition largely followed the examples first offered by Emerson, and then James, and then Dewey, though there were plenty of nonpragmatists, nonphilosophers, and nonacademics with whom all three were in competition. How quickly all that changed. The ideal of the American scholar rapidly shifted from the figure of the public intellectual to the model of the professional intellectual. Today, we Americans do not really have our Emersons, our Jameses, and our Deweys, nor do the English have their John Stuart Mills and their Bertrand Russells (at least not in their former abundance). It is thus that contemporary public intellectuals like Rorty are rightly disconcerted by the fact that "hopelessness has become fashionable on the Left—principled, theorized, philosophical hopelessness" (Rorty 1998b, 37).[11] Rorty traces this sudden shift to the ascendance of the new leftism during the sixties. I do not wish here to engage supposed answers to difficult questions about the causes of these changes. Without risking explanations, we can still affirm the obvious: today our public thought is far narrower both in scope and output than it was during the golden years of early pragmatism.

Rereading pragmatists such as Rorty, Dewey, James, and Emerson as public thinkers might perhaps help usher along a renewal of the once proud tradition of public thought. At the very least, such a rereading should enable us to understand the relevance of their pragmatism to our contemporary cultural problems as well as to the epistemic, ethical, and political problematics within which these problems can often be located. The result of pragmatism's transitionalist reconstruction of philosophy is a form of melioristic cultural criticism that gathers together most of the traditional philosophical concepts within the orbit of hopeful projects of reconstruction. In this sense, pragmatist transitionalist philosophy reworks knowledge, ethics, and politics such that the true, the good, and the just are together reconstructed as conceptualizing melioration. The point of truth and good and justice, the fact that they constitute valuable work performed, is to improve the realities in which we find ourselves in some definite way. Their point is not, as philosophers obsessed with certainty and ill disposed to hope have long argued, to gain an accurate picture of some reality that transcends our mere powers such that we might chain ourselves to that power and thereby gain our freedom—the old and untenable picture of freedom as obedience to the profound. Truth, good, and justice are our achievements—not some gift bestowed upon us by some reality or power that works on our behalf regardless of the work we do.

This proposed rereading of pragmatism under the guidance of the once prominent vision of philosophy as cultural criticism is enabled by emphasizing the centrality of meliorist transitionalism for all the great pragmatists. These two conceptions of philosophy—meliorist transitionalism and cultural criticism— are tuned to one another. The crucial upshot of both of these conceptions is that they enable us to see philosophy as a reconstructive response to our cultural, scientific, moral, and political predicaments. When approached as a distinctively philosophical project, this cultural-critical pragmatist meliorism is at once traditional and innovative. It is traditional insofar as it focuses attention on the deep problems forming obstacles to cultural growth. It is innovative insofar as it does not address these problems as universalistic issues but rather as pragmatic difficulties rooted in the experience of historically situated cultures. This exercise in conceptualizing new possibilities for philosophy helps us recognize the distinctive advantages of pragmatist philosophy and the persisting problems it must continue to address.

Despite my proposing a rereading of pragmatism as a project of philosophical cultural critique, the present book does not offer all that much in the way of the sort of philosophical cultural criticism I am cheering. I do not here engage the pressing epistemic, ethical, and political issues of our day: globalization, geneticization, Internetization, new social movements, the fragile balance of environmental and industrial technologies, and the other shifting sands of our political, ethical, and scientific landscapes. This is because my purpose here is of a different order. I aim to explicate both what a philosophical cultural criticism might look like when taken up through a pragmatist sensibility and what that pragmatist sensibility might look like when deployed for the purposes of a philosophical cultural criticism. The result is a conception of the practice of reconstruction. I take it as an important task to describe with rigor what the practice of reconstruction involves even if I take it as an even more important task to actually undertake the work of reconstruction itself. Accordingly, in this and the following two chapters, my aim is to locate this conception within the history of the tradition of pragmatism. In the middle chapters, I describe how pragmatism departs from traditional philosophical inquiries in epistemology, moral philosophy, and political theory by approaching our epistemic, ethical, and political practices as transitional in a way that calls for close cultural-critical reconstructions. And in the final chapter, I describe how pragmatism might integrate itself with other transitionalist philosophical traditions for the purposes of engaging in connected and adjacent critical inquiries that would clarify the contours of our cultural landscape. But throughout, I do not aim to explicate or orient any particular critical reconstructions of our contemporary cultural moment. That would be a rather different project(s) yielding a rather different book(s). The best I can do at present is to admit that some of the old tensions haunt me too. (But I can clue the reader in that I am at work on one such project concerning the quintessential liberal distinction between public and private with a focus on how certain contemporary practices, including some of those mentioned above, are rendering such a distinction increasingly fraught.)[12]

Adjacency and Connectedness in Cultural Criticism

So that my conception of philosophical cultural critique might not appear as provincially pragmatist, I now briefly turn to two other contemporary thinkers in whom I discern similar visions of the work of thought as a project of cultural melioration. This helps me provide a broader cultural-critical platform on which to base my interpretation of pragmatism. The reason for increasing the breadth of my conception is that it helps emphasize the rich harvest yielded by bringing pragmatism into conversation with other traditions of thought. This is a central aim in later chapters, where I intend to show how a transitionalist interpretation of pragmatism enables us to develop connections to the work of some of the centermost figures in late twentieth-century Analytic and Continental philosophy. And insofar as the public thought of cultural criticisms is now on the wane, it must be admitted that the handful of thinkers in whom I detect an engaged cultural criticism are an embattled minority. This is all the more reason for airing their distinctive voices.

I begin by situating my construction of meliorist cultural criticism by reference to a conception that some may regard as located on rather surprising terrain. The hope is that surprise will lead to provocation and then provocation to experimentation. Experimentation, in any event, is how I found myself situated in this terrain. I was led to it by experimenting with a conjunction: I was engaged simultaneously in the work of reflection on the thought of the pragmatist

philosophers and in the work of collaborating with a small group of genealogical anthropologists. These anthropologists were themselves engaged in reflection on the thought of the pragmatists, and that is more or less how I became
engaged with them. This led to our occupying positions in our research that can
be described as adjacent to one another. We were not quite inside of one another's intellectual cocoons, but we were clearly adjacent to one another's intellectual instrumentalities. This adjacency resulted in the familiar experiences of
surprise, provocation, and experimentation. All of these experiences have left
an inerasable impression that the work of thought is an enormous challenge.

This little introductory narrative illustrates the concept of adjacency. It is
in relation to this concept that I want to situate meliorism as the form of pragmatist cultural criticism. I borrow this concept from one of the anthropologists at the center of my little narrative. Paul Rabinow is an anthropologist
whose work and thought are firmly planted in both traditions of pragmatism
and genealogy. He has over the past decade been focused on the elaboration of
an ethos of the contemporary that I find remarkably valuable for situating
meliorism: "The ethos of the contemporary contrasts with that of the modern;
it is not fascinated with the new per se but concerned with the emergence and
articulation of forms within which old and new elements take on meanings
and functions" (Rabinow 2008, 24). This is the transitional space at the confluence of old and new also occupied by pragmatism.

A crucial concept for Rabinow's work on the contemporary is that of adjacency. Adjacency, for Rabinow, is "a distinctive double reversal, a kind of ethical and epistemological conundrum in which and through which many of us
find ourselves perpetually seeking our way—and giving form to our selves and
to our work" (2008, 34). I follow Rabinow in understanding adjacency as sig-
naling an ever shifting space that our critical inquiries might inhabit. It is a
space whose time is emergence, and so a space where old and new confront.
Adjacency is a process of provocation, and it provokes by holding to the characteristically pragmatist position of being in between. Being in between means
being in transition. How might we describe this philosophical, historical, and
anthropological adjacency? Rabinow's answer: "Neither the overdrive of the
universal intellectual nor the authoritative precision of the specific. Rather: a
space of problems. Of questions. Of being behind or ahead. Belated or anticipatory. Out of synch. Too fast or too slow. Reluctant. Audacious. Annoying"
(2008, 39). I think of adjacency as somewhere between universal and specific

but also as somewhere between outside and inside or external and internal. This location is one from which thought can be offered up as experimental. The adjacent critic gains distance from their object of criticism—but not too much distance. Theirs is the distance of William James's "margin" or "fringe." The adjacent critic lives on edges.

Here is, for my purposes at least, the most useful of Rabinow's descriptions of his concept of adjacency: "[Anthropological inquiry's] goal is identifying, understanding, and formulating something actual neither by directly identifying with it nor by making it exotic. Rather, it seeks to articulate a mode of adjacency" (2008, 49). One way of thinking about adjacency is in terms of a metaphorical image of the relation between the critic and the cultural object of their criticism. Imagine the critic's culture as occupying the space of a room. Then picture this critic as neither inside the room, though they came from the room, nor outside the room, though they are heading there. Picture the critic in those fleeting moments during which they are passing through the threshold from one room to whatever lies beyond. This critic occupies a vague space of adjacency, both physically on the edge of the room and temporally on the edge where the culture might transition from the past that is their little room to some better future outside that little room. The adjacent critic is a figure who stands on thresholds as liminal. They open the door through which the light of some possible future begins to suffuse the present. This light is not the truth of the best possible future. It is the light of some better future that is actually visible for those within the room. The work of the adjacent critic is thus that of provoking those within the room to find their way into some better room that is connected to the room they already inhabit. The adjacent critic opens doors that lead between all those little boxes we love to inhabit. Adjacency is like pragmatism in that it provides inviting corridors that enable movement, interaction, and engagement.

The critic occupying the space of adjacency is in between the rooms of the past and the rooms of the future. Their aim could be to assist the difficult political work of getting from here to there. Rabinow refers to adjacency as "a mode of virtual untimeliness" (2008, 49). I am not sure how to take this remark, because I find this form of untimeliness particularly timely. But so, apparently, does Rabinow: "if one is committed to untimely anthropological work then being a bit late may well be timely; and being ahead of things, or slightly beside the point, is worth our while" (2008, 50).[13] As I understand and use it, then, adjacency is a temporal location occupied by the transitional critic. This temporality enables a certain form of critique, inquiry, and reconceptualization that pragmatists might find valuable. Adjacency is thus a mode of critique that enables what Dewey calls reconstruction or what Rabinow, following Dewey, here calls remediation. Adjacency is that untimeliness in which cultural critique, understood as a meliorist project, is best situated.

I can further situate my conception of an engaged pragmatism with a model of critical inquiry that bears some resemblance to the practice of adjacency just considered. I take the notion of criticism as connectedness from Michael Walzer as explicated in his history of what he calls connected criticism. As Walzer explains it, the connected critic is someone who is not quite apart from the social practices they criticize and yet also not quite wholly inside of them either. Walzer says of his critic that "he never quite stands free and freely chooses his commitments, but struggles instead to sort out the commitments he already has" (1998, 226). The critic is not best thought of as impartial or neutral. The critic, rather, is already situated, which is to say that their criticism is adjacent. It is both internal to practices in which the critic finds himself or herself and at the same time external to those very same practices in achieving the distance needed for sorting them out. Connectedness is not identification and adjacency is not internality. But connectedness is not wholly apart nor is adjacency wholly external. Their mode is that of being between, both conceptually and temporally.

Walzer stresses that the connected critic is an oppositional figure but one that does not descend to the bad faith of absolute opposition: "He is in opposition here, and here, and here; he is never in absolute opposition." This is because criticism can only be effective if it stands with some particular set of people and against some other particular set of people who are acting unjustly toward them. The opposition of connected criticism is, in short, a connected or adjacent opposition: "For criticism will never shake the world unless it is directed against specific features of the world that other people besides the critic recognize as wrongful, oppressive, brutal, or unjust" (1998, 237). The critic is thus situated between not only conceptually and temporally, but they are also between different groups or forces or factions. They are connected both to the group to which they are committed but also to the group to which they are opposed. Their oppositions and their commitments, in short, must matter to someone and must maintain connection to the groups to which it is directed.

Particularly notable for my purposes here is the connection Walzer draws between the connected critic and the attitude of hope, referring at one point to "critical occasions" as "occasions for hope." As first elaborated by the pragmatists, meliorism was simply another name for the philosophy of hope, that is, for the philosophy of human effort and energy in the here and now directed toward the improvement of our political and ethical realities. Walzer similarly states this "one common mark of the critical enterprise" in terms of the historicist implications of ameliorative criticism: "[Criticism] is founded in hope; it cannot be carried on without some sense of historical possibility" (1998, 239, 17). Connected criticism, in other words, is criticism with a historicist sensibility. The connected critics attach, or connect, themselves to actual political conditions by locating their criticism along the precise historical trajectories that define these conditions. They do not stand against historical reality in the name of some ahistorical ideal. They stand against some specific historical reality in the name of some specifiably better, and actually possible, historical reality. Melioristic connected criticism occupies historical time and as such assumes a temporal form. It reaches out of the present both backward into the past and forward into the future. In this way, it manages to be both connected to the present yet also adjacent to it, so as to gain that fine edge of critical distance.

Centers and Margins of Pragmatist Cultural Criticism

I have been urging that we regain a focus on pragmatism as a practice of philosophy that is adjacent and connected to the cultural present in which it finds itself. I now want to consider how this way of bringing pragmatism into focus might help me respond to lingering questions raised by my selection of Emerson, James, Dewey, and Rorty as exemplars of transitionalist pragmatism. These questions concern certain rather prominent exceptions from my selection of exemplary pragmatists. Among these prominent exceptions we must include a small handful of important classicopragmatists, including Jane Addams, Randolph Bourne, Walter Lippmann, W. E. B. Du Bois, Alain Locke, and George Herbert Mead, as well as a small number of important neopragmatists, including Cornel West and Robert Brandom. I have no intention of denying that all of these thinkers are relevant to the wider project I am here announcing, and I happily bestow the title of pragmatist on each of them. Yet despite

their undeniable importance for the vitality of pragmatism, all of these thinkers remain more marginal to my particular conception of pragmatism than do
the four pragmatists I reckon as central. My four pragmatists offer a unique,
because difficult to achieve, combination of cultural critique and theoretical
reflection on the status of philosophy as cultural critique. Other pragmatists
have forged similar combinations at times, but none have done so with quite
the depth and breadth exhibited by my four pragmatists. Other pragmatists
thus remain more marginal for me in that their work does not often attain
both pitches of cultural-critical engagement and philosophical rigor, which I
am arguing constitutes the central strength of the tradition.

Similar reasoning motivates my explicit marginalization of the figure who
is surely the most glaring exception from my mantle of canonical pragmatists.
Charles Santiago Peirce assumes on my accounting a far more marginal status
in pragmatism than is counseled by prevailing wisdom. This is justified by my
conceptualization of transitionalist pragmatism as a philosophical project of
cultural critique. But many will no doubt contest this marginalization and its
supporting conceptualization, so allow me to explain.

Peirce was simply not invested in the philosophical project of cultural critique to anywhere near the degree evident in the work and writings of Emerson, James, Dewey, and Rorty. If Peirce addressed himself at all to issues of his
day, then he did so only obliquely, in contributing to the raging debates over
the increasing prominence of scientific worldviews in the midst of the still
religious culture of late nineteenth-century New England.[14] But even here
Peirce did not address these debates as a cultural problem so much as a tangled philosophical perplexity. So it is that Peirce almost nowhere directly engaged what Cheryl Misak (2004c) calls, riffing on a quip James made to Peirce
in a letter, "vital matters." Misak's discussion is meant to help motivate the
project of using Peircean insights for the purposes of moral and political philosophy. It strikes me as quite an odd move to try to construct a moral and
political theory on the basis of the epistemological writings of a philosopher
who never seriously devoted himself to moral or political melioration (I return to this issue in Misak in chapter 6). Such a move seems even odder in
light of the superabundance of philosophical resources provided by other
thinkers who have engaged these topics. Peirceans are entitled to make of his
work what they will, of course, but we are entitled to point out that they are
the ones making the moral and political theories, not Peirce, because he never

attempted such a thing. But what troubles me much more than minor manners of pedigree is that even where scholars have extended Peirce's thought
along these rails, they have often done so very much as Peirce himself might
have. The result is too often a treatment of vital matters not as pressing cultural problems but rather as abstracted instances of philosophical systems.
Surely such work is worthwhile, but it too often and too easily turns matters
brilliantly vital into dim and lifeless statues. Such work is not, in short, in
keeping with a conception of pragmatism as a project of engaged cultural
criticism. I suspect that most Peirceans would in fact agree with me in this
assessment, for their work is generally more classically philosophical in comparison to the engaged cultural criticism offered by Emerson, James, Dewey,
and Rorty.

To get a sense of the relatively ill fit of Peirce's thought for vital matters, we
need only gain a glimpse of the systematic impulse that ever pervaded his
thought. No one has ever faulted Peirce for not being an ambitious thinker.
But too often Peirce's ambitions were too precisely ordered to enable him to
engage with vital matters as topics in their own right rather than as exemplary
instances of a complex system. In some of his earliest writings, we can indeed
discern a Peirce whose ambitions are less systematic, more modest, and thus
much more inviting, at least to a pragmatist such as myself. But even in these
writings Peirce neglected to turn his thought toward the pressing issues of his
day. Cultural melioration was simply not on Peirce's agenda. And if early
Peirce freely chose not to engage in cultural criticism, then later Peirce practically forbade himself from descending to the tangled roots of reality. As time
pressed on, Peirce became more resolutely immodest as he spun out one of the
most fascinating intellectual cocoons a philosopher has ever attempted. Here
is a sampling of vintage Peirce at the height of his systematic ambition:

> What I would recommend is that every person who wishes to form an opin-
> ion concerning fundamental problems, should first of all make a complete
> survey of human knowledge, should take note of all the valuable ideas in
> each branch of science, should observe in just what respect each has been
> successful and where it has failed, in order that in the light of the thorough
> acquaintance so attained of the available materials for a philosophical the-
> ory and of the nature and strength of each, he may proceed to the study of
> what the problem of philosophy consists in, and of the proper way of solving
> it (1891, 286).

In this recommendation is concealed the dangerous bravado of a philosopher all puffed up and raring to go. Needless to say, I favor the early and more modest Peirce. The later Peirce is just too breathtakingly big. But in both periods Peirce never saw fit to engage the realities in which his thought was suffused and so he never directly contributed to the melioration of the cultural vistas informing his invention of pragmatism.

To bring some of these differences into focus, consider Peirce on truth, since this is the topic I used above to discuss the melioristic contribution of my four pragmatist exemplars. In contrast to Emerson, James, Dewey, and Rorty, it is undeniable that Peirce was more preoccupied with a philosophical conception of truth than he was with a cultural critique of the role that truth plays in our lives. To be sure, Peirce did often theorize truth in terms of a progressive inquiry that seems to fit well with pragmatist meliorism. Even so, Peirce's conception was ultimately reliant upon extrahuman powers that pull inquiry toward its end. This is clear where Peirce describes truth as something "determined by nothing human, but by some external permanency" (1877, 120). Contemporary Peirceans have generously emphasized this theme in calling truth "something stable and independent of what this or that person or community might think" (Misak 2004a, 15).[15] The problem with this view is that it employs a theory of truth that eviscerates philosophy of its meliorating impulse. A most telling instance of this is found in a June 12, 1902, letter from Peirce to James: "No doubt truth has to have defenders to uphold it. But truth creates its defenders and gives them strength" (in Perry 1935, 286). This passage measures that long distance between Peirce's view on truth and those of the other pragmatists I have here considered. Peirce finds in truth stability, externality, independence, and a source of possible salvation. Emerson, James, Dewey, and Rorty, by contrast, all urged that we look to our selves for our salving and said that truth might be but one of the names for our self-saving.

Peirce once wrote that "if philosophy is to be made a science, the very first price we must pay for it must be to abandon all endeavor to make it literary" (1905b, 360). This is true enough, but more important is that it raises the question of whether or not philosophy should strive after a self-image as a nonliterary scientific endeavor or if it might instead cede its claims to being a full-blown science in order to achieve a more general relevance to its culture. This question is not easily settled, but it is easy enough to see how we could classify the pragmatists in its terms. Peirce's systematic and rigorous conception of philosophy left little room for countenancing those exercises of thought required to give philosophy vitality and currency in its culture. My four pragmatists craved at every turn that literary literacy requisite for turning severe thought into a philosophy of culture.

I suspect that most Peirceans will agree with my not counting him as a canonical pragmatist given my definition of pragmatism as primarily a project of cultural criticism. I also suspect that most Peirceans will then reply that pragmatism is hardly best stipulated in the terms that I would have. Those who admire Peirce often do so because they admire the classical philosophical ambitions of his pragmatism more than the seemingly base ambitions of a cultural-critical pragmatism. It is not clear how we might resolve this impasse between two prominent ways of conceiving the work of philosophy through pragmatism. On both views, in any event, the debate can only be resolved in the forthcoming hereafter, because our conceptions of pragmatism, like all our other conceptions, will only pay out down the road. But allow me to at least sharpen the swords. I can do so by making use of a contrast between Peirce and Dewey offered by Joseph Margolis, who specifies the contrast between these two classicopragmatists as follows: "the Deweyan version is no more than an unguarded doctrine of *hope* regarding progressivism; the Peircean version is a *metaphysics* of inquiry" (1998, 539). If we accept the terms of this contrast, and I think we should, then the pressing issue becomes a matter of which pragmatism is the best pragmatism, which pragmatism we should take up in our philosophical work, and which pragmatism will yield the most copious, sane, gigantic offspring. On one side we have a hopeful cultural criticism and on the other a robust philosophical metaphysics. I am urging that we ought to prefer the former conception to the latter. This does not require that we dispense with all the robustness and rigor usually attendant in philosophy. Nor does it require that we evacuate philosophy of metaphysics. But it does require that our metaphysics, just like our epistemology, moral philosophy, and political theory, yield priority of place to our cultural-critical engagements. Metaphysics et al. ought to accept a more humble role as just one more way of ameliorating the pressing problems we find ourselves facing.[16]

At the center of the meliorist mood and transitionalist perspective is a view of every human accomplishment—from our epistemic accomplishments we refer to as "truths" to our moral accomplishments of "goods" and "rights" to our political accomplishments of "justice"—as an achievement that develops in a field of practice whose form is temporal and whose contents are historical. Meliorism develops within this broader transitionalist perspective in a way that explicates the orientation toward practical success characteristic of pragmatist perspectives on knowledge, ethics, and politics. Transitionalism captures the philosophical orientation toward temporality and historicity at the heart of this perspective. Meliorism captures the cultural-critical mood of hope that enables us to better navigate these transitions.

America as a Context for Cultural Critique

To conclude my discussion of melioristic cultural criticism as a model of transitionalist pragmatism, I would like to offer a few thoughts about that experimental culture which forms the context for American pragmatism, what makes that context distinctive, and why pragmatism is particularly suited to it. This requires making explicit the interconnections between the projects of pragmatism and the projects of democracy as they have together evolved in America. These interconnections reveal an inborn American commitment to meliorism, a commitment that America is once again learning to take seriously, braced as many of us are by a prominent proclamation of that American creed: "Yes we can."

Another pragmatist cultural critic, Cornel West, puts the point I aim to make this way:

> The evasion of epistemology-centered philosophy—from Emerson to Rorty—results in a conception of philosophy as a form of cultural criticism in which the meaning of America is put forward by intellectuals in response to distinct social and cultural crises. In this sense, American pragmatism is . . . a continuous cultural commentary or set of interpretations that attempt to explain America to itself at a particular historical moment (1989, 5).

Contemporary pragmatists like West have rightly argued that pragmatism in the melioristic cultural-critical sense in which I am putting it forward here can be usefully understood as a distinctively American project. I agree with this view, though it needs careful qualification. What is right about the view is that pragmatist meliorism is organic with the distinctive American context within which pragmatism originated and continues to find its most inspired contributors. Following the precedent set by Henry Steele Commager's (1950, 97) declaration that pragmatism is "almost the official philosophy of America," David Hollinger (1980, 43) describes pragmatism as an "emblem for America," John McDermott (1965, 42) writes of a "philosophical revolution that is structured by the development of American culture," H. O. Mounce (1997, 1) claims that "pragmatism is the distinctively American philosophy," and Richard Bernstein (1992b, 834) stresses the "rootedness of the pragmatic tradition in American culture." Robert Westbrook usefully summarizes the common thread running through all of these philosophers and historians of pragmatism: "What most distinguishes the American hope of the pragmatists from that of others—and makes it so intriguing—is that it is hope without transcendent foundations. It is underwritten by neither God, nor nature, nor providential history. It is, like pragmatic truth, wholly a human artifact" (2005, 139).

All of these commentators can be seen as suggesting that pragmatism is American insofar as America itself anticipates pragmatism in emblematizing hope. It is thus far from idiosyncratic for contemporary pragmatists such as Rorty to write of James and Dewey as "Americanizing philosophy" by "replacing certainty with hope" (1994a, 32). For Rorty, "both pragmatism and America are expressions of a hopeful, melioristic, experimental frame of mind" (1994a, 24). In calling attention to America as the best context for pragmatism, thinkers such as Rorty and West strive to articulate a complex relation to their America as well as to their pragmatism. Their critics, unfortunately, have all too often mistaken this articulation for a myopic nationalism when it is in fact better seen as a potentially global democratic optic. We ought to note carefully that Rorty's and West's melioristic tone betray nothing incompatible with a plurality of modes of democratic self-governance taking place outside of the American orbit. West's view is that "the deep democratic tradition did not begin in America and we have no monopoly on its promise. But it is here where the seeds of democracy have taken deepest root and sprouted most robustly" (2004, 68). It is neither contradictory nor confused both to affirm the value of a multiplicity of democratic projects and to devote oneself carefully to the democratic history in which one finds oneself flowing. In the case of Rorty and West, their history is the democracy of the American experiment. If this American experiment is so congenial to the pragmatist experiment, then it is because, as Westbrook notes, America is like pragmatism in its emphasis on a melioristic hope whose only home is its history.

Contemporary intellectuals, who by and large are more comfortable with national self-shame or national self-promotion than they are with national self-respect, can learn from Rorty's and West's example of drawing generously on our native democratic energies. This is in part because Rorty and West stand in a tradition of courageous public thinkers who have sought to retrieve from America's past the requisite resources for America's future. We all know the familiar litany of great names. Allow me to consider just one, James Baldwin, who has offered a particular inspiration to meliorist pragmatists in recent years. Rorty borrowed the title for his American meditations in *Achieving Our Country* from one of the last lines of Baldwin's *The Fire Next Time*, West has described Baldwin as "the most fully Emersonian of democratic intellectuals in our history" (2004, 78), and other pragmatists have eagerly taken up Baldwin in their work.[17] Baldwin's importance for pragmatism is his steady knowledge that the American project in his day demanded neither scorn nor celebration but a careful and considered transformation. Baldwin's cultural critique thus forms part of the roots of that transitionalist engagement with America so boldly celebrated by West and Rorty. This engagement is indeed bold, because for a very long time now it has been the fashion to opt for either a cheap self-congratulatory nationalism or an easy self-hating anti-Americanism. Confidence in America is dear today. It is only with well-chosen hopes that we shall build a better America, not a holy America nor an evil America, but simply a better form of our striking experiment in self-governance. Baldwin reminds us in *The Fire Next Time* that "freedom is hard to bear" in part because it requires a project of historical transformation that Baldwin calls "change in the sense of renewal." Baldwin's transformative criticism aims to re-new the past in the present: "To accept one's past—one's history—is not the same thing as drowning in it; it is learning how to use it." Baldwin's strength is that he recognizes in the past of his peoples a remarkable and necessary resource for the future of America: "this past . . . yet contains, for all its horror, something very beautiful." Captured here is the characteristic melioristic attitude toward America so needful again today. Baldwin's short book excellently exemplifies a strain of reflective engagement that neither denies the sins of our democracy nor feels the need to denigrate that democracy itself. Baldwin ends his book by noting that it falls only on us to make of ourselves what we will: "And here we are, at the center of the arc, trapped in the gaudiest, most valuable, and most improbable water wheel the world has ever seen. Everything now, we must assume, is in our hands; and we have no right to assume otherwise" (1963, 120, 124, 111, 132, 141). What we may yet make of ourselves can be carried only by a careful hope informed by a considered history.

When we pragmatists locate our work as a contribution to the ongoing American experiment in democracy, we situate ourselves neither provincially nor geographically but rather historically and temporally. Our America is not primarily a place so much as it a hope, a project, a generous past and a fragile future. It may have been Emerson (1844, 320) who first celebrated America as just such a never fully present process—"I am ready to die out of nature and be born again into this new yet unapproachable America." An essentially transitionalist concept, prospective in its being yet retrospective in its strengths, America is a challenge we can meet only with the confidence inspired by hope. Hope credits the effort required for self-creative and self-governing energies. Our America exists on margins of itself—pressing always for increase—ever spilling beyond the edges of its former selves. Hope, like Walt Whitman's America, always looks out from itself to some beyond: "Nor is that hope unwarranted. Today, ahead, though dimly yet, we see, in vistas, a copious, sane, gigantic offspring. For our New World I consider far less important for what it has done, or what it is, than for results to come" (Whitman 1867, 488).

Far from claiming pragmatism as a provincial philosophy, my approach is to seek in pragmatism's meliorism a unique and insightful tradition of cosmopolitan philosophy. Such a project is viable just insofar as America has itself always been an experiment in democratic pluralism, that is, an experiment in bringing together once disparate cultural strands so that they may mutually improve one another. My placement of pragmatism in the American grain should not be mistaken for a provincial self-congratulating nationalism. America is but a conceptual shadow haunting extant political geographies. The pragmatist idea of democracy encourages a renewal of American hope and in doing so counters prevailing tendencies in our United States. Pragmatism's prioritization of hopefulness thus offers a much needed philosophical response to the unique challenges presented by the increasing malversation of American hope in our United States.

Two

TRANSITIONALISM IN THE PRAGMATIST TRADITION

An Intellectual History of Pragmatism

By playing up the emphasis on transitionalism and meliorism found in various pragmatisms, I aim to focus on what is best throughout the tradition: a commitment to understanding how we humans can ameliorate our lot by drawing on and improving resources already found within that lot. Focusing on pragmatism in this way, I want to argue that transitionalism is the key philosophical perspective elaborated not only by my four pragmatists but by every other leading pragmatist as well. Motivating this thought will require a lengthy tour through the intellectual history of pragmatism. In this chapter, I explicate the transitionalist themes featured in all these previous pragmatisms. In the next chapter, I show that despite the clear presence of these themes all previous statements of pragmatism have proposed some other idea as the unifying thread of the tradition. Taken together, these chapters offer an intellectual-historical motivation to play up transitionalism and play down other themes more prominent in the thinking of previous pragmatists. I aim to neither rehearse pragmatism nor to break away from it. In reenvisioning pragmatism through this intellectual historical lens, I can present a variation on a repetition, or a repetition with a difference. This chapter shows how my approach is quite in keeping with the previous pragmatisms that I here repeat with a difference. In the following chapter, I then explicate the differences with which I inflect this repetition.

I begin this chapter by featuring transitionalism as it was inaugurated by Ralph Waldo Emerson, moving forward quickly and at greater length to its availability in William James, John Dewey, and certain of their contemporaries, including Charles Santiago Peirce, George Herbert Mead, and Jane Addams. I then read transitionalism forward along two lines: first by way of Wilfrid Sellars and Willard Van Orman Quine to Richard Rorty, Robert Brandom, Hilary Putnam, Cornel West, and others; second by way of John Herman Randall and John McDermott to Joseph Margolis, Larry Hickman, John Stuhr, and others.

Throughout this chapter, my expositions will be on the rather atmospheric side, which is to say that they are not offered as rigorously argumentative. This is a matter of intention. I do not aim to demonstrate that all previous pragmatists were transitionalist through and through. That would be contrary to my point. I aim to show that we can detect tones of transitionality struck throughout their writings. It will be the job of later chapters to rigorously rework these tones into a more harmonic sequence. Here I merely wish to seed the idea that transitionality is indeed worth taking seriously as a genuinely pragmatist perspective. The best way of doing this is to shower the reader with quotations.

Transitionalism in Classical Pragmatisms

In searching for transitionalist themes in classicopragmatism, we are met with an incredibly rich harvest in the writings of William James and John Dewey. They inherited these themes from Ralph Waldo Emerson, though they did much to transform their intellectual inheritance. As for Emerson, his thought could perhaps be decently summarized as a philosophy of transitions, though we should also remember that Emerson does not easily admit of summary. In envisioning pragmatism as transitionalism, I have returned often to a quintessential Emersonian statement of transitionalism, which I find crucial: "Old and new make the warp and woof of every moment. There is not a thread that is not a twist of these two strands" (1868, 1028). This thought abides throughout much of Emerson. In "Art," he explicated a transitionalism in these terms: "Because the soul is progressive, it never quite repeats itself, but in every act attempts the production of a new and fairer whole" (1844, 274). And in "Circles," an energetic transitionalism is concisely captured in this line: "Nothing is secure but life, transition, the energizing spirit" (1841, 261). Here was a thought which James and Dewey could, in good Emersonian fashion, pick up and run with in order to really get somewhere.

Although a philosophy of transitions is by no means the most explicit controlling idea to be found in the works of James and Dewey, I nevertheless believe that a philosophical focus on transitionality is almost everywhere evident in their work. So although James and Dewey never explicitly articulated their pragmatism in transitionalist terms, they could hardly fail to inflect nearly every aspect of their philosophy with notions of temporality and historicity. It turns out that even though James and Dewey did not always explicitly describe their own thought in terms of the transitionality I ascribe to it, this notion nevertheless offers a valuable vantage from which to understand the most central aspects of their thought. I would like to offer a perspective on the great variety of contexts in which transitionalism appears in the work of James and Dewey.

In *Some Problems of Philosophy*, the book he was writing at the time of his death, James returned one last time to what he had called in *Pragmatism* "the most central of all philosophic problems, central because so pregnant" (1907, 64), namely the debate over monism and pluralism. James concluded in his unfinished final book that the views separating these two great philosophical traditions could be telescoped down into the issue of novelty. He wrote that "towards this issue, of the reality or unreality of the novelty that appears, the pragmatic difference between monism and pluralism seems to converge" (1911, 74–75). Pragmatism, it turns out, takes novelty as its central philosophic problem. This means that pragmatism takes change, or transition, as its central philosophic problem.

The central place of transitionality in James's pragmatism can be seen acutely in his discussions of experience, surely one of the central concepts in his philosophy. For James, experience is not a thing; it is an event or a process. Experience is in transition; it is a stream "made of an alternation of flights and perchings" (1890, I.243), in James's phrasing. This suggests that the present, for James, is not a presence.[1] It carries along no substantial identity within itself insofar as it is wholly constituted by relations between past and future. But for me, James's best evocation of the transitionality internal to the human condition is offered in a memorable passage written in the signature style of American philosophy's greatest poet:

> Life is in the transitions as much as in the terms connected; often, indeed, it seems to be there more emphatically, as if our spurts and sallies forward were the real firing-line of the battle, were like the thin line of flame advancing across the dry autumnal field which the farmer proceeds to burn. In this line we live prospectively as well as retrospectively. It is "of" the past, inasmuch as it comes expressly as the past's continuation; it is "of" the future in so far as the future, when it comes, will have continued it (James 1904b, 212–213).

We are, James is here suggesting, constantly unstilled, ever in motion, always streaming. This was a recurring theme of James's career, and it found its earliest and clearest expression in his famous chapter on "The Stream of Thought" in *The Principles of Psychology*. The key idea of James's metaphor of the stream of thought was that of consciousness's continuous change. Consciousness ever assumes two notable characteristics: it is in constant change and it is continuous (1890, I.229ff., I.237ff.). Thought, like a stream, "flows." This means that the present does not constitute a presence so much as a focal point for experience's constant retrospective and prospective dartings:

> The knowledge of some other part of the stream, past or future, near or remote, is always mixed in with our knowledge of the present thing. . . . These lingerings of old objects, these incomings of new, are the germs of memory and expectation, the retrospective and the prospective sense of time. They give that continuity to consciousness without which it could not be called a stream (1890, I.606).

Once one starts looking for this transitionalism elsewhere in James's writings, it begins to appear everywhere, almost as a kind of unstated master theme of his work. It appears in the subtitle of his book *Pragmatism* and in the account of truth set forth in its pages: Truth "marries old opinion to new fact so as ever to show a minimum of jolt, a maximum of continuity" (1907, 35). It later turns out to be a key element of his radical empiricism as explicated in the preface to *The Meaning of Truth*: "the parts of experience hold together from next to next by relations that are themselves parts of experience" (1909a, 7). In sketching a metaphysics in *A Pluralistic Universe*, James wrote of a "distributed and strung-along and flowing sort of reality which finite beings swim in . . . and by reality here I mean reality where things *happen*, all temporal reality without exception" (1909b, 558). In speaking on some of life's ideals in his *Talks to Students*, James noted that "there must be *novelty* in an ideal" (1899b, 656), which he explains in terms of evolving our moral universe from older into newer forms. A particularly insightful example of James's transitionalism occurs in his "The Moral Equivalent of War" (1910), where he argues that we ought to move from an older moral ideal of violent militarism toward a newer moral ideal of peaceful militarism. This can be contrasted to less historically attuned calls for replacing violence with peace. Such demands offer little in the way of concrete strategies, as they present no third term that performs the temporal integration of the other two terms. In moving from violence to peace, where do we find the connection between the two that actually enables us to get from here to there? James's alternative is valuable precisely because it offers a way of actually transitioning from violence to peace by way of reforming the mediating impulse of militarism. James does not simply tell us where we should end up, but rather he shows us how to get from here to there—this is clearly the more pragmatic approach.

Transitionalism was also central for Dewey's thinking. In an essay entitled "Philosophy and Civilization," Dewey stated his transitionalism in terms that renew Emerson's phrasing of a confluence of old and new: "The life of all thought is to effect a junction at some point of the new and the old, of deep-sunk customs and unconscious dispositions, brought to the light of attention by some conflict with newly emerging directions of activity" (1928, 7/LW3.7). Indeed, of life itself Dewey wrote that it is "a thing of histories, each with its own plot, its own inception and movement towards its close" (1934, LW10.42). This transitionalism can be found throughout Dewey's writings, most notably in his ethics, his epistemology, and his logic.

In his *Ethics*, Dewey wrote that "at each point there is a distinction between an old, an accomplished self, and a new and moving self, between the static and the dynamic self" (1932, LW7.306). Dewey located morality as a process that consists in moving from a past problem to a future resolution. This approach to ethics was perhaps most fully worked out by Dewey in relation to his conception of democracy as a way of life.[2] That conception attempted to foreground, above all, the sense that democracy is a politics that begins and ends with persons who are neither substances nor static founts of rationality but are rather themselves "a history, a career" (1940, LW14.102). In his work on knowledge, Dewey evinced the same focus on process, transition, growth, and development as we find in his work on morality. In *The Quest for Certainty*, Dewey wrote that "the object of knowledge is eventual." By this he meant that "'real' things may be as transitory as you please or as lasting in time as you please; these are specific differences like that between a flash of lightning and the history of a mountain range. In any case they are for knowledge 'events' not substances" (1929, LW4.136, LW4.103). Dewey's view was that knowing is an event that takes place between an organism and an environment rather than a static quality of either mind or reality or their correspondence. Elsewhere, he wrote that "knowledge appears as a function within experience" such that "its work and aim must be distinctively reconstructive and transformatory" (1903a, MW2.296). The point of knowledge is not to copy unmoving facts but to change rushing realities. And in his work on logic, Dewey poignantly insisted that "a philosophical discussion of the distinctions and relations which figure most largely in logical theories depends upon a proper placing of them in their temporal context" (1916b, 1/MW10.320). Thus thought itself is thoroughly historical insofar as it "comes between a temporally prior situation . . . and a later situation, which has been constituted out of the first situation by means of acting on the findings of reflective inquiry" (1916b, 18/ MW10.331). The very structure of logic, on Dewey's account, must be articulated in terms that match the transitional quality of our experience.

So it was that all inquiry (ethical, artistic, scientific) was for Dewey a transitional affair—a matter of moving an organism out of a problematic environment into a more stable situation. And so it was that all aspects of his thought bear out the central observation of *Reconstruction in Philosophy*: "change rather than fixity is now a measure of 'reality' or energy of being; change is omnipresent" (1920, 61/MW12.114).

These remarks culled from across the works of James and Dewey demonstrate that throughout their careers and in a variety of contexts, both thinkers gave temporal transition a leading role in their presentations of pragmatism. Having featured the richness of transitionalist themes in James and Dewey, I shall consider now other classical pragmatists who I take, for reasons explained in the previous chapter, as more marginal to the tradition. Considering these less central figures is certainly worthwhile insofar as it begins to open up a perspective on just how widely transitionalist themes run throughout pragmatism. For even at the margins of classicopragmatism we find the tone of transitionality at which I am aiming.

In the previous chapter, I mentioned the names of a small number of classicopragmatists who I claimed were important for the vitality of the tradition and yet not exemplary of my conception of pragmatism. Transitionalist themes appear in the work of all of them, including Randolph Bourne, Walter Lippmann, W. E. B. Du Bois, and Alain Locke. A particularly steady emphasis on history and time is especially pronounced in the work of two other classical pragmatists who deserve more attention than I can here lavish on them, namely Jane Addams and George Herbert Mead. Addams and Mead, though admittedly not as central to my pragmatism as James and Dewey, left a rich legacy of works and writings that earnestly exhibit transitionalist themes. As such, both Addams and Mead offer a distinct inflection of pragmatism that is well positioned to make important contributions to my proposal for a refocusing of pragmatism through a transitionalist lens.

Considering Addams, I offer just one small sample of the way in which she treated time and history as crucial for the work of pragmatist melioration: "Our conceptions of morality, as all our other ideas, pass through a course of development; the difficulty comes in adjusting our conduct, which has become hardened into customs and habits, to these changing moral conceptions" (1902, 13). Addams's influence on Dewey's pragmatism proceeded from both her written contributions to social philosophy and from the example offered by her work at Chicago's Hull-House settlement. It has not been noted often enough that Dewey himself recognized Addams's influence on his thinking. It has been even less noted that he recognized this influence in a distinctly transitionalist tone. In a foreword written for one of Addams's books, Dewey quotes as the key to her philosophy this line by Addams: "social advance depends as much upon the process through which it is secured as upon the result itself" (Addams 1922, 316; quoted in Dewey 1945, 195).

A similar transitionalism inflects the work of another thinker whose influence on Dewey should not be discounted, namely G. H. Mead. Issues of temporality and historicity appear throughout Mead's writings. An exhaustive survey is beyond my scope here, so once again a small sample will have to suffice: "I wish to make as emphatic as possible the reference of pasts and futures to the activity that is central to the present. . . . The presents, then, within which we live are provided with margins, and fitting them into a larger independent chronicle is again a matter of some more extended present which calls for a wider horizon" (1932, 88). It is easy to pass over pragmatist claims that we inhabit the present as a sort of truism. Yet such a claim is not at all trivial, for it serves to focus attention on the idea that our lives are shot through with a temporality whose point of reference is the flowing present in which we find ourselves.

Turning finally to the third figure in the usual triumvirate of classical pragmatists, these themes are no less noticeable in his work. I explained above why I do not include the name of Charles Santiago Peirce on my list of canonical transitionalist pragmatists. But despite his cultural-critical deficiencies, it is undeniable that the impressive cocoon that was Peirce's philosophical system provided no small amount of intellectual incubation for ideas that James and Dewey would later repackage into concepts that I find at the core of pragmatism. This is true not only of most of the familiar textbook themes long emphasized by commentators but also of the transitionalist themes that I am arguing should be seen as an index of that entire textbook. Peircean expressions of temporality, historicity, and evolutionism can be found in many aspects of his admittedly disorganized corpus of writings. Indeed, one rather general way of summarizing Peirce's lifelong philosophical project is to say that he was concerned to preserve the philosophical core of realism in such a way as to show how reality itself is capable of transformation. Another way of putting this point is to say that Peirce hoped to update scholastic realism so as to make it consistent with modern evolutionism. It is not clear that Peirce ever fully succeeded in this project, but he said a great many interesting things in trying. For my purposes here, it is certainly worth noting that transitionality and transitions played a central role in nearly every aspect of Peirce's work. His famous model of inquiry as the transition from a state of doubt to a state of belief, for example, simply would not make sense outside of the transitionalist framework of pragmatism. The same can be said of much else in Peirce, including his more abstract notion of thirdness as mediation, his synechistic cosmology, and his speculative hypotheses concerning the expansion of the universe in the form of evolutionary love. Perhaps historicity and temporality are most profound in Peirce in his semiotic conception of all purposive thought and action as temporally developing on the basis of historically sedimented prior such processes. Some of the most telling indications of transitionalism in Peirce's writings are to be found in his often cited *Cognitions Series*, published in the *Journal of Speculative Philosophy* in 1868. In these essays I find Peirce at his debunking best. The primary target of attack is Descartes, and Peirce ably fells the most prominent statement of the high-modern program. The resulting philosophy is a hearty transitionalism: "thought cannot happen in an instant, but requires a time" (1868a, 24). The strong affirmations of historicity and temporality inflecting this series of essays would remain at the core of Peirce's thought for the rest of his life. It is still evident in his 1892 contribution to his *Monist Metaphysical Series*: "consciousness must essentially cover an interval of time" (1892a, 315). Despite reservations that I above expressed about Peirce's work, I wish to note in fairness that Peirce always retained a commitment to transitionalist themes. As such, I regard his work as enormously instructive for the transitionalist lessons I here aim to learn.

This classical pragmatism with historicity at its heart has, the familiar wisdom has it, experienced something of a resurgence over the past few decades. In almost every respect, this resurgence has been a good thing, even if it has meant some straying from theses held dear by James and Dewey in order to keep pragmatism fresh with the times. Indeed, contemporary pragmatists of the last three decades have strayed considerably from James and Dewey on innumerable points. But transitionalism is one point, ironically, where things remain unchanged. Transitionalism remains both crucial to contemporary pragmatism and crucially unrecognized as such a crucial element therein. Just as James and Dewey never explicitly identified themselves as transitionalists, most contemporary pragmatists have developed their thought without explicitly calling attention to themselves as transitionalists. And yet just as with James and Dewey, if one goes looking around for transitionalist themes in the writings of contemporary pragmatist thinkers, one is bound to find much. Transitionalism is there, and it is deeply there.

Transitionalism in Contemporary Pragmatisms

The recognition of a tradition-wide transitionalism that runs throughout pragmatism can, in combination with a coherent statement of pragmatist transitionalism itself, function to bring together all hitherto disparate threads in the tradition. By recognizing a common inflection of historical and temporal themes, thinkers otherwise quite disparate can come to recognize in one another important points of contact that reach much deeper than mere mutual claim to the pragmatist banner.

The most notable contemporary pragmatist in whom I recognize a strong, though often understated, focus on transitionality is Richard Rorty. Take *Contingency, Irony, and Solidarity*, the most typically Rortyan of all of Rorty's books because the most constructive of all of his work. One way of reading this book is to see it as attempting to show how the "historicist turn" that Rorty thinks is the consequence of the last two hundred years of intellectual history can be embraced without eviscerating modern cultures of a normative sense of progress. The upshot of this "general turn against theory and toward narrative" is, in Rorty's view, that "we try to get to the point where we no longer worship *anything*, where we treat *nothing* as a quasi divinity, where we treat *everything*—our language, our conscience, our community—as a product of time and chance" (1989a, xiii, xvi, 22). The great cultural sea-change resulting in the temporalization of everything poses an important question, which Rorty thinks we moderns would do good to address: how can the historicist turn be squared with the valuable parts of our liberal democratic tradition without reducing the latter to a worthless relativism? Rorty's well-known, and well-criticized, defense of the liberal split between public and private is a response to this question, which is a question motivated by taking historicism, or transitionalism, seriously.

Rorty's thought that historicism is crucial for pragmatism, or at least his version of pragmatism, stretches back at least as far as *Philosophy and the Mirror of Nature*. Here Rorty argued that "the common message of Wittgenstein, Dewey, and Heidegger is a historicist one" such that, given the centrality of these three thinkers to his argument, "the moral of this book is also historicist" (1979, 9–10). Rorty went on from here to restate this historicist moral in the *Contingency* book as just described. Going forward from there, Rorty continued to employ themes of historicity and temporality on a wide range of topics in later work. We find Rorty discussing Dewey's relation to Hegel and Darwin in terms emphasizing their common historicism (1992, 292ff.). We find him boldly proclaiming that "Dewey's philosophy is a systematic attempt to temporalize everything, to leave nothing fixed" (1998b, 20). We find him cashing out his distinction between truth and justification "in terms of the contrast between future audiences and present-day audiences" (2005, 40). These themes also inform his political and cultural contributions. We find him explicitly describing a pragmatist politics as a historicist project: "Pragmatists are entirely at home with the idea that political theory should view itself as suggestions for future action emerging out of recent historical experience, rather than attempting to legitimate the outcome of that experience by reference to something ahistorical" (1998c, 272). And in one of his most recent essays, noticeably titled "Philosophy as a Transitional Genre," we find Rorty touting pragmatism as helping usher in the kind of culture that "is always in search of novelty . . . rather than trying to escape from the temporal to the eternal" (2004b, 12). Just as pragmatism is entirely at home with historicism, so too is the kind of liberal democratic culture that Rorty hopes we shall have the courage to realize. Such a culture, Rorty suggests in the last line of this essay, "will have taken fully to heart the maxim that it is the journey that matters" (2004b, 27).

Rorty's self-descriptions as historicist have rarely been the focus of even his most sympathetic commentators. One notable exception is an essay by Rorty's favorite contemporary philosopher and also former student Robert Brandom (2000b). Brandom portrays Rorty as achieving a synthesis of naturalism and historicism that enables him to replace representationalism with pragmatism. In swinging between this naturalism and historicism, Rorty effortlessly alternates between internal accounts of the way our practices actually work and external accounts of the way in which they may potentially develop. This exposition of Rorty's pragmatism sits well with Brandom's own take on classical pragmatism as an evolutionary philosophy of "mutabilism" (2004, 3).

Brandom applies these pragmatist insights in developing his own expressivist-inferentialist account of normative rationality: "Every claim and inference we make at once sustains and transforms the tradition in which the conceptual norms that govern that process are implicit. . . . *Applying* conceptual norms and *transforming* them are two sides of the same coin" (2000b, 177). Brandom's view of normative rationality as inherently transformational and mutable clearly exhibits transitional themes. At the heart of Brandom's philosophy, we find these three crucial theses: all awareness is conceptual, all concept use is linguistic, and language is "a paradigm of the sort of thing that must be understood historically" (2000c, 26–27). It would seem to follow that the best place to look in Brandom for an emphasis on historicity and temporality would be in his account of semantics. Indeed, this would be no minor point given the weight

Brandom accords to semantics in his reading of the history of modern philosophy as beginning with Kant's "shift from epistemology to semantics" (2002, 21ff.). When Brandom inflects semantics with developmental ideas that lean heavily on pragmatism, we should pay careful attention. Such a transitionalist semantics is clearly called for in Brandom's *Between Saying and Doing*, a book notably generous in its usage of Dewey: "This pragmatist privileging of process over relation in the order of semantic explanation is worth looking at more closely" (2008, 178). Brandom privileges process over relation by developing a semantics that begins with the pragmatist insight that meaning (saying) cannot be understood apart from use (doing). As he elsewhere explains, "This *pragmatist* strategy looks to the *development* of concepts through their use" (2002, 386n12).[3] All of this goes toward showing the tight link between Brandom's provocative even if contestable interpretation of pragmatism and his crucial even if understated deployment of transitional themes of temporality and historicity.

Transitionalism can also be located in the work of other important contemporary neopragmatist philosophers. Hilary Putnam, Richard Bernstein, and Jeffrey Stout have all amply developed transitionalist themes, by extending pragmatist thought to a wide variety of philosophical contexts where neopragmatism has been enriched by and in turn enriched other philosophical traditions. Cornel West and Eddie Glaude have charted yet another path for contemporary neopragmatism, in which the quintessential pragmatist commitment to cultural criticism is impressively foregrounded. In leading pragmatism back to its cultural-critical roots, West (1990, 183) crisply situates pragmatism as "part of a more general turn toward historicist approaches." Glaude (2007, 7) then follows West's "prophetic pragmatism" in order to envision the work of pragmatism as an effort to "express a profound faith in the capacity of everyday ordinary people to transform their world."[4] There are countless examples of such transitionalism among these and other neopragmatists. Employing them as my data, I take Rorty as the best representative of a much wider tendency of neopragmatist engagement with historicity and temporality.

The presence of transitionalist resources in both classicopragmatism and neopragmatism indicates an important continuity between these two strains, despite clear differences separating them. The distinctively neopragmatist transformations of many of the inaugural themes of classicopragmatism can be explained in part by the fact that the neopragmatists inherited much of their pragmatism from a handful of midcentury philosophers in whom classical pragmatism was combined with the full force of logical positivism. This includes two thinkers situated at the pragmatist-positivist crossroads who also happen to be two of the unsung heroes of Rorty's *Philosophy and the Mirror of Nature*: Wilfrid Sellars and Willard Van Orman Quine. As it turns out, transitionalism is also present in Sellars and Quine. Sellars, whose work is pragmatist in no more than an anticipatory fashion, generously offered up transitionalist themes. In a little-noted passage in his much discussed "Empiricism and the Philosophy of Mind," Sellars noted of the myth of the given that, "Above all, the picture is misleading because of its static character" (1956, 78). Sellars went on to expressly endorse a conception of knowledge, and science, as an ongoing self-correcting enterprise. Similar insights regarding the historical-temporal revision of knowledge are also featured in Quine's epistemology. A subtle transitionalism crops up in the most unexpected places in Quine. We find it in an important essay on Carnap:

> The lore of our fathers is a fabric of sentences. In our hands it develops and changes, through more or less arbitrary and deliberate revisions and additions of our own, more or less directly occasioned by the continuing stimulation of our sense organs. It is a pale grey lore, black with fact and white with convention. But I have found no substantial reasons for concluding that there are any quite black threads in it, or any white ones (Quine 1963, 406).

Although it is undeniable that Quine was more interested in confronting the positivist dichotomy between facts and values than he was in developing the pragmatist insight that our webs of belief are interactions between the old lore we inherit and the new sentences we furnish, it is not remarked often enough that Quine's repudiation of core positivist theses proceeded precisely on the basis of his acceptance of core pragmatist theses, including that of transitionalist historicity and temporality. Quine's "more thorough pragmatism" as espoused in the last paragraph of his famous "Two Dogmas of Empiricism" repudiates a narrow positivist frame in decidedly transitionalist terms: "Each man is given a scientific heritage plus a continuing barrage of sensory stimulation; and the considerations which guide him in warping his scientific heritage to fit his continuing sensory promptings are, where rational, pragmatic" (1951, 46). Transitionalism appears to be one of the most notable advantages that Quine drew from pragmatism.

The work of the diverse set of neopragmatists I have been discussing is not the only form of pragmatism on the scene today. Neopragmatists such as Rorty have been subjected to a great deal of critical scrutiny by other contemporary pragmatists who present themselves as the primary expositors and developers of the pragmatisms of Peirce, James, and Dewey. Many of the differences these critics detect between classicopragmatism and neopragmatism can be accounted for in terms of the latter's more thorough confrontation with positivism. But these differences, however real they are, should not outweigh the commonalities, which I find of much greater moment today. It would turn out to be quite an event for the tradition of pragmatism if one could demonstrate substantial points of contact between contemporary neopragmatists such as Rorty and Brandom and the contemporary classicopragmatists who are devoted to carrying forward the thought of James and Dewey while being strongly critical of their neopragmatist cousins. It is my view that transitionalism provides one such important point of contact. That, among other reasons, is why it merits consideration just now.

Evidence of transitionalism in the thought of leading contemporary Deweyan and Jamesian pragmatists is surprisingly widespread once one goes searching for it. To build up to this claim it is useful to first note that transitionalism can be found in the writings of many influential midcentury thinkers who carried the banner of pragmatism from the 1940s to the 1970s, during pragmatism's years of eclipse. These midcentury classicopragmatists in whom we find important statements of transitionalist themes include John Herman Randall, who was Dewey's student at Columbia, and H. S. Thayer and John E. Smith, who studied at Columbia after Dewey's retirement but while Randall was still on the faculty. Also deserving of mention in this crowd for both his influential scholarship and invaluable editorial work is John McDermott.

Of this group, the single pragmatist most devoted to pragmatism's engagement with temporality and historicity was John Herman Randall. Randall's transitionalism is most evident in his view that "cultural change must be taken as a basic subject-matter" by philosophy such that philosophical "understanding must be in terms of the problems set by cultural change itself." This means, as Randall (1935, 4) explained, that "we must inquire into our world in its temporal dimensions." He reiterated the same point again, twenty-three years later, in terms of the transitional tension between the old and the new: "Since most men concerned are committed to both old and new, the tension between the two, which is generating these other internal tensions in each, becomes a central problem" (1958, 104). Although he was more devoted to and engaged with the impact of temporality and historicity on pragmatism than any other thinker of his time, Randall is not the only midcentury pragmatist to have taken transitions seriously. Others furnish additional resources, though it bears repeating that no other thinker of generation matches Randall's contributions in this area, and the contemporary neglect of his thought is unfortunate and perhaps symptomatic of certain losses that pragmatism has withstood in recent decades.

H. S. Thayer characterizes "the notions of time, contingency, development, and continuity" as "serious and basic subjects in the philosophizing of pragmatists" (1968, 452). John Smith likewise regards as "basic" to pragmatism its "insistence on the reality of time, of change, of novelty and organic development" (1992, 3). And John McDermott, who I will have occasion to return to later, offers a pragmatism in which "the manifestations of living occur in time" (1976, 102). I should also briefly mention here a study of the concept of time in American philosophy by Bertrand Helm, which may seem to anticipate my transitionalism in its argument that with pragmatism, "attention fell upon the temporal stream of events" (1985, 6). But Helm's focus is on what the pragmatists have to contribute to traditional philosophical issues about time and temporality rather than on what time and temporality contribute to the philosophy of pragmatism. Helm's study is thus rich in resources for anyone interested in pragmatist transitionalism, but it is not itself a study of pragmatist transitionalism.[5]

Other more recent work in classicopragmatism bears ample evidence of having learned a lesson in transitionalism from these and other second-generation pragmatist students of Dewey. Indeed, transitionalism is so widespread in contemporary classicopragmatist scholarship that an exhaustive survey would be rather tedious. The important thing is the atmosphere of thought from which contemporary classicopragmatism continues to draw breath. I will consider only three leading contemporary classicopragmatists in whose work is evidenced a thorough attention to issues of temporality and historicity: Larry Hickman, John Stuhr, and Joseph Margolis. I take these three as collectively exemplary of a much larger trend afoot in contemporary classicopragmatist scholarship.[6] Despite the growing richness of transitionalist themes featured in this scholarship, there remains much else that continues to pass under the banner of pragmatism but that has lost the crucial bearings provided by temporality and historicity. Part of the aim of the present study is to recall certain regions of pragmatism from this atemporal and ahistorical aimlessness. In embarking on this venture, my three representative classicopragmatists provide the best orientation I can find.

Larry Hickman's valuable reconstruction of pragmatism as a philosophy for our modern technological culture urges that we take quite seriously that "Dewey repeatedly insisted that his account of inquiry was based on a genetic method that took development over time as an essential component" (1990, 10). For Dewey, in Hickman's view, "inquiry was characterized as linking past and future" (1990, 32) such that pragmatist inquiry can be fairly described as "the genetic analysis of conceptual tools" (2001, 36). In like manner, John Stuhr argues that a primary task for pragmatism today is that of furthering its historicist sensibility. Stuhr's subtle argument is that "there is a need not to invent from scratch but to recover and reappropriate a pragmatic theory of time" (1997, 182). In initiating this recovery effort, Stuhr claims first that "experience is intrinsically and irreducibly temporal" and second that "time is intrinsically and irreducibly experiential" on a pragmatist view (1997, 184). Working outward from these general philosophical theses, Stuhr then outlines versions of pragmatist ethics and politics that take time seriously.

But surely the most impressive and fully developed account of philosophical historicity in contemporary pragmatist circles is offered in Joseph Margolis's rich and expanding body of work. Margolis has been developing an impressive version of a "radically historicized pragmatism" (1986, 206) for more than two decades now. While much in Margolis's version of pragmatism is his own, he is clear that his historicism comes straight out of the pragmatist tradition. Speaking of his primary predecessor in pragmatism, he boldly claims that "everything [Dewey] features would have made perfect sense in historicized terms" (2004, 243) such that, conjectures Margolis, "the only conception that's missing in Dewey . . . is an up-to-date paraphrase of Hegel's notion of historicity" (2002a, 129). It is precisely such an account that is the central aim of Margolis's own pragmatism, which postulates "that the world is a flux, that thinking is historicized, and that selves are socially constructed or have histories rather than natures" (1999a, 338). I will have the opportunity to return to Margolis's fluxist pragmatism at the end of the next chapter, where I describe some of the ways in which it anticipates my own attempt to fashion a transitionalist pragmatism out of materials supplied by both classicopragmatists and neopragmatists. There I will suggest that crucial aspects of my arguments in the pages that follow can be profitably seen as taking up Margolis's suggestion that "pragmatism would be greatly strengthened by the addition of an account of historicity" (2002a, 114).

I have been arguing that a philosophical stream of transitions runs through American pragmatism from James and Dewey in two streams: on the one hand through Quine and Sellars down to Rorty, Brandom, Putnam, and West, and on the other through Randall, McDermott, and others down to Margolis, Hickman, and Stuhr.[7] All of these thinkers are usefully approached as *transitionalist* pragmatists, due to the centrality of historicity and temporality in their conceptions of pragmatism. This highest common denominator running through all of these pragmatisms is summarized by Vincent Colapietro when he notes "the deeply *historicist* cast of the very best in American philosophical thought" (forthcoming). Yet despite the viability of this transitionalist interpretation of their work, no pragmatist has explicitly set forth a detailed conception of pragmatism in transitionalist terms. This yields a considerable tension. All of the pragmatist philosophers to whom I have referred make claims to the effect that transitional concepts are central for pragmatist philosophy and yet all of them offer their pragmatism under some other banner that they take be the central factor in pragmatism: experience, language, practice, instrumentality, intelligence, semantics, purpose, thought, meaning, action, growth. All of these concepts are indeed central for pragmatism. But I would argue that what enables this diversity of pragmatisms to fit together under a single philosophical canopy is the pragmatist reconstruction of each of these concepts as transitional. What I hope to provide in the pages that follow is a more complete explication of pragmatism in light of my many predecessors' boldly proclaimed but underdeveloped suggestions for a pragmatist transitionalism.

Transitionalism in Pragmatisms Beyond Philosophy

My account of pragmatist transitionality serves as a node that establishes fruitful points of contact among the shifting networks tying together the classical pragmatisms of James and Dewey, the neopragmatisms of Rorty and Brandom, and the contemporary classicopragmatisms of Margolis and others (as well as a diversity of midcentury pragmatisms). Transitionalism also functions as a fruitful point of contact between pragmatist philosophers and other contemporary pragmatists working largely outside the confines of the discipline of philosophy. In fact, I would argue, pragmatism's transitionalist themes have thus far been better discerned by historians and literary theorists than by philosophers. This point bears special consideration insofar as pragmatists, quite against the calling of their own mantle, do not often enough cross disciplinary boundaries in order to see what pragmatism can do not only philosophically but also critically, historically, anthropologically, and so on.

In literary theory, Richard Poirier and Jonathan Levin have explicitly developed pragmatism along the lines of transitionalism. Levin (1999) writes of pragmatism as the intellectual source of a "poetics of transition," which he finds best realized in literary modernists such as Gertrude Stein and Wallace Stevens. This argument in its essential structure is largely derived from Levin's former teacher, Poirier, who throughout his career and in an excellent short book on pragmatism and poetry emphasized pragmatist themes in literature having to do with transition and related themes such as the renewal of literary tradition (Poirier 1987, 1992, 1998). Poirier's work has been crucially important in my own process of coming to recognize just how central transitionalism is for pragmatism. It is my hope that future years may yet counterbalance the unfortunate neglect of his work among pragmatist philosophers.

Another literary theorist who has made extensive use of pragmatism and its transitionalist thematics is Stanley Fish. I offer just one quotation drawn from Fish's early work, during which time he described his views in terms of a theory of interpretive communities that borrowed generously from reader-response theory, whose origins in at least one prominent form were explicitly pragmatist. Though Fish here did not yet self-identify as a pragmatist, we can already discern pragmatist themes of transitions in his work:

> It is often assumed that literary theory presents a set of problems whose shape remains unchanging and in relation to which our critical procedures are found to be more or less adequate. . . . It seems to me, however, that the relationship is exactly the reverse: the field of inquiry is *constituted* by the questions we are able to ask because the entities that populate it come into being as the presuppositions . . . of those questions (Fish 1980, 1).

In his more recent and more explicitly pragmatist writings, including his editorials and blog entries for the *New York Times*, Fish readily emphasizes themes of historicity and temporality in his musings on interpretation, law, and culture.

In the historical discipline, a number of prominent intellectual historians of pragmatism have explicitly described pragmatism in terms consonant with my concept of transitionalism. Transitionalism was particularly apparent in the first intellectual-historical accounts of pragmatism, which began to emerge in the middle of the twentieth century. In the 1940s, Morton White asserted that pragmatism locates "the life" of the mind in "not logic but experience in some streaming social sense" (1947, 11). Philip Wiener (1949) later in that decade authored an impressive intellectual history of the crucial role played by evolutionary conceptions in the development of pragmatism, thus fleshing out an important thesis suggested a few years earlier by Merle Curti (1943). With these intellectual histories in his back pocket, Jacques Barzun in his wonderful book on William James was thus able to confidently refer to James as "the historian among philosophers" whose characteristic philosophical attitude could be described in terms of "mind possessing a sense of history" (1983, 124). Barzun's description of James precisely and concisely captures the sensibility I am here imputing to pragmatism more generally.

More recent work on the intellectual history of pragmatism ratifies the first-generation assessments concerning the importance of temporality and historicity for the pragmatist way of philosophizing. David Hollinger set the tone for recent scholarship with his claim that "nothing is more essential to an understanding of James than recognition of his commitment to the critical revision of existing traditions" (1981, 20). James Kloppenberg soon followed up by detailing a "historical sensibility" in early pragmatism that fully "excluded the possibility of any non-historical existence or idea" (1986, 110). James Livingston, writing almost a decade after Hollinger and Kloppenberg but at greater length on my favored theme of transitions, finds pragmatism at its most influential in James's and Dewey's reconstitution of modern personality as a "transitive subject" such that "the self is not just in the transitions—it just is the transitions" (1994, 289, 293). In assessing this reconstitution, Livingston remarks that "time is the key to [the] argument" (1994, 268). The upshot of the argument from time is a tight embracing of "the continuities as well as the discontinuities of historical time" such that "every moment, every event, becomes intelligible only in retrospect or prospect, in the 'continuous transitions' between them" (1994, 288, 290). Some philosophers, of course, may object that it is rather convenient for historians to understand pragmatism as a philosophy that forces us to take history seriously. And historians, of course, may reply that it might just prove inconvenient for a bunch of philosophers to start nosing around in history. However convenient or inconvenient it may end up being, historians are nevertheless correct to discern in pragmatism a special focus on transitions.

Transitionalism Beyond Pragmatism

Not only does transitionalism establish contact between different camps of pragmatist philosophy and between different conceptions of pragmatism in philosophy, literary criticism, history, and elsewhere, but it also establishes contact between different philosophical traditions. In explicating transitionalism in the chapters that follow, I shall call attention to such points of contact. Indeed, it is obvious that many of the core themes featured in what I am calling transitionalism are not unique to pragmatism alone. An emphasis on these themes is readily apparent in a host of other philosophical traditions: genealogy, critical theory, hermeneutical phenomenology, psychoanalysis, process philosophy, vitalism, and even in some (quite prominent) corners of analytic philosophy. My claim is thus not that these themes are the exclusive purview of pragmatism alone. Clearly, historicity and temporality are crucial features of important work in each of these traditions. These traditions could thus, fairly I think, be referred to as transitionalist in my sense. Nevertheless, in what follows I take transitionalism as mostly referring to the uniquely pragmatist way of inflecting these themes of historicity and temporality. While history and time are by no means unique to pragmatism among philosophies, I urge that pragmatism does bring a unique perspective to bear upon these themes. The results are conceptions and uses of historicity and temporality uniquely pragmatist in character.

That transitionalism is uniquely pragmatist in this way is not meant to suggest, however, that we cannot find rich connections between pragmatism and other philosophical traditions precisely as concerns those themes that contribute to the construction of transitionalism. Indeed, one of the central aims of many of the chapters to follow is to point out the rich connections between pragmatism, interpreted through transitionalism, and other strands of philosophical thought prominent in contemporary Analytic and Continental philosophy. I am keen to lavish attention on connections between pragmatism and the work of Pierre Bourdieu (on knowledge), Stanley Cavell (on ethics), Bernard Williams (on politics), and above all Michel Foucault (in developing effective experiments in philosophical critique and inquiry). If pragmatism is to remain philosophically viable, then it must cultivate not only its internal points of contact but also its shared roots with leading thinkers in other leading philosophical traditions. Bourdieu, Cavell, Williams, and Foucault all offer a great deal to pragmatism. Pragmatism in turn can offer a great deal back to the traditions in which these thinkers are situated.

This suggests that the transitionalist themes of historicity and temporality I here present are not after all the exclusive province of pragmatism. This is as it should be. Pragmatism should not be developed as a theory that lays exclusive claim to this or that piece of intellectual property. Pragmatism should rather be developed as a rich matrix of theories and concepts that enrich our practices of inquiry. There is no loss to these inquiries if the theories and concepts enriching them are furnished by intellectual traditions other than pragmatism.

Why, then, do I devote so much effort here to a distinctively pragmatist conception of transitionalism? One reason is because I think transitionalism helps us better understand, so that we may then go on to deploy, the theoretical, conceptual, and practical resources of pragmatism. While transitionalist themes are not pragmatism's exclusive property, these themes are nonetheless featured in pragmatism and in a way that has as yet to be fully developed. This furnishes an opportunity. My hope is to develop these underdeveloped resources in such a way as to strengthen pragmatism. This suggests that this work itself is an effort in transitions: I am here attempting to develop a tradition of thought by, first, locating where it has come from and where it is today and, second, by developing the resources made available in its historical and present forms so as to fashion more usable future iterations of this tradition. My concern is not to imagine some ideal form of pragmatism, located either in the past or the future, but to take pragmatism as it works now and transition it over the course of the pages that follow into a new form of pragmatism that does its distinctive work even better. My aim is to enliven pragmatism rather than to pin it down. Philosophies should be critiques, not curiosities. Picture philosophy as a butterfly or a bird—must we cage it up to know it in those dim details that only confinement will enable us to discern, or might we let it free so that we may yet realize those of its potentialities that we can witness only in its generous flights?

Allow me, then, to insist upon the importance of developing new forms of pragmatism that seek out new pragmatists, marginal pragmatists, barely pragmatists, and almost pragmatists. The full range of pragmatist thinkers I have referred to in this chapter, especially when combined with those thinkers from other intellectual traditions in whom I detect crucial similarities with pragmatism, form a rather motley crew. I invoke the flexibility and diversity of pragmatism itself in offering transitionalism as a carapace under which all of these thinkers can comfortably gather together. Disagreements will surely persist among various parties to this crowd. But this is as it should be insofar as philosophical traditions achieve their unity not by way of doctrine so much as by way of debate. I agree with each of the pragmatists referred to above on numerous crucial issues, but I also disagree with each of them just as often. That helps explain why I am here attempting to develop, rather than merely reiterate, the philosophical tradition in which pragmatism participates. James thought that pragmatism was a new name for some old ways of thinking. I assume that he also meant to suggest by this that pragmatism might itself become an old name for some new ways of thinking. I hope that this may yet be the case.

Three

THREE WAVES OF PRAGMATISM

Experience and Language in the First Two Waves of Pragmatism

Having shown that temporality and historicity inform the core of previous pragmatisms, I wish to now turn around and show that previous pragmatists have rarely taken these as the constitutive themes of their philosophies. Transitionalist pragmatism is a differentiation from the tradition as much as it is a repetition of it.

The history of pragmatism up to the present moment can be described as having developed in two waves. The first wave of classicopragmatism placed its primary emphasis on the concept of experience. The second wave of neopragmatism placed its primary emphasis on the concept of language. This yielded a philosophy of experience and a philosophy of language, respectively. A philosophy of transitions was at best an afterthought in each instance. Having described in the previous chapter the core transitionalist themes of my third-wave pragmatism, I will in this chapter turn back to the first two waves in order to showcase their persisting internal deficits and tensions with one another. On the basis of the brief intellectual history comprised by these two chapters, I can then go on in following chapters to show how transitionalist pragmatism offers the best way of focusing the distinctive advantages yielded by the previous offerings of experiential pragmatism and linguistic pragmatism. Transitionalism can then be seen as a third wave of pragmatism that cumulatively washes in upon the other two waves rather than disaccumulatively draining them away. This helps reposition pragmatism as an again rising tide.

Contemporary pragmatist philosophy is quite clearly riven. The recent revival of pragmatism by neopragmatists like Richard Rorty, Hilary Putnam, and Robert Brandom has generated a wealth of intramural debates with contemporary scholars of classicopragmatism devoted to the work of Charles Santiago Peirce, William James, and John Dewey. Of all the internecine conflicts that have raged in recent decades between these neopragmatist upstarts and the classicopragmatist establishment, perhaps the most ink has been spilled over issues concerning the relative priority of language and experience in pragmatism. Defenders of classical pragmatism locate experience as the conceptual center of pragmatism; Rorty and many of the neopragmatists drop the concept of experience altogether in favor of a thoroughly linguistic pragmatism. Although this is certainly not the only debate burning between upstart neopragmatists and contemporary classical pragmatists, it is very much a flash point for pragmatism today, according to a number of recent surveys by esteemed intellectual historians including James Kloppenberg (1996), Robert Westbrook (2005), and Martin Jay (2005). This is one issue on which nearly everyone agrees that there is an important split within the heart of pragmatism itself.

My transitionalist pragmatism is offered as a proposal that we now begin to view this debate in a different manner, namely from the perspective of its forthcoming resolution. Rather than understanding experiential classicopragmatism and linguistic neopragmatism as two opposed camps, it is time to consider the possibility of yet another stage in pragmatist thought that will combine the best insights of each of its predecessors. This would require reinterpreting this intramural debate such that classicopragmatism and neopragmatism could be seen as two moments in a broader pragmatist sweep. This revision would be in keeping with the temperament of pragmatism itself, insofar as it would prove pragmatism capacious enough to house both of its major moments. This attempt at a resolution need not, of course, involve denying that there are other important areas of conflict separating Rorty and Brandom from Dewey and James. Certainly there are. My goal here is only to reconcile some of the central issues concerning language and experience. It is my hope that this will then allow other points of disagreement, which are potentially of far greater moment, to come to the foreground.

It is worth clarifying at the outset the relevance of these matters to other debates taking place outside of the context of pragmatism. The intramural debates among the pragmatists I am here considering recapitulate larger debates central throughout much of modern philosophy. These debates concern, for example, traditional epistemological issues of the relation between our knowledge and the realities that this knowledge is about. These debates have returned time and time again to the familiar stand-off between those who hold that any claim to truth stands in need of some final extrahuman arbiter that makes truths true (foundationalists, realists, externalists) and those who adopt the view that internal factors such as coherence among beliefs is all we could ever need to settle any practical dispute regarding competing truth claims (nominalists, antirealists, internalists). The latter camps affirm, while the former camps deny, that our beliefs do not really aim at a truth adequate to reality so much as a justification of these beliefs to other rational beings. This debate has loomed large in a variety of contemporary philosophical scenes, from contemporary analytic epistemology, to the *hermeneutikstreit* between Habermas and Gadamer, to scholarship on the status of discourse and language in the work of thinkers such as Foucault and Wittgenstein. In the context of moral and political theory, these debates are featured in the recent contests between, for example, language-centric varieties of deliberative democracy and experience-centric varieties of communitarianism.[1] Also worthy of note is the centrality of this debate for work taking place in other disciplinary contexts, including history and anthropology.[2]

I point out these resonances so as to indicate the breadth of many of the philosophical issues featured in the debates between the pragmatist philosophers of experience and the pragmatist philosophers of language. Of course, there remain important differences such that the internecine pragmatist debates will not always result in consequences that will be useful elsewhere. All this goes toward stating the obvious: the transitionalist solution I offer for overcoming the impasse between the two pragmatist camps is by no means a complete answer to the larger philosophical problems at the heart of other domains of contemporary philosophy, yet at the same time a resolution of these issues internal to pragmatism still offers at the very least a promising new approach to these problems as they arise elsewhere. Another reason for mentioning these resonances is to note up front that the debates between experience pragmatism and language pragmatism are not confined to epistemological issues alone. This reminder is so needful because it often seems as if epistemology constitutes the primary context for pragmatism's impasses today. This is perhaps due to the fact that epistemology has over the past century so often been positioned as the primary vehicle of philosophy itself. I think this has more to do with the particular constraints on professional(izing) philosophy during the heydays of the first two waves of pragmatism than with anything else. In both periods (roughly 1900 to 1930 and 1970 to 1990), professional philosophy tended to be identified overwhelmingly with epistemology and its attendant disciplinary subfields (first psychology and metaphysics and then later cognitive science and philosophy of language). This led to ready opportunities for formulating these successive waves of pragmatism in epistemological terms. But epistemology is not the only domain where the experience-language debates have shaped up, nor is it by any means the only domain where these debates are relevant. In the following expositions of these two waves of pragmatism, I will aim to give an indication of the full breadth of both pragmatisms. Yet the scholarly duty to follow the arguments themselves as they played out will at times require that I hone in on the specifically epistemological dimensions of classicopragmatist experientialism and neopragmatist linguisticism.

The Classicopragmatist Defense of Experience

Rorty's revival of pragmatism under the auspices of the linguistic turn has put contemporary defenders of classicopragmatism in a defensive posture from which they have yet to wiggle free. Contemporary classicopragmatists have found Rorty's attempt to replace experience with language a threat to the philosophical core of pragmatism. In order to save this philosophical core, they have rallied around the concept of experience, so as to demonstrate both its centrality for a correct, scholarly interpretation of the classical pragmatists and its vitality for contemporary philosophy in contexts as diverse as epistemology, ethics, and political theory.

The great risk involved in a revival of an experience-centric pragmatism is that of backsliding into some of the philosophical dead ends that language-centric neopragmatism has helped philosophy see its way out of. Chief among these are the dreaded dead ends of representationalism and foundationalism, which in their most subtle forms are invited by what Wilfrid Sellars (1956) called the myth of the given. The main risk facing pragmatists is that experience will be theorized in such a way as to make too many concessions to givenism, thus opening the door to representationalism and foundationalism. Allow me to briefly explicate the relations among these various philosophical perspectives. Representationalism is the thesis that our mental events are adequate (true or good or just, depending on the context) insofar as they accurately represent some reality outside of themselves. Foundationalism is the thesis that there exist incorrigible representations that can act as a foundation for (epistemic, moral, or political) practice. Now, typically, these foundations are supplied by experiential immediacies or basic beliefs that are recognized as items of noninferential awareness that are immediately "given" to consciousness. Their incorrigibility in being immediately given to consciousness is what qualifies them to play a foundational role. Givenism can thus be understood as a combination of two theses: first, that we have noninferential qualitative experiences, and second, that these qualitative immediacies play some important role in our knowings, doings, and sharings. In criticizing the conception of epistemological givens, Sellars was taking on one of the last strongholds of empiricist foundationalism and representationalism. If givenism goes, then so too go foundationalism and representationalism, at least in their most viable incarnations.[3]

All this suggests that when classicopragmatists argue that there are items immediately given to us in experience that play some important role in our practices, they have already gone a long way (though surely not quite all the way) toward a position that may prove difficult to distinguish from representationalist foundationalism. Conceptions of immediate and direct experience are precisely the sort of epistemic item that philosophers like to press into service as a foundation. To avoid this foundationalism, contemporary pragmatists who are eager to retrieve the classicopragmatist accounts of experience must be on guard to not treat experience as a kind of ultimate given-ness against which we might be able to measure our practical knowings, doings, and sharings (that is, our epistemic, ethical, and political practices).

Unfortunately, the classicopragmatists prove frustratingly ambiguous about givenism. In certain moments, they appear theoretically committed to avoiding the pernicious errors of givenism. Yet in certain other moments, they warmly invite subtle forms of givenism that exhibit pernicious connections to representationalist foundationalism. This ambiguity is present throughout much of the work of Dewey, James, and Peirce. Contemporary pragmatists returning to these headwaters of classical pragmatism can indeed retrieve a concept of experience without reverting to foundationalism, but they can do so only after first absorbing some of the downstream insights of the neopragmatists that helped motivate the shift away from conceptions of experience inflected by givenism.

The classicopragmatists themselves, of course, could not have anachronistically benefited from the criticisms of foundationalism offered by Sellars and Rorty. The decades of philosophical innovation that intervened between the development of classicopragmatism and the crystallization of neopragmatism helps explain why earlier pragmatists may not have seen themselves as fully clear of representationalist foundationalism as did later pragmatists. The simplest explanation of this historical gap is to say that it took the linguistic turn to get the full extent of the problems of representationalist foundationalism into proper view. The linguistic turn was eventually pressed into service as one crucial element in a broader philosophical revolt against foundationalism that Peirce, James, and Dewey, along with others in Europe, including Nietzsche, Bergson, and Heidegger, helped mount. The classical pragmatists were writing at the beginning of that revolt, and from that position they lacked the tools and metaphors that would later prove necessary for gaining an appropriate grip on the role played by experience in practice. It was only near the end of this revolt, in the final stages of the linguistic turn, that philosophers began to develop the concepts necessary for eschewing the most subtle forms of givenism, representationalism, and foundationalism in favor of alternative compelling accounts of our knowings, doings, and sharings.

My argument is best seen as offered in the following modality: I am not chastising the classical pragmatists for certain failings in their thinking; rather, I am issuing the reminder that the intellectual-historical situation of classicopragmatism did not enable them to effectively confront certain intellectual problems that emerged into full view only decades after their pragmatisms broke onto the philosophical scene. I am not arguing that classical pragmatism was foundationalist and representationalist; I am suggesting that classicopragmatism was never in a very good position to understand how we might go fully antifoundationalist and antirepresentationalist in the right kind of way. A claim by the French philosopher-turned-sociologist Pierre Bourdieu

(1980, 5) can help me elucidate the modality of my critique: "In what is un-thinkable at a given time, there is not only everything that cannot be thought for lack of the ethical or political dispositions which tend to bring it into con-sideration, but also everything that cannot be thought for lack of instruments of thought such as problematics, concepts, methods and techniques." Dewey, James, and Peirce lacked a full appreciation of the problematic of givenism because it was not until later decades that this problematic was rigorously laid out in all its thorny detail. This should not, of course, discourage us from re-calling that these later formulations of givenism as a problematic were deeply if not always consciously indebted to the philosophical innovations urged much earlier by the classical pragmatists. Now, in addition to lacking the philosophical problematic of givenism, the classicopragmatists themselves also lacked a sense of the general type of response to this problematic that might be adequate. I will urge that an adequate response must involve turning a good amount of our philosophical energies over into collaborations with social scientists and practitioners. Since social science remained underdevel-oped in the years during which the classicopragmatists formulated their views, they could not have seen themselves all the way toward an adequate solution. Once again, however, this observation should not discourage us from noting that the burgeoning of the social sciences was in many ways indebted to the pragmatisms of especially James and Dewey. In a sense, then, the argument I will be making should be seen as a call to return to key classicopragmatist interventions in order to complete what was begun but could really never get finished on its own—fulfilling this vision requires reconstructing classico-pragmatism in light of the problem of givenism and the response of social science, both of which are fortunately very much a part of the pragmatist legacy.

From our perspective today, where we are in fuller possession of both the problematic of givenism and a series of possible responses to it, we ought to find particularly troublesome James's and Dewey's numerous, even if some-times merely casual, references to such notions as "primary experience" and "perceptual immediacy." James troublingly described his concept of pure ex-perience in terms of "a chaos of experiences" (1904a, 175) or "the immediate flux of life" (1905, 215). Dewey made loose references to such experiential giv-ens as "the immediate qualitative 'feel'" suggesting a "dumb, formless experi-ence" and expanded on his central concept of "primary experience" in terms of its "heterogeneity and fullness" and its "coarseness and crudity" (1925, 36/ LW1.227, 298/LW1.300, 401/LW1.39). All of these descriptions suggest that sort of primary awareness of raw givens that can serve well as the grounding term in a foundationalist epistemology. All of these descriptions are therefore difficult to distinguish from claims for some immediate experiential content that we can lay our conceptual schemes over as the grounds of our knowledge.

But what of the practical role attributed by the classicopragmatists to the content of our experience as they conceptualized it? The crucial thing about givenism is not after all the mere existence of the raw feeling of immediate and dumb experience but is rather the practical role we assign to primary experience in our second-order philosophical inquiries into knowledge, ethics, and politics. If the concept of primary experience can be shown to play no important or offensive role in classicopragmatist epistemology, ethics, and politics, then the concept might yet emerge vindicated. As we will see, this is in fact Rorty's own considered view, though it was probably not Sellars's. But is this option available to classicopragmatism? More importantly, is it explicitly made available by classicopragmatism?

In favor of this suggested strategy is an idea Dewey stressed quite often, namely that we must distinguish between primary experience as "had" and reflective experiences as "known."[4] However, despite such distinctions as this, it is really not in the spirit of Dewey's classicopragmatism to regard primary experience as playing no important role in our practical activity. Dewey did not merely admit the existence of primary experience as a concession but rather labored to conceptualize it, because he thought it would offer a large amount of insight into our practices and their conditions of possibility. Despite a distinction between the "had" and the "known," Dewey expended enormous energy precisely specifying the havings of primary experience in his epistemology and ethics, and this can only be attributed to his holding that such primary havings are meant to play some role in his conception of epistemic and ethical practice. The problem Dewey thus ran up against time and time again was that of specifying these epistemic and ethical roles without describing primary experiences as givens capable of functioning as epistemological or moral foundations. We must be prepared to admit that Dewey generally failed to resolve this problem. Consider his claim in *Experience and Nature* that primary experience "furnishes the first data of the reflection which constructs the secondary objects" such that "test and verification of the latter is secured only by return to things of crude or macroscopic experience" (1925, 4/LW1.16). Subsequently, in the essay "Qualitative Thought," he repeated the same error in arguing that "the immediate existence of quality" is "the point of departure and the regulative principle of all thinking" (1930b, LW5.261). These and other quasi-foundationalist formulations in Dewey suggest that we ought to be very cautious when traveling around in the territory of primary experience.

The same story can be told about James's conceptualizations of pure experience. In theorizing knowledge as an affair of "leading," James consistently argued that knowledge can only terminate in perception immediate and direct.[5] In recognizing this, we need not deny that there were isolated occasions, surfacing in parts of James's later work, in which he more cautiously suggested that the terminal point of the cognitive relation can be any item of practical significance.[6] James, like Dewey, exhibited an unfortunate unresolved ambiguity in his thinking on these matters.

Some will be inclined to suggest that we can find a more sophisticated treatment of these matters in Peirce. Although he is not a central figure in my account of classicopragmatism for the important reasons discussed in chapter 1, Peirce is worth considering at this juncture insofar as his pragmatism is sufficiently distant from Dewey's and James's to warrant the suspicion that he may have seen past certain difficulties on which the other classical pragmatists got stuck. I admit that this suspicion is reasonable, but I also insist that it ultimately proves indefensible. This is because conceptions of experiential givens simply run amok in certain core aspects of Peirce's pragmatism. These conceptions are hardly innocent if they rambunctiously open doors to foundationalism and representationalism, even if only inadvertently. Despite all his brilliant recognition of the historical-temporal mediation of all human experience, there remains in Peirce more than a lingering whiff of immediate experiential givens.

Peirce analyzed experiential unity into three regulative categories of Quality (firstness), Relation (secondness), and Representation (thirdness). Though he frequently changed his preferred terminology for these categories, Peirce always held to the view that these three together form the conditions of possibility for any unified experience. It is not clear that Peirce ever found a way of distinguishing this categorial conceptualization of the unity of experience from a pernicious form of Kantianism according to which experience consists in the reduction of a raw sensible manifold into unity by way of concepts. But it is clear that Peirce—at least the early Peirce for a little awhile—grasped the pernicious-ness of something not altogether unlike the problem of givenism. Peirce, in the first article in his first seminal series of philosophical contributions, clearly argued against both the existence of a faculty of intuition and the idea that we possess noninferential cognitive content not traceable to some previous cognitive content (1868a, §1, §7). He offers here a fairly concise case against intuitionism, foundationalism, representationalism, and what appears to be something quite like givenism. In the second article in the series, Peirce is bold, compelling, and I think right in claiming that "no present actual thought (which is a mere feeling) has any meaning, any intellectual value" (1868b, 42; cf. 47). His much better preferred alternative was that thoughts have value only insofar as they are part of broader inferential processes in which they are articulated to a whole network of other thoughts.

But even from early on, Peirce was in the grip of an ambiguity that he would later resolve in the wrong kind of way. Throughout Peirce's writings, we find endorsements of givenism in varying strengths implicit in his various conceptualizations of Quality or firstness. In many of Peirce's formulations (he was always shifting his terminology and reapplying his system in different ways), this conception appears to countenance both core theses of givenism. First, that of our awareness of experiential immediacies, as for instance when Peirce says that "the quality of feeling is the true psychical representative of the first category of the immediate as it is in its immediacy, of the present in its direct positive presentness" (1903, 150). Second, that these immediacies play some important role in our (epistemic) practices, as suggested by Peirce in such claims as "it follows, then, that our perceptual judgments are the first premises of all our reasonings and that they cannot be called in question" (1903, 191). The combination of these two views in a single lecture series is ample evidence (and there is more) that Peirce was at least in some moments in the grip of a subtle form of givenism. Despite early hesitations, Peirce's later work exhibits in fuller colors the givenism that had always lingered in his long-running defense of the first thesis asserting the awareness of raw qualitative feels.

A relatively simple argument helps us see why we should avoid the givenism implicit in Peirce's theorization of a raw feeling of qualitative immediacy as a categorial component of every unified experience. Concerning the question of our access to such Qualitative feels, Peirce must accept one of two approaches: either we have direct experience of Quality or we do not. Peirce denies the viability of the first option of feelings as self-standing for at least three reasons. In that case, a manifold of raw feeling could constitute a unified experience on its own such that the other regulative components of experience (Relation and Representation) would not be universal categories of other experience. Further, self-standing raw experiences of unmediated immediacies seem to be accountable for only by reference to a faculty of intuition, the existence of which Peirce is committed to denying. Last, if raw feeling were self-standing and directly available, we would be at a loss as to explain its relation to the other components of experience by which alone unified experience is possible, at least on Peirce's account. These three reasons force us to turn to the second option, according to which we can never experience qualitative feeling directly but rather only indirectly. But on this view, it is as hard to explain our access to these qualitative feels as it is to account for our confrontations with the noumena posited by Kant. If this is his considered view, then perhaps Peirce is best seen as offering, like Kant, a transcendental argument for the given.[7] But more would certainly need to be said here, because it still needs to be shown that we cannot get by with a more economized picture of practical experience as determined by historical conditions without referencing a controversial story about transcendental conditions. Facing the failure of these two approaches, we might be encouraged by Peirce to consider a third way, according to which we indirectly experience Quality by way of prescension. This seems to have been Peirce's own favored view. But this approach does not enable Peirce to evade the dilemma I am attributing. The proposal for prescinding Quality only pushes the dilemma back one step. Quality prescinded is either directly experienced or is always already mediated by Relation and Representation. If, on the one hand, prescinded Quality is immediately available, then Peirce owes an account of how, without the unity of experience provided by Relation and Representation, we can experience, say, prescinded redness without relating it to or differentiating it from anything else (and given Peirce's own clever arguments against intuition, I doubt that this is possible on his account). But if, on the other hand, prescinded Quality is thoroughly mediated, then it follows that we can never have experiential access to it and can only ever posit it as transcendental.

Subsequent commentators who have wrestled with Dewey's discussions of primary experience, James's of pure experience, and Peirce's of qualitative firstness have found it extraordinarily difficult to say just how it is that we can deploy these conceptions of experience without specifying them in terms of the outworn metaphysical dualisms of mind and reality or subject and object that pragmatism was meant to help us overcome. Commentators have also (when they have bothered to consider it) had a difficult time of saying just how it is that these conceptions do not yield a pernicious form of givenism that opens the door to representationalist foundationalism. This occasional proximity to such troubled philosophical paradigms has led critics from Santayana (1925) to Rorty (1977a) to worry that the pragmatist conception of experience is particularly problematic when put forth in the form of a metaphysics that attempts to describe the context-transcendent traits of all human experience. Even if we can reasonably dispute the accuracy of Santayana's and Rorty's occasionally idiosyncratic interpretations of pragmatism, it is still difficult to deny the force of their common point that there is more than just a whiff of givenism in the pragmatist metaphysics of experience. This criticism need not be formulated in positivistic terms such that the concept of experience is problematic simply because it is metaphysical, but it can more plausibly be stated as the worry that classicopragmatists too often put forth their metaphysics in the wrong kind of way, such that their metaphysics resembles first philosophy more than it resembles a postulated tool of inquiry. The lesson we should draw from these standing criticisms is that pragmatists need to employ special caution in focusing their pragmatism in terms of experience. My claim is not the strong thesis that James and Dewey (and Peirce) were foundationalists but only the more modest thought that they were not equipped with a sophisticated enough antifoundationalist repertoire to ensure that their descriptions of experiential givens would not play into the hands of foundationalism. James and Dewey (and Peirce), simply put, were not always cautious enough, even if we can find plenty of places in their writings where they were on sufficient guard against givenism. This is the tension between a pragmatism committed to a conception of raw experience and a pragmatism committed to a historicism that sees its way clear of even the most subtle forms of representationalist foundationalism.

One of the most perspicuous examples in the entire pragmatist literature of this burdened tension is offered in Dewey's 1915 essay "The Logic of Judgments of Practice." This is an important work because it offers one of the first full statements of Dewey's mature pragmatism, and in so doing it clearly highlights both the advantages and disadvantages of that mature view. Particularly clear in this essay are the tensions between Dewey's recognition that pragmatism must not cave in to a position resembling givenism and Dewey's difficulties in adequately following up on that recognition. Dewey is here clear that pragmatism should not countenance epistemic givens or what he calls "a kind of *knowledge* or simple apprehension (or sense acquaintance) implying no inference and yet basic to inference" (1915a, 406/MW8.60). Dewey's strategy for avoiding such foundational givens is to argue against any epistemically relevant function of immediate perception: "every proposition regarding what is 'given' to sensation or perception is dependent upon the assumption of a vast amount of scientific knowledge which is the result of a multitude of prior analyses, verifications, and inferences" (1915a, 413/MW8.64). His view seems to be that perceptions are not raw givens but are rather mediated forms established by and as ongoing transitions. This is a view Dewey should have cultivated. Yet Dewey never clearly saw his way to the full implications of this vantage. For in the very same essay, Dewey writes of perception that it "just exists physically" and of knowledge that it begins in "an incomplete situation" such that "the *given* is itself indeterminate" (1915a, 398/MW8.54, 337/MW8.15). From these and other remarks, it is clear that Dewey had not yet seen himself all the way clear of the givenism that he was careful to avoid in some forms. Indeed, it seems fair to claim that Dewey here had not yet fully recognized givenism as a problematic, because if he had done so, then he would not have so easily gone back and forth between unfavorable and favorable explications of the idea. As this problematic had not yet emerged into its later fullness when this essay was written, givenism could creep back into Dewey's theory of knowledge by way of his conception of those initial indeterminacies that in his mature epistemology and logic play the role of motivators for inquiry. Here is Dewey in another essay published in the same year: "In this case, the elementary data, instead of being primitive empirical data, are the last terms, the limits, of the discriminations we have been able to make. That knowledge grows from a confusedly experienced world to a world experienced as ordered and specified would then be the teaching of psychological science" (1915b, 299/MW8.95). Givenism lurks here too, if not in the form of primitive sense qualia, then in the form of an immediate experience of indeterminacy or confusion. A givenism of this subtle form would continue to shadow Dewey's pragmatism throughout the remainder of his work (I return in the final chapter to this point in hopes of repairing the errors in this view).

Dewey's work in the years in which these essays were published nicely showcases the way in which he went back and forth between two quite different interpretations of pragmatism, unclear as to how to pull pragmatism away from givenism and toward transitionalism. Dewey, like James (and also like Peirce), could never quite get clear on the idea that in being already mediated by ongoing practical transitions all the terms of inquiry (every object of perception and conception) are not given but are rather on the way as mediated mediations between projecting actions and their eventual outcomes. Yet Dewey, again like James (and again like Peirce), does elsewhere offer useful leads for how pragmatism can avoid givenism: focus on the ways in which knowledge is transitionally mediated all the way through. These are the leads contemporary pragmatists should follow rather than trying to salvage insolvent classicopragmatist concepts of immediate or primary or qualitative experience. By following these leads out, we can focus our efforts on other moments in the writings of the classicopragmatists where they fare far better. These leads encourage us to note well that James wrote in 1904 that "there is no *general* stuff of which experience at large is made. There are as many stuffs as there are 'natures' in the things experienced" (1904a, 179). They also motivate us take seriously that Dewey too proffered this point in 1905 in writing that we have "no need to search for some aboriginal *that* to which all successive experiences are attached," because, quite simply, "Experience is always of *thats*" (1905, MW3.164).

As we pragmatists today are informed by the antigivenist interventions of philosophers from Sellars to Davidson to Rorty, we are particularly well positioned to follow the leads of these more transitionalist aspects of classicopragmatism. I thus find it particularly unfortunate that many contemporary classicopragmatists have not been inclined to realize our positional benefits. In fact, a number of contemporary pragmatists have come dangerously near to foundationalism in relying on a metaphysics of experience to guard themselves against the linguisticism of Rorty's pragmatism. The proximity of these guarded contemporary classicopragmatisms to foundationalism is indeed firmly rooted in much textual evidence, in virtue of which its expositors can rightly claim titles as loyal to the leading classical pragmatists. But such claims to this title owe too much to the fact that James and Dewey themselves were not always on sufficient guard against various philosophical conceptions that are difficult to dissociate from the foundationalist notion of an experiential given. Pragmatists at the beginning of the twenty-first century have at their disposal the tools necessary for being more vigilant against these errors than James and Dewey could have been at the beginning of the twentieth century, prior to several decades of refining these tools. A quick review of classicopragmatist work from the past few decades shows how important it is that we pragmatists should now avail ourselves of these tools.

Ralph Sleeper's work is probably the most spirited defense of Dewey's pragmatism against Rorty's attempted appropriation. His work is still quoted often by those opposing Rorty's use of Dewey. But Sleeper was, unfortunately, more concerned to salvage Dewey's concept of experience from Rorty's critiques than he was to eliminate foundationalism from his own account of pragmatism. Sleeper was explicit that he did not wish to revive foundationalism, but in prioritizing the rescue of Dewey's concept of experience from Rorty's linguisticism, he came dangerously near to it. This prioritization of experience over antifoundationalism is signaled in such ripostes to Rorty as this: "by concentrating almost exclusively upon the antifoundationalist consequences of pragmatism, Rorty's account is all too 'deconstructionist'" (Sleeper 1985, 12, 13). Sleeper's attempt to work out a more viable pragmatism went as follows: "The foundational function of epistemology is denied by assigning the task of accounting for what explains knowledge jointly to logic and metaphysics," which can together provide a complete "system in which the divergent elements all hang together" (1986, 6, 201). Rorty's (1985) convincing reply to this maneuver was to argue that Sleeper's emphasis on a logic of experience and a metaphysics of existence simply places too much weight on certain notions, such as method, which exhibit too many of the trademarks of familiar forms of foundationalist philosophy. In Sleeper's version of pragmatism, logic and metaphysics turn out to be something quite more than merely postulated tools that may occasionally be useful—they assume the form of special philosophical accounts that promise to offer something like a groundwork of experience and existence.

A number of contemporary pragmatists similarly give metaphysics pride of place in their accounts of pragmatism, including Richard Bernstein (1966), Thomas Alexander (1987), and James Gouinlock (1972). Despite the many merits of their work, there is a clear tension in these authors' attribution of both a strong metaphysical and a strong antifoundationalist strain to Dewey. In too many cases, this tension gets resolved by prioritizing the metaphysics of experience in a way that risks turning experience into a foundation. Metaphysics can be consistent with antifoundationalism, but only if the antifoundationalism comes first and the metaphysics follows later as a pragmatic tool to be provisionally employed only where it comes in handy. Rather than prioritizing metaphysics in a way that opens the door to foundationalism, pragmatists should prioritize antifoundationalism as the most general context for a reconstruction of experience such that metaphysics gets invoked as just one among the many tools we postulate in describing and developing experience. The dangers of taking metaphysics too seriously in this way are most clearly evidenced in Gouinlock's defense of Dewey against Rorty. Gouinlock (1995, 86) claims that "Dewey's metaphysics is an attempt to characterize the inclusive context of human existence in such a way that we might learn how to function in it as effectively as possible." He describes this attempt as "the discrimination of traits common to all contexts, or situations, of experience" (1972, 2). I worry that when the skeptics roll into town and start bullying pragmatists about being relativists, these universal traits common to every experience will get drafted into service as invariant givens capable of functioning as philosophical foundations. We will defeat the bully skeptics, but only by purchasing protection with the dangerous weapons of foundationalism.

It is worth noting that such foundationalist tendencies are not restricted to commentators on Dewey alone. While Charlene Haddock Seigfried (2001; 1990, 347–350) carefully guards her own pragmatism against substantive metaphysics and strong foundationalism, her description of James's pragmatism nevertheless locates the "organizing center" of James's thought in "the establishment of a secure foundation in experience" explicable in terms of the "priority of lived experience" (1990, 2, 300).[8] In Peirce's pragmatism, too, talk of foundations continues to surface in debates over whether or not Peirce was a foundationalist, an antifoundationalist, or closer to some middle position such as Susan Haack's (1993, 1996) Peircean foundherentism.

Turning to some of the most recent classicopragmatist scholarship, the secondary literature seems to indicate that pragmatists are indeed increasingly comfortable with endorsing nuanced forms of givenism. Responding to Rorty's suggestion that we move everything over from experience to sociolinguistic practice, Deweyan pragmatist David Hildebrand is right to note that "there are still cases, Dewey would maintain, in which neither an appeal to social practices nor human needs will do." To what do we appeal in such cases? Hildebrand's answer is that we appeal to "the problematic situation" itself insofar as "experience is 'prior' to practices and needs." He backs this up with the claim that "our very ability to reassess 'needs' and 'social practices' depends upon our ability to measure the meaning of these abstractions against something more intimately present, namely the lived moments to which they supposedly apply" (2003, 107). In a similar vein, John Shook's excellent book on the development of Dewey's theory of knowledge attributes to Dewey, or at least to one stage of his thought, the view that "human experience must be the ultimate philosophical ground of appeal" (2000, 121). And, as a final example, Gregory Pappas's fine book on pragmatist ethics begins with an observation about Dewey's attempt to "base philosophy in experience" in which experience is "where things are present in their brute and direct qualitative 'givenness' and 'thereness'" (1997a, 524, 527). Givenism lurks wherever epistemic, ethical, or political roles are attributed, as they are here, to experiential concepts of "gross qualitative givenness in a situation" (2008, 22). This and other work seems to indicate that contemporary classicopragmatists are growing increasingly comfortable with conceptions of a direct and immediate form of experience despite the fact that such conceptions are extremely difficult to distinguish from a conception of experiential givens. This is reflected in other recent scholarship that is admirably forthright about the givenist residue countenanced by classicopragmatist conceptions of experience. Scott Aikin argues that the noninferential cognitive awareness of givenism is "entailed by a pragmatic theory of experience" (2009, 19). And Hugh Miller echoes the increasing prevalence of quasi-foundationalist conceptions of the given in contemporary classicopragmatisms in arguing that "Dewey did not completely fumigate the heavy scent of foundationalism that permeates objectivism" (2005, 367).

In view of these trends in recent scholarship, it bears repeating at the present moment that a conception of experience as an "ultimate ground of appeal," a "more intimate measure," or a "direct qualitative 'givenness'" serves to make experience virtually indistinguishable from a fount of givens. Though most contemporary pragmatists would want to deny that their endorsements of experiential givenism entail foundationalism and representationalism, it is decidedly difficult to understand how we might fully detach the doctrine of the given from foundationalist and representationalist theories of knowledge, morality, and politics. Some pragmatists may wish to follow Dewey in insisting that these experiential givens are but raw feels that can be carefully distinguished from mediated knowings, doings, and sharings. But it still needs to be spelled out exactly why pragmatists are so insistent on a notion of primary experience if they concede that this notion does not play any important epistemic, moral, or political role in our practices. This forces a choice to which classicopragmatists must reply: *either* primary havings hold no relation to reflective practice and so do not play any important epistemic, ethical, or political role in our practices, *or* primary havings indeed provide the basic stuff out of which reflective practice is developed and against which we test our actions, in which case classicopragmatists are obliged to provide a thoroughly nonfoundational account of the relations that hold between these havings and the knowings, doings, and sharings they inform. Classicopragmatists tend to grab hold of the second alternative and in so doing affirm a givenism that courts representationalism and foundationalism. I prefer to grab hold of the first alternative, in order to freely dispose of the idea that primary havings are in any way important for an account of practical experience, thus dispensing with any pernicious form of givenism.

I can elaborate on this point by returning to Bourdieu, not to once again orient my modality of critique but to further my critique. Bourdieu helps us understand how we can explanatorily engage human practices without explicating these in terms of an experiential immediacy that can be abstracted from its historical contexts: "if the agent has an immediate understanding of the familiar world, this is because the cognitive structures that he implements are the product of incorporation of the structures of the world in which he acts; the instruments of construction that he uses to know the world are constructed by the world" (Bourdieu 1997, 136). The classicopragmatists were interested in explicating practice in terms of its experiential (Dewey and James), phenomenological (James and Peirce), or even just logical (Peirce) conditions of possibility, where these would refer to immediate or qualitative feels through which agents negotiate practice in coordination with other instrumentalities and media obviously involved in every practice. By contrast, I am much closer to Bourdieu in being interested in explicating practices in terms of historical (including cultural, social, and individual histories) conditions of possibility, where these refer to the accumulation of practical exercises, skills, and beliefs over time. Classicopragmatists also acknowledge historical conditions of possibility, but these remain in tension with the immediate experiential conditions of possibility they also feature. I am suggesting that we pragmatists go fully historicist in asserting that the conditions of our practices are always historically and temporally mediated.

A pair of examples will help illustrate the difference I am insisting upon. The classicopragmatist position perhaps makes a little sense if we focus on primitive examples, like feeling the pain of a headache or discriminating blotches of color. Here it seems as if an explanatory account can do a great deal by referring to immediate awareness of differences in color. I insist, on the contrary, that we would do better to dispense with such an idea of awareness in favor of a thoroughgoing historical account that emphasizes long and short histories of practical exercises involving color differentiation. Such a historical account might refer to our built environments in virtue of which color discrimination takes on added importance and to the skills and exercises we develop in learning how to negotiate these environments. The advantages of such an approach emerge more clearly in considering more complex examples, such as discriminating good wine from very good wine. I confess that I have no talent and little familiarity when it comes to such discriminations. In consideration of my lack of ability to make these qualitative discriminations, my hunch is that such discriminations are developed on the basis of accumulations of practical exercise and training. Learning to make these discriminations is not a matter of recognizing a qualitative distinction that one is somehow already dimly aware of—I can assure you that I possess no such dim awareness, which a simple experiment could prove, nor would I even know how to go about developing such delicacies of taste, except of course by calling in some expert to help me. Making these discriminations is a matter of training oneself to employ such qualitative distinctions in the context of practices where they count for something. This learning process occurs on the basis of and as a historical accumulation of practical exercise. And as for relatively complex tastes, so for relatively simple colors. So says Sellars:

> Even such "simple" concepts as those of colors are the fruit of a long process of publicly reinforced responses to public objects (including verbal performances) in public situations . . . we now recognize that instead of coming to have a concept of something because we have noticed that sort of thing, to have the ability to notice a sort of thing is already to have the concept of that sort of thing, and cannot account for it (1956, 87).

In sum, classicopragmatists from early to late have made generous use of conceptions of primary experience and qualitative immediacy without being on sufficient guard against the foundationalism conjured by these concepts. There is a great deal that we can learn from the work of all of the philosophers, classical and contemporary, whom I have quoted over the past few pages, but we should not turn to their work for lessons about how pragmatism can success-fully avoid the pitfalls of foundationalism, representationalism, and givenism. For that we must turn to the neopragmatists, such that any successful recu-peration of classicopragmatism now requires bringing neopragmatist insights on board. Absorbing the full force of the threat of givenism, which neopragma-tists such as Rorty can help us do, will disabuse classicopragmatists of some of their more problematic ritual incantations as well as the need to do battle with the foundationalist specters these spells conjure.

The Neopragmatist Linguistic Turn

Rorty has described the linguistic turn as a way out of the all-too-common philosophical errors of foundationalism, representationalism, and givenism. By concentrating exclusively on the use of language publicly available to us all, Rorty argues, we can rid ourselves of any hankerings for an authoritative sky-hook on which our claims to knowledge, morality, and justice could conceiv-ably be hung. As in the writings of the classicopragmatists, in Rorty's neoprag-matism the argument for focusing on language is most fully developed in the context of epistemology, even if it also applies to moral and political philoso-phy. In my discussion, I will once again aim for breadth, but following Rorty's argument will often requiring honing in on the specifically epistemic dimen-sions of his neopragmatist linguisticism.

Rorty, one of our most insightful intellectual historians of twentieth-century philosophy, noted that the philosophical push in the early twentieth century to move everything over from consciousness to language was a "rather des-perate attempt to keep philosophy an armchair discipline." This push, often referred to as the linguistic turn, was thus originally thought of as a way of rescuing philosophical foundationalism:

> The idea was to mark off a space for *a priori* knowledge into which neither sociology nor history nor art nor natural science could intrude. It was an attempt to find a substitute for Kant's "transcendental standpoint." The re-placement of "mind" or "experience" by "meaning" was supposed to insure the purity and autonomy of philosophy by providing it with a nonempirical subject matter (Rorty 1993, 337).

Philosophy had always promised a nonempirical foundation for empirical inquiry, but it had never delivered one. It was this promise (as convincingly pledged by Descartes, Locke, and Kant) that had secured philosophy its place in the modern world. So at the very moment when it began to look like empirical inquiry could take care of itself without any need for philosophical foundations, the philosophers reissued their bold promise to state the conditions of the possibility of empirical knowledge by removing these conditions of possibility from experience in order to place them in language. This saved them from the imminent encroachments of the psychologists—only to put them later on in the path of encroaching linguists and sociologists.

Rorty notes two crucial premises that lay behind the philosophers' attempt to replace "experience" with "language": "First, the two terms had an equally large scope—both delimited the entire domain of human inquiry, of topics available to human study. Second, the notions of 'language' and 'meaning' seemed, at the beginning of the century, immune to the naturalizing process" (1993, 340). Armed with these two premises, the first generation of language philosophers (Frege, Russell, and the early Wittgenstein) argued that language could at last provide that foundation through which philosophy could specify an ultimate court of appeal for all truth claims. But it soon became apparent that once you move everything over to language, the foundationalist project begins to seem pointless. And so the second generation of language philosophers (the later Wittgenstein, Sellars, Quine, and Davidson) began to experiment with hooking up linguisticism to the antifoundationalism launched by James and Dewey. They eventually concluded that the second premise, language's immunity against naturalization, would fail to hold. Over time it grew increasingly disreputable, as the analysis of words gave way to the analysis of sentences, which gave way to the analysis of coherent sets of sentences or vocabularies, which finally gave way to naturalized sociological accounts of language use, of which empirical researchers had already developed adequate descriptions. This premise had been requisite for keeping philosophy an independent armchair discipline. So philosophy, it turned out, had lost its special status as an independent area of research.

Rorty's first book, *Philosophy and the Mirror of Nature* (1979), is usefully read as an intellectual historical account of this move from the foundation of philosophical explanation to the nonfoundation of sociological description.[9] The book made such a splash among philosophers in part because it carefully traced the history of a doubt about philosophical research that every philosopher had been feeling the force of for at least a few decades: philosophy had somewhere taken a turn that was leading it down the path of its own ultimate extinction. Thomas Nagel poignantly expressed one form of this then-familiar skepticism in a preface to a book published in the same year as *Philosophy and the Mirror of Nature*: "I am pessimistic about ethical theory as a form of public service. . . . Philosophy is best judged by its contribution to the understanding, not to the course of events" (1979, xiii). Nagel was like most philosophers in that he happily practiced a form of philosophy that could easily be recognized as irrelevant to the actual practices he was theorizing. At some point, Rorty started everyone worrying that this recognition might entail that philosophy had somewhere along the way lost its reason for existence. Most of Rorty's readers (many of them secondhand gleaners at that) were predictably frightened by his gloomy outlook on the profession. The response to Rorty's book among the leading lights of the profession was to stage a quick retreat from their former pessimism in order to host an unending series of pep rallies in defense of their conception of philosophy. Only twelve years later, Nagel was already confidently asserting a view that was the very opposite of his previous skepticism about philosophy: "Political philosophy . . . has its role, for some of the apparently practical problems of political life have theoretical and moral sources" (1991, 6). Nobody seemed to notice these increasingly common metaphilosophical switcharoos—or if they did they preferred to keep them quiet—yet they remain there, most conspicuous in those casual first pages of introductions to all number of philosophy books, even if they have yet to find their official recognition in an intellectual history of the era. What these metaphilosophical shifts indicated was an increasing anxiety among philosophers about the intellectual viability of work, which they worried had little actual impact beyond, and perhaps even inside, the classroom. While others worried, Rorty traded in his philosophical anxieties for concerns more explicitly public. Armed with the confidence of a well-deserved MacArthur Prize, Rorty left his stony McCosh Hall office at Princeton in order to take up a University Professorship down on the sprawling greens of Thomas Jefferson's University of Virginia. Here he grew increasingly impatient with canonical philosophical problems and increasingly fascinated by the moral and cultural problems of living in a liberal democracy, the very same problems that had obsessed his pragmatist forebears James and Dewey and such of his liberal forebears as John Stuart Mill. One way of interpreting the clear shift indexed between *Philosophy and the Mirror of Nature* and *Contingency, Irony, and Solidarity* is to view Rorty as trading in a rather private self-image of the rigorous professional philosopher for a more public self-image of the hopeful American pragmatist, a view that Neil Gross (2008) explicates in detail as Rorty's adoption of an "intellectual self-concept" of "leftist American patriot." This shift is what eventually led to the provocative view of philosophical inquiry expressed in the title of Rorty's final volume of collected papers, *Philosophy as Cultural Politics*. Of course, in reality things were not quite so clear. There was always a metaphilosophical tension in Rorty such that half the time he saw philosophy as a potential contributor to our liberal democratic culture and the other half the time he saw it as increasingly trite kibitzing between overgroomed eggheads.

But given pragmatism's typical insistence on the role of experience, how did Rorty ever find his way to a pragmatist cultural criticism in the mold of James and Dewey by way of the linguistic turn? The very premise of the linguistic turn, after all, was the obviation of the concept of experience, the very concept that was at the center of so much of classical pragmatism. In one of his final essays, Rorty explained that he both repudiated the foundational yearnings of the original linguistic turn and at the same time held the view that "the linguistic turn was useful nevertheless, for it turned philosophers' attention from the topic of experience toward that of linguistic behavior." This shift is what "helped break the hold of empiricism—and, more broadly, of representationalism" (2007b, 160). The crucially important thing about the linguistic turn for Rorty was that it led the way out of representationalist foundationalism and all its attendant metaphors of the given, of mind as mirror, and of some way that the world really is. Rorty saw the linguistic turn as a move toward pragmatism in that it let us stop giving accounts of the experiential grounds of human knowledge and start focusing instead on the sociolinguistic field in which knowledge develops in a self-correcting way.

The central message of pragmatism according to Rorty is that it enables us to give up the search for some deep-seated thing that lies behind all human practices and that ties them together in some neat package by explaining all of them. Rorty's view was that pragmatism helps us give up the search motivated by what he once referred to as "a sense of humility, or a sense of gratitude, toward something which transcends humanity" (1993, 351). This yearning is motivated by a thought that Rorty found severely debilitating, namely "the thought that there is something nonhuman that human beings should try to live up to" (2000b, 29). The shift from foundationalist humility to pragmatist hope is to be achieved by focusing on the way in which justifications develop internally within an epistemic field rather than foundationally upon an epistemic ground such as experience.

For Rorty's money, the best available account of the relation between the field of linguistic usage and the knowledge that develops within that field is Robert Brandom's inferentialist pragmatism.[10] Rorty took Brandom as having shown why we do not need to search beyond our practices of knowing for something capable of grounding knowledge. Brandom shows that we should instead recognize that knowledge is justified by nothing deeper than just more knowledge as it develops over time in the field of sociolinguistic practice. At the core of the Brandomian account is a rejection of the concept of experience that is Rortyan in inspiration and implementation. Brandom quite frankly puts it this way: " 'Experience' is not one of my words" (2000c, 205n7).

I believe that contemporary pragmatists ought to pay more attention to Rorty's and Brandom's neopragmatist strategies for overcoming foundationalism. They fashioned a clever way of giving up the quest for the grounds of knowledge by favoring instead the project of specifying the field in which knowledge operates. This approach is likely to prove invaluable for the future of pragmatism. To see this, consider not pragmatism's futures but pragmatism's pasts. Note again that Rorty's pragmatist strategy for avoiding the most subtle forms of representationalist foundationalism did not even come into view until philosophers in midcentury began to seriously question the once innocent relation between language and experience. But once philosophers began interrogating this relation, it was only a few decades before it was the primary problem animating the tradition of analytic philosophy into which Rorty initiated himself in the early years of his career. Although this relation was clearly of some interest to James and Dewey, it was not the primary object of concern in the larger philosophical milieu in which they developed their pragmatism. As such, they were not always pressed to formulate their pragmatism as a response to those problems that would become of primary concern only later on, with Rorty's generation. The result was that they did not sufficiently focus on developing the philosophical metaphors and conceptual tools necessary for avoiding the subtlest forms of foundationalism. This does not mean that the classical pragmatists were foundationalists. It only means that they did not equip themselves with the kind of philosophical repertoire necessary for overcoming foundationalism in all its varieties. This helps us see why contemporary classicopragmatisms risk backsliding into foundationalism if they do not reformulate their epistemic conceptions in light of the later antifoundationalist vocabulary that came into proper view only with the linguistic turn. Fortunately, all of the central themes of classicopragmatism lend themselves quite readily to antifoundationalism: fallibilism, antiskepticism, antiauthoritarianism, and of course meliorism and transitionalism. If pragmatism is to remain a viable philosophical tradition, it must focus on developing these antifoundationalist resources.

This brings us to a crucially important question facing all brands of pragmatism today: Is the Rortyan-Brandomian linguistic turn the best way to make the move to a rigorous antifoundationalism? The question is whether or not Brandom is on the mark in suggesting that "what one misses most" (2004, 15) in James and Dewey is that they did not buy into "the distinctively twentieth-century philosophical concern with *language*" and whether or not Rorty is right in arguing that the classicopragmatists "should have dropped the term 'experience,' not redefined it" (1992, 297). The question before us now is how far pragmatists must go down the road of the linguisticism that Rorty and Brandom adopted from Sellars in order to steer fully clear of givenism, representationalism, and foundationalism. At the end of that road, we find Sellars articulating linguisticism at its extreme: "*all* awareness of *sorts, resemblances, facts*, etc., in short, all awareness of abstract entities—indeed, all awareness even of particulars—is a linguistic affair" (1956, 63). It is not clear that pragmatists need to go this far in order to develop an adequate conception of practice that does not resort to the errors of empiricist givenism, representationalism, and foundationalism. But certainly we must go further in this direction than classicopragmatists have thus far been inclined.

The positive upshot of the Sellarsian rejection of experience in favor of language is a nonfoundational conception of knowledge as arbitrated not by subjective mental certainty but by intersubjective conversational consensus. The idea that intersubjective conversational consensus is all that we need has been defended by Rorty with as much cogency and commitment as anyone else. In rigorously defending this controversial view, Rorty has offered a tremendous service to contemporary philosophy by laying his thought out as a coherent field upon which others could dispute the important issues featured therein. This should be applauded insofar as Rorty has hereby enabled an enormous output of productive philosophical scholarship, much of it at the expense of his views. By considering certain of the criticisms of linguisticism furnished by that scholarship, I can show why pragmatists may want to now begin looking for a route to antifoundationalism other than that offered by linguisticism. My conclusion will be roughly as follows: contemporary pragmatists ought to adopt Rorty's strategy of shifting from foundationalist talk of philosophical grounds for practice to pragmatist talk of historical fields of practice, but we ought to do so without adopting Rorty's view that linguistic practices by themselves constitute the totality of these fields of practice.

Rorty's philosophical linguisticism is nicely summarized in his claim that "there are no constraints on inquiry save conversational ones—no wholesale constraints derived from the nature of the objects, or of the mind, or of language, but only those retail constraints provided by the remarks of our fellow-inquirers" (1980, 165). One common criticism of this sociolinguistic theory of practical achievement is that it cannot see its way clear of relativism. Can sociolinguistic consensus provide criteria of truth, goodness, and justice any stronger than the manifest noncriterion defended by the relativist? John McDowell thinks not and so urges against Rorty that we should conceive of "inquiry as normatively beholden not just to current practice but to its subject matter" (2000, 115) as well. McDowell's criticism rests on the intuition that "if our freedom in empirical thinking is total . . . that can seem to threaten the very possibility that judgments of experience might be grounded in a way that relates them to a reality external to thought. . . . Surely there must be such a grounding if experience is to be a source of knowledge" (1994, 5). The difficulty facing McDowell's position, which McDowell of course takes as his challenge, is to tell a convincing story about how these relations between our judgments and something external to them might function in a way that is not equivalent to the foundational and representational function that these relations typically play. Rorty's reply to critics like McDowell has always been that we philosophers ought to stop waiting around for this sort of philosophical story to write itself.

A number of other critics have pointed to the seemingly obvious problem that Rorty's linguisticism is unable to come to terms with nonlinguistic experiences.[11] But these critics too often overlook Rorty's affirmation that he can accept experiences outside the realm of sociolinguistic consensus without contradiction by simply urging that these experiences have nothing to do with practical honorifics like knowledge, morality, and justice. This move would probably not have been endorsed by Sellars, but Rorty deftly makes it by urging a seemingly plausible distinction between practices requiring justification and practices that proceed without such a requirement. Replying to Richard Shusterman's criticism on this matter, Rorty writes that "we can agree with Gadamer that 'being that can be understood is language' while remaining aware that there is more to life than understanding." Some parts of life are irrelevant to social practices of justification and others are relevant to these practices. Rorty's strategy is to claim that these two sides of life "do not stand in a dialectical relationship, get in each others' way, or need synthesis in a programme or theory" (2001, 156–157).[12] This point happens to line up quite nicely with Rorty's arguments elsewhere for a split between public and private spheres in liberal culture. Think of quintessentially public practices like particle physics and probate law as places where we cannot get along without justifications and quintessentially private practices like poetry and painting as places where demands for justification are more often than not indicators of obtuseness. Rorty's strategy with both distinctions consists in arguing for a deep bifurcation in our practices, which he thinks does not stand in need of any reconciliation.

Rorty's strategy here, though perhaps ingenious, will not work if it can be shown that we sometimes engage in social practices of justification without formulating these justifications linguistically in terms of explicit reasons and rules. Bourdieu's work is once again helpful insofar as it is exemplifies an important commitment to rooting out the "rationalism" that lingers in such philosophical postures as linguisticism. Bourdieu argues that it is important to avoid theoretical perspectives incapable of acknowledging that, "as Dewey reminds us, appropriate practice (speaking a language or riding a bicycle, for example) is knowledge and that it even contains a particular form of reflection" (1997, 80). Bourdieu helps us recognize just how pernicious philosophical rationalism can be when applied to explicating practice itself. (It is worth recalling, in this regard, that Brandom [2000c] explicitly offers his view under the banner of "rationalist pragmatism.") There are, it is Bourdieu's point, logics of practice that the theoretical perspective of reason-exchange and language-interaction are unequipped to recognize. Bourdieu's signature concept of *habi-*

tus is explicitly intended to avoid these errors. The idea of *habitus* "has the primordial function of stressing that the principle of our actions is more often practical sense than rational calculation" (Bourdieu 1997, 64). It is notable in this context that Bourdieu often invokes the temporality and historicity (that is, transitionality) of practice to make this point.

Having now seeded discontent with neopragmatist linguisticism by way of Bourdieu, allow me to now turn to another critic who explicitly develops such a line of argument against neopragmatist linguisticism. Barry Allen (2000a, 2000b, 2004) argues that Rorty's sociolinguistic epistemology fails to capture not only the full range of human experience (which is the usual critique offered by contemporary Deweyans and Jamesians) but more importantly knowledge itself (which is the more useful critique, similar to that developed by Bourdieu). Allen's point rests on two claims also featured in Bourdieu's work, though in a rather different sense. The first claim is that there are a diverse set of skills, performances, and technologies that make an essential contribution not only to our actual knowledge but also to the concept of knowledge itself and the very possibility of our sensibly deploying this concept. The second claim is that these skills, performances, and technologies cannot be reduced in their entirety to linguistic, propositional, or doxastic entities. Allen's view is that knowledge is better understood in light of complex artifactual achievements than in terms of either linguistic or mental states. A well-made bridge is a better example of human knowledge than some justified true belief about some cat on some mat. I take Allen's point to be that the cat on the mat is more like a parody than a paradigm of knowledge and that philosophers would do well to note this.

The Rortyan reply to this line of thought is that bridges can be well-made and thus exemplary of knowledge only in virtue of the sociolinguistic practices in which alone we can justify or warrant such assertions. But Allen (2000b, 142) thinks that Rorty misses "the crucial difference between the accomplishment of knowledge and the conventional, social weight of institutional authority." Allen's critique is that Rorty's linguisticism about knowledge fails to account for some of our best epistemic achievements as well as some of our worst epistemic failures. How, Allen asks, can Rorty account for that incredibly narrow but infinitely important gap between agreeing that we know and actually knowing? In that narrow gap lies the enormous difference between our saying that we have got it right and our actually getting it right. Allen argues that this gap is real (he cites examples where all the certified experts said we had it right and it turned out later on that we had it wrong) and that it should "disabuse philosophers of the notion that knowledge is nothing but the consensus of disciplinary or professional peers" (2000a, 233).

Similar concerns emerge when we shift contexts from knowledge to ethics or politics. Just as linguisticism fails to confront artifactual and embodied instances of knowledge, so too does it fail to confront embodied and otherwise nonpropositional aspects of politics. A hunger striker is not only endorsing a propositional expression even if they are doing that too. I will return in later chapters to these problems with the ethical and political consequences of linguisticism, remaining content for now to merely mention the difficulty.[13]

For my purposes here, the important point raised by critics from Allen to Bourdieu is that linguisticism comes up lacking not just in terms of an account of human experience (after all, Rorty never really cared about that) but in terms of an account of human practices including knowledge practices, ethical practices, and political practices (the very stuff to which Rorty tailored his accounts). Allen and Bourdieu thus manage to effectively criticize the linguistic turn on its own grounds. They show how the linguistic turn leaves us feeling a lack precisely where it promised a plentitude. This intervention goes much further than the classicopragmatist anxiety that the linguistic turn leaves us feeling a lack precisely where it insisted we do feel a lack. Allen and Bourdieu both argue, albeit in quite different ways, that we can respond to this deficit in linguisticism without returning to foundationalism. The promising possibility that their work thus raises is that of a conception of practice that is neither purely linguistic nor grounded in an ultimate appeal to human experience.

Furthering the Pragmatist Sequence

What conclusion can we draw from this brief intellectual-historical review of the two waves of experience-centric and language-centric pragmatism? If certain critics of foundationalism and linguisticism have valid concerns, as I have urged they do, then these debates clarify the central problem facing pragmatism today: *we must find a way of developing the core epistemological, ethical, and political insights of pragmatism without reliance on either an experience-centric or a language-centric philosophical framework.* The idea that best fulfills the requirements of this third-wave pragmatist renewal is what I am calling "transitionalism," with its ready insistence on temporality and historicity.

At the heart of this transitionalist perspective is the philosophical exercise of bringing our epistemic, ethical, and political practices into focus by way of the mediating transitions in terms of which these practices themselves have developed and continue to develop. These practices are to be treated in terms of the temporality that forms them and the historicity that yields their specific content. Engaging our practices in this way means a lot less explanation offered in terms of experiential or semantic conditions of possibility and a great deal more explanation offered in terms of the historical, anthropological, and sociological analyses of the practices themselves. My invocations of Bourdieu above were meant in part to motivate this sort of cross-disciplinary perspective at the heart of transitionalist pragmatism. I used Bourdieu both because he helps me state the problems fueling the need for routing around the experientialism-linguisticism divide and because he helps me point the right way in developing a pragmatist conception of how to engage our historical-temporal practices. Bourdieu serves as a convenient reference point that can help us understand how philosophy, in order to do its work, must involve itself in sociology, anthropology, and history. But it is worth noting that for these purposes one could just as well invoke any number of other thinkers as a reference point, for instance Michel Foucault, Bernard Williams, or Jürgen Habermas as well as Ian Hacking, Paul Rabinow, or Michael Walzer. All of these thinkers, though each in very different ways, help point us toward what is needed for a revitalized third-wave pragmatism today. The sorts of historico-sociologico-anthropologico philosophical critiques featured in their work will better reveal the conditions of our practices than either a philosophy of experience or a philosophy of language. This is because they will in almost every instance yield a greater abundance of material to work with in our ongoing efforts to transitionally meliorate the situations in which we find ourselves.

Whatever reference points and conversation partners we choose, the task before pragmatism today is to move beyond the impasses of past pragmatisms. These impasses have left the tradition in a holding pattern for at least the past decade. The result is that pragmatists of all stripes now readily acknowledge the pressing need for a third-wave pragmatism. But to do justice to the insights of both previous pragmatisms, such a third wave will need to be developed in a way that productively furthers the historical sequence. It will not do, in other words, to attempt to overcome previous iterations of pragmatism by distancing the tradition from them. A third-wave pragmatism must avail itself of insights from both the classicopragmatists and the neopragmatists. Transitionalist pragmatism explicitly aims for this.

Thus aiming for sequential advance does not entail that third-wave pragmatism must define itself in terms of the experience-versus-language debates that have been so central for the swelling impasse in pragmatism. As noted above, the seeming centrality of these debates is probably an effect of the contingent fact that, during the high years of the previous two waves of pragmatism, philosophy gave pride of place to epistemology and its attendant subfields. This contingency has unfortunately led many commentators to the incautious conclusion that pragmatism is primarily a contribution to epistemology when in fact it is best seen as primarily a contribution to a broad-based cultural criticism that wraps together philosophical reflections on knowledge, ethics, and politics. This has further led to the marginalization of other important debates among previous pragmatists in moral and political contexts. A viable third-wave pragmatism ought to have something to say about all of these debates in each of these philosophical contexts. Different contexts, of course, carry different constraints. In some contexts, a third-wave pragmatism must address the experience-language impasse, but in other contexts no such requirement will be pressing. Although this impasse is surely relevant to issues throughout epistemology, moral philosophy, and political theory, it is not always the most major impasse blocking advance in each of these areas. The sole thread of continuity that runs throughout the ensuing discussions is the idea of transitions as the best part of a pragmatism that now moves beyond these debates. This thread can weave all three waves of pragmatism into work on knowledge, ethics, and politics.

Although pragmatists today widely acknowledge that a renewed third-wave pragmatism is now needed, we ought to be proceed carefully here, because there are different ways of envisioning how this might shape up. There are as yet very few well-developed proposals for a third-wave pragmatism on offer. I would like to briefly consider two other recent pragmatist offerings positioned as a third option for pragmatism today. One of these offerings I find misguided and the other I take as an inspiration. Contrasting the two enables me to further elucidate what I am aiming for in offering my own pragmatism as a third wave that washes fresh life over the remnant foam of the first two waves.

One of the most influential and enticing third pragmatisms arriving on the scene in recent years is developed by Cheryl Misak (2007), in her call for a "New Pragmatism" that would convene a rather disparate set of philosophers under the banner of Peircean epistemology. The work of Misak and others in her *New Pragmatists* anthology at once returns to classicopragmatism by borrowing core ideas of truth and objectivity from Peirce and at the same time involves itself in neopragmatism by translating these ideas into the medium of linguisticist analytic philosophy. Two problems are immediately evident. First, although these "new pragmatists" revive some ideas taken from Peirce, they altogether refuse to engage with the role played by the concept of experience in classicopragmatism. Richard Bernstein thus rightly laments that "not a single one of the papers in *New Pragmatists* treats what was perhaps the most central concept for the classical pragmatists—the concept of experience" (2007, 32). Indeed, Misak even saw fit to leave this word out of the index. Neglect of experience suggests that the "new pragmatism" will from the perspective of classicopragmatism be seen as simply a furtherance of neopragmatism. That may prove philosophically sound, but it does not answer to anything that might motivate the need for a "new" pragmatism today. A second problem in combination with the first bankrupts the project entirely. Misak's pragmatism really does not involve itself all that fully with many of the insights offered by the neopragmatists either. Many of her contributors prefer instead to draw different lessons from the teachings of the linguistic turn. Misak describes herself as "reclaiming the label 'pragmatism'" from the Rortyan view that "there is no truth or objectivity to be had" (2007, 1). This statement is far too polemical to entertain as a serious criticism of Rorty. Rather than evincing any insight about neopragmatism, it shows more importantly that Misak's New Pragmatism is explicitly antineopragmatist. It is clearly not meant as an attempt to dialectically advance pragmatism in light of the insights of her predecessors in the tradition.

The problem I am pointing out is already visible in the metaphor that leads Misak's offering. She urges the need for a "new" pragmatism. But in her avant-gardism Misak forgets what came before. This is decidedly against the grain of the historical and temporal continuity sought by the transitionalist. A better metaphor than "new-ness" is that of "renewal," in which we can hear the connotations of both repetition ("re-") and difference ("-new"). The task before us now is accordingly to "re-new" pragmatism.

A renewed third-wave pragmatism of this sort has been offered by Joseph Margolis in a number of stimulating writings in which he fully and fairly engages the work of both the classico- and the neopragmatists. Margolis describes his third-wave pragmatism with the metaphor of "reinvention," which is much closer to my reformist "renewal" than it is to Misak's avant-gardist "new." This metaphor suits Margolis's project perfectly, in that his aim is to develop a "'third' way of viewing pragmatism" that would take account of the insights of both Deweyan and Rortyan pragmatism. Why is this called for? "To 'revive' pragmatism within the terms of nothing more recent than whatever Dewey wrote in his best moments is to confirm pragmatism's demise, though I have the greatest regard for Dewey's achievement; by contrast, to go beyond Dewey, to address the entire force of the analytic tradition . . . is to make room for the intervening serendipity of Putnam's and Rorty's quarrels." It is clear that Margolis favors classicopragmatism over neopragmatism, but he is always more than fair to Rorty, and this alone qualifies him as among a very small handful of critics who genuinely and charitably engage both classicopragmatism and neopragmatism. Not only does Margolis's third-wave fluxist pragmatism offer a useful way of orienting the tradition vis-à-vis its previous two waves, but it also provides an orientation precisely along those conceptual contours that are central to my transitionalist pragmatism. Margolis's fluxism makes much of the very themes of historicity and temporality that inform my transitionalism. A leading metaphor found through much of Margolis's work is that of "the flux," which he offers in decided opposition to the metaphor of "invariance." The point of playing up the metaphorical "fluxive account of nature" is to emphasize that "all invariances will be judged to be the artifacts of flux" (2002a, 132, 12, 130, 22).[14] This is an incredibly precise formulation when you think about it—what it might be taken to imply, for example, is that the Kantian categories would be judged artifacts of a Hegelian dialectic and yet be no less categorical for it. The result of all this is helpfully summarized by Margolis in a forthcoming piece: "Pragmatism *is* the leanest form of naturalism committed (often too vaguely) to the post-Hegelian analysis of historicity and encultured life. Yet it never pursued these themes forcefully or adequately enough during or even since its classic days." This neatly summarizes Margolis's contribution to the project of a renewed pragmatism in terms of two key ideas: pragmatism is at core a philosophy of flux, and it has yet to adequately develop its core fluxist themes. Both of these insights are also at the heart of my transitionalism. In combination, they offer the prospect for a renewal of pragmatism that may yet overcome the impasses of the present.

At this point, some readers will begin to suspect that my transitionalist pragmatism merely follows along rails already laid down by Margolis. (I would take this suspicion as a compliment, though I cannot say if Margolis would.) There are, however, some rather substantive differences that, in all fairness to both offerings, deserve mention. I shall air two (merely noting as a third divergence the fact that Margolis takes Peirce as far more central for pragmatism than I am capable of).[15] First is Margolis's (1986) attempted use of pragmatism as a strategy for historicizing transcendentalism. Transitionalism and transcendentalism offer two quite different images of philosophy. I agree with Margolis that pragmatism is best understood as a post-Kantian philosophy heavily invested in certain core features of the Kantian project especially as it was transformed by the Hegelian intervention. But I would insist that the pragmatists, for all their Kantianism, were not at all invested in transcendentality, because they saw historicity and temporality as a way of routing around the need for anything like transcendental thought. This is a point I cannot argue for here, but I may as well state the idea in its baldest form: pragmatists take from Kant the idea of critique as an inquiry into conditions of possibility of present practices, but they detach this idea from a transcendental application of critique whereby these conditions of possibility form limits that are both universal in scope and necessary in modality—critique is henceforth an inquiry into the complex and contingent conditions of possibility constitutive of our present. A second difference between my third-wave pragmatism and Margolis's offering is that he situates pragmatism as primarily an epistemological conception and in so doing defines it largely by way of contrast to other prominent strains of epistemology, chief among them contemporary analytic naturalism.[16] My pragmatism is, for all the reasons previously laid out, primarily a cultural-critical conception according to which the labor of philosophical thought devotes itself to clarifying and amplifying the meliorative reconstructions already underway in our present cultural moment. Epistemology is crucially important for my pragmatism, but equally crucial are ethics and politics such that it is not helpful for my purposes to bring pragmatism into focus as a primarily epistemological view whose chief import consists in its being an alternative to naturalism. Such debates with naturalism and transcendentalism are important, but they are not the proper core of pragmatism.[17] Despite these and other differences in orientation, I find that Margolis's "flux pragmatism" offers a replenishing stream of insights that are altogether bracing for my transitionalist pragmatism, particularly so in comparison to other recent pallid attempts to advance the tradition of pragmatism.

A transitionalist-fluxist approach is so attractive for pragmatism just now because it can be constructed out of notions of temporality and historicity that are, as I showed in the previous chapter, central across the entire tradition from classicopragmatism to neopragmatism. Thus it is that transitionalism and fluxism are in a unique position to re-new or re-invent pragmatism rather than tailor it of wholly original cloth. Both renewals turn to historicity and temporality to blend the best of both waves of previous pragmatism.

In the case of transitionalism, this works as follows. From James and Dewey, it takes a commitment to the present experiences we find ourselves in the midst of as the only possible resource for overcoming the problems presented by these experiences. From Rorty and Brandom, it takes the crucial antifoundationalist strategy of replacing the search for practical grounding with an account of practice as a differentiated field of interaction. Transitionalism plays up these elements in previous pragmatisms so as to play down other more pernicious elements: it dispenses both with Rorty's argument that antifoundationalism requires linguisticism and with lingering foundationalist tendencies that still hinder James's and Dewey's conceptions of experience as sometimes given. The result is a transitionalist view according to which the temporal flow of practice is both broad enough and flexible enough to accommodate all of what we should want to count as successful human practice, without forcing this practice to conform to a pattern that would evade the contingencies of the human condition.

What I thus propose is a third pragmatism that makes peace. We no longer need see the first two waves of pragmatism as opposed factions vying for control of the pragmatist banner. These two pragmatisms can rather be seen as two coherent moments within the broader development of a resynthesized or renewed pragmatism. Some will complain that this version of pragmatism strays too far from its sources by freely taking those parts of James, Dewey, and

Rorty that I like and discarding other parts that do not suit my purposes. They will worry that this is just too much intellectual poaching. Perhaps. My reply is that we should take our pragmatism from where we need it, not worry too much over the parts we find troublesome, and judge the resulting product by its flowers and their fruits.

Four

KNOWLEDGE AS TRANSITIONING

The Temporality and Historicity of Knowledge

Having laid out the basics of my conception of transitionalist pragmatism and its place in the broader intellectual history of pragmatism, I turn now to explicating this transitionalist pragmatism as it functions with respect to the core philosophical concerns of knowledge, ethics, and politics. My aim is to show how the central transitionalist themes of historicity and temporality offer the best light for discerning the distinctive advantages of pragmatist perspectives on these core philosophical areas. This requires showing that the third-wave transitionalist pragmatism at once preserves the previous two waves of classicopragmatism and neopragmatism while also advancing beyond their shortcomings. In the territory of epistemology, the experience-language debates dominate the conceptual landscape. I will accordingly continue in this chapter to navigate by means of the conceptual devices laid out in the intellectual history offered in the previous chapter. Later chapters roam through different territories and will be explored with different maps.

One useful way in which philosophers have thought about epistemic concepts is to suppose them as explaining epistemic relations. Approached in this way, the whole point of epistemology is to explain those relations holding between judgments (or beliefs, or propositions) and their objects in virtue of which the judgments (or beliefs, or propositions) are true or false. Whereas philosophers have typically treated these relations as atemporal, a better approach might be a form of pragmatism that treats temporality as internal to epistemic relations. Foundationalist empiricism takes knowledge to be a static relation between a judgment and an immediate percept: knowledge is an accurate representation. Linguisticism takes knowledge to be a static relation holding between a judgment and the broader sociolinguistic mass of beliefs in which that belief is articulated: knowledge is what we have consensus on. Both foundationalists and linguisticists can of course accept that bodies of knowledge change, but such changes have no effect on what they view as the certifying epistemic relation insofar as this is in every instance a static or tenseless relation. By explicitly temporalizing the epistemic relation, transitionalist pragmatism redescribes knowledge in terms of a concurrence between prior parts and future parts of an unrolling field of practice. We thus get a full-enough account of the epistemic relation without either leaning on experiential givens or restricting ourselves to linguistic practice alone.

Here is the core of a transitionalist epistemology: *the epistemic relation holds between prior practical projections (for example, beliefs, skills) and the future practical eventualities at which they aim (for example, the objects of beliefs, the aims of skilful action).* Knowledge just is what this relation is—a temporal-historical relation between anticipations and emanations but not a static relation between, say, minds and matters. The mark of epistemic achievement (which can be variously analyzed in terms of justified true belief, warranted assertability, epistemic reliability, or some other theoretical apparatus— I abstain from committing to any particular analysis in the present exposition) is neither agreement with experience nor with sociolinguistic consensus but is rather the process of getting from here to there. The knowledge relation is that which carries us through time from prior practical initiations to their anticipated practical outcomes. The transitionalist view thus holds knowledge as thoroughly temporal and historical. It is temporal because it is in its form a process of being guided through time from a past to a future experience. It is historical because the process is made up of only that historical content involved in being so guided.

On this transitionalist account, the basic stuff out of which our epistemic practices are formed are the practical engagements within which we find ourselves always already enmeshed. It follows from this that we can get a full-enough account of our epistemic practices on the basis of historical, sociological, and anthropological inquiries that take into account the full complexity and contingency of these practices. In this way, pragmatism circumvents the traditional philosophical attempts (and failures) to offer universalizing philosophical explanations of the (singular) knowledge relation across the (plural) social, cultural, and historical contexts in which our epistemic practices develop.

The thought that history, sociology, and anthropology provide crucial orienting instruments for a pragmatist epistemology is part of what motivated my invocation of Pierre Bourdieu's theory and practice of critique in the previous chapter.[1] For like the transitionalist pragmatist, Bourdieu strongly affirms "the historicity of reason" and its corollary that "practice is inseparable from temporality" (1997, 93; 1980, 81). My view is that we pragmatists should turn toward detailed historicist critiques of epistemic practice like Bourdieu's once we accept that there is nothing in general, neither experiential givens nor linguistic usage, that makes our epistemic practices work the way that they do. Recognizing that there is nothing in general underwriting every epistemic practice helps us recognize that there is a vast storehouse of contingently accumulated practical materials that we have somehow managed to cobble together into successful epistemic practices. The materials constitutive of our practices are historical-temporal beginnings and outcomes. For this reason, epistemic success (and failure) is best accounted for in terms of detailed inquiries into the relation between our practical projections and the practical outcomes anticipated (or not) by these projections. Epistemologists will be best equipped to study these practical processes if they involve themselves in the sociological, anthropological, and historical inquiries that bring the rich detail of our historical-temporal transitions into adequate focus.

There are, of course, numerous approaches here with which pragmatists can profitably partner for these purposes. These partnerships will be most productive where the sociologico-anthropologico-historico critique in question does all it can to explicate our knowledge as historical accumulation and temporal relation. Bourdieu's social science is thus of particular value for pragmatist purposes because of its uncompromising explicit methodological commitment to historicity and temporality: "Social science, which is obliged to make a critical break with primary self-evidences, has no better weapon for doing so than historicization. . . . It is clear how damaging it is to reject historicization, a rejection which, for many thinkers, is constitutive of philosophy itself and which gives free rein to the historical mechanisms that it claims to ignore" (1997, 182). Bourdieu overcomes this refusal by articulating practices as historical processes and temporal interplays between habitus and agent. This is not the place to digress into an explication of Bourdieu's enormously complex theory of practice. I simply wish to note the privilege Bourdieu accords to historicity and temporality in his work: "The *habitus*, a product of history, produces individual and collective practices—more history—in accordance with schemes generated by history" (1980, 54). I have to admire any theorist who finds an intelligent way to use the word "history" three times in one sentence.

According to a transitionalist epistemology, the determination of whether or not past and future agree must be drawn up in terms of particular historical contents. What outcome past practice predicted is specified in that practice's terms such that agreement with the future is also accounted for in wholly practical terms. It follows that epistemic success and failure are internally attributed wholly within practices. This helps us see why there is little need for general philosophical accounts of what form knowledge must assume or what contents it must abide. And this is why we can now confidently dispose of those overarching conceptions of experiential immediacy and linguistic consensus so familiar to pragmatists of diverse orientations. What we need in the place of these overarching conceptual edifices are thick conceptual and empirical elucidations of our practices explicating what would be adequate for discriminating relations between past projections and future realizations. Bourdieu's work offers a valuable model of this sort of practice of a thick elucidation that is neither antiphilosophical nor overphilosophical in its willingness to blend the conceptual and the empirical. The outcomes of Bourdieu's inquiries are not overarching philosophical invariants but rather a wealth of practical material that enables us to articulate, understand, and engage with the epistemic practices under investigation. These inquiries thus reveal a practical material sufficiently complex as to enable the stabilization of valuable relations of knowing. It is in virtue of this complexity that our practices are historicist but not relativist: "It is in history, and in history alone, that we must seek the principle of the relative independence of reason from the history of which it is the product" (Bourdieu 1997, 102). So though it is historical through and through, knowledge is a relation that bears definite connections we can inquire into, test, and certify. It is a relation, internal to practice itself, between past projections and future anticipations.

At this point, more than a few philosophers will begin wondering whether these sorts of thick conceptualizations are really adequate for the difficult task of determining whether or not we actually achieve knowledge in the practices under consideration. They will object that these conceptualizations fail to bring into focus the knowledge relation itself and instead only enable us to come to terms with the effects of knowledge, whose true core lies elsewhere. If the transitionalist view is that knowledge consists merely in the process of transitioning from past practical projections to the future practical outcomes they predict, then critics may ask how we would ever know that we have arrived at the outcomes at which our beliefs or skills aim. If I have a belief about where a building is and then go to the building itself, how do I know that I am at the building that I believe I am at? How do our beliefs compare to their objects when both are copresent? This question has fueled a great deal of epistemological attention. One familiar answer has been that beliefs and their objects must correspond to one another in order for the beliefs to be true and justified (and hence known). Another has been that beliefs must cohere with a greater mass of beliefs in order to be true and justified (and hence known). Another has been that beliefs must be formed by reliable processes in order to be true and justified (and hence known). The pragmatist view is that this little riddle does not deserve the great deal of attention that it has received from philosophers. We do not need a general account of the way in which we go about certifying all of our beliefs. Instead we need the diverse accounts of different ways in which different practitioners certify their beliefs. This is why we need thick historical, sociological, and anthropological accounts of certification practices rather than blown-up philosophical theories of certification, verification, and confirmation. The more detailed inquiries better help us realize when we can and cannot accept that we have arrived at the objects of our belief—they help us, that is, discriminate the known, the unknown, and the unknowable. Where doubts persist, as they always will in practice, our only recourse will be to keep muddling through the temporal intermediaries that lead us from beliefs to their objects. Never will we arrive at some philosophically unassailable coincidence between beliefs and objects. Unassailability may be achieved in practice, but never is it secured through philosophy. Pragmatism, which is at home with uncertainty, is bracing for this thought.

One metaphor particularly suitable for a transitionalist conception of knowing is that of betting. Knowing is an instance of articulating relations between past projections and future outcomes. So according to my metaphor, it is not like a direct apprehending but rather like a mediated betting. The betting metaphor usefully calls attention to the fact that knowing is an instance of a relation that is wholly mediated by what comes between its being placed and its being paid out. Taking this seriously as a metaphor for knowing suggests that knowing is a matter of inquiring into the situations in which we find ourselves so as to find out if our hypotheses pay off whenever we follow them out. The thorny philosophical issue of whether or not our projections are true or false before they are actually verified can be left to the side, as it has no bearing on actual practical conduct. What matters for knowing is not whether projections about the future are true now but whether they will be true in the futures that they are about. Indeed, the only thing that could matter is whether or not our projections actually get things right in the futures of which they are predictive. You bet on a horse in the first race tomorrow. What matters for your bet is how that horse does tomorrow. If it turns out tomorrow that your horse loses, then it will have done you no good had it been true today that the horse will win tomorrow. All that really matters and all that you are really betting on is whether or not it will be true tomorrow that your horse wins the race. All our beliefs—remember that for the pragmatist beliefs are rules for action—are like bets. Truths, says James, must "*pay*" (1907, 104). What counts is not how our beliefs and bets stand right now but how they will pay out for us when their appointed hour is upon us. This is the characteristically pragmatist attitude, and Peirce was accordingly right to appropriate the term "pragmatism" from Kant as the name for this view. Kant defined "pragmatic belief" as "such contingent belief, which yet forms the ground for the actual employment of means to certain actions" (1781, A824/B852). In other words, a bet. Kant went on to explain that "the usual touchstone . . . is *betting*. . . . Thus pragmatic belief always exists in some specific degree." We would do well to note more often that pragmatism was born in the crucible of probabilities.

The critics I mentioned before are likely to reply at this point that a view of all knowing as betting clearly runs afoul of simple logical platitudes. My view is that what matters for a bet is whether it will be true or false tomorrow that the horse wins the race such that it matters not one bit if it is true today that the horse will win tomorrow. Critics will bear their logical teeth at this point, insisting that "it is now true that x will p" entails "x will p." But the transitionalist view is only that "it is now true that x will p" is in every instance a bet about the future. The realities such beliefs are about, and that alone can settle their truth or falsity, have not yet obtained (since the belief is a bet about a future that has not yet obtained), and so such beliefs are neither true nor false, though they may be claimed as such. Critics of pragmatism have long worried about this result. Both Bertrand Russell and Josiah Royce laid into James early on over these matters. Russell (1908, 123; 1946, 846) thought James's view entailed that truth is a mere fancy unconstrained by hard facts. Royce, who was more intimate with James's thought than any other of his contemporaries, expressed similar worries, which he put to James in 1899 in a letter: "Do you mean to assert any of the following propositions? An astronomer's present assertion about the eclipses of the year 2000 is neither true nor false until these eclipses occur? . . . Neither truth nor falsity? Nothing real?" (Royce, cited in Richardson 2006, 387). Royce was worried that James had denied himself the possibility that truths about the future can hold now. James did not share the worries of his critics. In replying to Royce, he bit the bullet: "Neither true nor false, in the strict sense! For the facts that could make these hypotheses either true or false are non-existent as yet" (James, cited in Richardson 2006, 387). Of course, we can act as if such beliefs are true. We can and do, and rightly, bet on them. Yet they are not true, strictly speaking, until they are certified by future experiences. This worries critics like Royce and Russell because it requires denying any significant epistemological role to postulates like the idealist's Absolutes or the empiricist's space-time unity. The pragmatist need not deny that these postulates might play a role in our metaphysics but they are happy to deny that they must play some important role in our epistemologies. Even if the full path of the future is already laid out in actual fact, such that a perfect space-time unity in the mind of the Absolute stretches out into some golden forever beyond, we have no unfettered access to it, and so we must be content with muddling through in the temporally and historically conditioned ways to which we are accustomed.

Another way to defang critics is to flash bigger fangs back. In this case, such a strategy might involve arguing that it is actually the standard logical account of truth preferred by the critics that obscures our view in these matters. The transitionalist view is that truth articulates past to future and so is not applicable until the contents of that articulation can be investigated. This view has more to do with the value of truth than with the logic of truth. For the value of our true beliefs consists in their leading us into the realities that they predict: if we assert something but do not follow our assertion through to its object, then we have failed to realize the benefits of our assertion, whatever we may be logically entitled to attribute to it. The transitionalist approach is accordingly made more plausible by thinking of epistemic concepts like truth primarily in terms of their value and only derivatively in terms of their logic. This involves setting seeming logical platitudes about truth and their thorny conundrums aside until we have cleared up more pressing issues concerning the value of truth. This switch from logic to value is a quintessentially pragmatist move. For it is the pragmatist view that logic is normative only insofar as it is a derived artifact of best practice. Logic summarizes our best practices so as to enable us to improve them even further. The logic of truth should thus be derived from the value of truth. Otherwise logic can possess no normative authority.

This shift in perspective perhaps alleviates some of the thorny philosophical issues that have long plagued pragmatism. But it also raises a number of other thorny metaphilosophical issues that must be addressed. The conversion of philosophers such as Bourdieu and Foucault to disciplines such as anthropology and history, where they nevertheless continued to produce some of the most important philosophical work of their era, reveals a number of important metaphilosophical lessons. But counterdisciplinary converts like Bourdieu and Foucault were not often eager to explicate their implicit metaphilosophical commitments. So in reflecting on what we expect from our philosophical work it may be useful to turn instead to philosophers who remained philosophers in large part by turning to metaphilosophy. In the case of epistemological concepts like truth and knowledge, we can find few better guides than Bernard Williams.

Williams points out that the widespread assumption that a philosophical theory of truth must primarily aim to define what truth is has recently culminated in its inevitable result: there cannot be any philosophically interesting theories of truth. Williams (2002, 63) concludes a survey of the history of twentieth-century theories of truth from Tarski to Davidson with the thought that "we should resist any demand for a *definition* of truth." But denying this much does not mean that we must also deny a philosophical inquiry into the value of truth. This, as it happens, is the very sensible approach explored by Williams: "I shall be concerned throughout with what may summarily be called 'the value of truth' . . . to the extent that we lose a sense of the value of truth, we shall certainly lose something and may well lose everything" (2002, 6–7). The upshot of Williams's approach is to suggest that we philosophers should shift our attention from conceptual-definitional inquiries into the logic of truth to explanatory-moral inquiries into the value of truthfulness. Hence the title of his book, *Truth and Truthfulness: An Essay in Genealogy*.

A key feature of Williams's project involves undertaking a genealogy of various forms that truthfulness takes in the present—it was Williams's view that truth is best explicated by bringing philosophy into collaboration with other forms of inquiry including most notably history but also conceivably sociology, anthropology, psychology, and even literature.[2] A crucial philosophical advantage of Williams's intervention, which any transitionalist pragmatist ought to take very seriously indeed, is that he does not focus all of his attention on the kinds of sensible-sounding stipulations that lead to deflationary accounts of truth. This enables him to confidently explore the value that truthfulness has in our lives. Williams thus changes the metaphilosophical assumptions about what we might expect from a philosophy of truth such that we can change the philosophical questions we are led to ask in light of these assumptions.

Williams is best read as urging one very simple but crucially valuable point: an explanation of truth's value is today philosophically more important than a definition of truth's conceptual content. (This was, as Williams points out, Nietzsche's project, and it was also, as he does not note, James's.) Philosophers are likely to react with hostility to this point, but their fears are unwarranted. Williams's point is not that the definitional-conceptual project is misguided or incoherent so much as it is that this project is less philosophically important than the explanatory-moral project. An emphasis on what is important about, rather than what is logical of, truth elucidates a crucial feature of the way in which Williams is urging us to approach truth: think of truth as Nietzsche and James did, in moral terms as a species of the good. Keeping this perspective in view when thinking about truth goes a long way toward explaining why we may want to concern ourselves more with explaining what truth *does* rather than with defining what truth *is*. For we can rightfully declare that what truth *does* for us is supposed to be a good thing even if we find that what truth *is* to us remains a very mysterious thing. That thought can take philosophical work on truth a long way.

Williams's approach to truth can help us sort out an approach to knowledge. The analogy from truth to knowledge may seem a stretch insofar as truth and knowledge are not easily comparable when taken logically. But if instead we focus on their value in terms of the roles they play in our epistemic practices, it turns out that they are not nearly so dissimilar as some philosophers have insisted. If truth is best approached as a valuable process that *does* something for us, rather than as a quality that *is* something regardless of what we do, then perhaps knowledge too is better treated in the same terms.

Transitionalist epistemology holds that knowledge (like truth) is ever futural and so irreducibly temporal and historical. Knowledge is a tensed relation ever pointing from past to future. This does not mean that we can never know anything about the present. What it means, rather, is that the achievement of knowledge is a futural achievement. Knowledge is a bet made on a future reality. If one makes a bet on some rather obvious present fact (for example, that I am seated here in this chair before you), then the payoff is likely to be small. But if one makes a bet on some future fact (for example, that if I sit in the chair in such and such a way then I will not have back problems in a month), then the payoff is likely to be greater if I can indeed successfully transition through time from my belief to its object. The value of knowledge does not consist in our recognition of the obvious but in our being able to make successful bets about the unobvious. What mediates between projections and outcomes so as to certify knowledge are not static relations like correspondence, coherence, or the absolute but rather those humble temporal-historical intermediaries that lead us from the present through the past to the future.

These humble temporal-historical relations that lead from past to future can be construed as the subject matter of historical, sociological, and anthropological inquiries. This helps us see why pragmatists ought to eagerly extend collaborative invitations to those undertaking such inquirers. Fleshing out our epistemology in collaboration with such inquirers will enable us to dismiss troubled philosophical conceptions such as that of experiential givens of linguistic ubiquity. This point also helps clarify the relation between transitionalist pragmatism and previous pragmatisms. Pragmatist epistemologists have thus far tended to invoke experience or language in one of two ways: either as final arbiters that could explain how practice is invested with epistemic success or as the practical basis that we confront in practice. Transitionalist pragmatism routes around both by referring only to the complexity and contingency of practice itself in working up an account of our epistemic achievements and entitlements.

First, the transitionalist account has no need for final arbiters of disputes over how well we steer through our practices. This is because our practices themselves do not admit of any such final arbiters. We get by as we do by continually deploying and redeploying our storehouse of practical material in order to further our practical engagements. We should take it as an advantage that we have learned to develop practices that depend on nothing but the ongoing flow of the practices themselves. This yields practices that lean on nothing but their own forward motion. Inertia, it turns out, goes quite a long way in keeping everything moving forward, and the credit invested in the future by the past propels the present ever forward. Second, the transitionalist account also has no need for referring to experience and language as supplying the basis upon which practice is elaborated. Practice is elaborated only upon itself, that is, upon its own accumulated historical furnishings. It confronts only the ongoing stream of practice in its further constructions and reconstructions of itself. We do not require experiential immediacy because we can accept that our practices take shape not on the basis of the qualitative tone of raw experience but rather on the basis of our practical engagements with the world. We should not neglect the immense accumulation of practical experience involved in even the simplest acts. What matters most is this accumulation itself, as a process, rather than experiential immediacies or linguistic consensuses acting as supposedly static bases for these processes.

Relating Experience and Language in the First Two Waves of Pragmatism

Having laid out the core of a transitionalist view and its theoretical advantages over previous conceptions of pragmatist epistemology, I now turn in greater detail to one of the core issues of the impasse between the two waves of previous pragmatism: the relation between language and experience. It is one thing to show how a transitionalist epistemology can dispense with a problematic reliance on certain conceptualizations of experience and language; it is another thing to show how such an epistemology can then reconstruct the relation between these epistemic concepts.

The history of twentieth-century philosophy teaches us that the relation between experience and language proves enormously difficult to conceptualize if we take either of these terms as a primary philosophical focus. This is unsurprising. The classicopragmatists granted too much priority to experience and so found it difficult to appropriately relate language to what they variously dubbed primary, pure, or qualitative experience. The neopragmatists reacted to these difficulties by shifting all the philosophical weight to the other term. This enabled them to more clearly present all epistemic relations as historical rather than foundational. As Rorty claimed, "the effect of adopting Gadamer's slogan ['being that can be understood is language'] is to replace [foundationalist] metaphors of depth with [historicist] metaphors of breadth" (2000b, 24). Rorty's argument was that making this crucial move required abandoning the concept of experience, which in even its most rigorous historicist forms could not do the work we expect from a philosophy tailored to historicity and temporality. This saddled neopragmatism with the immense and as yet unresolved difficulty of accounting for the historicity of nonlinguistic experience from within their avowed purely linguistic perspective. Both of these options have left pragmatism at a bit of an impasse with respect to epistemology for the reasons adumbrated in the previous chapter: either experience is given as a certain immediate awareness that can be taken as a static foundation for knowledge such that language turns out to be a mere representation of experience, or everything that is relevant to our epistemic relations is dynamically linguistic all the way down. It is not difficult to infer how these deficits play out in the context of the relation between language and experience—indeed, much of the argument has been furnished above, so all that is needed here is to flesh out a few more details specific to this particular subissue.

The first option, that of experiential classicopragmatism, is problematic for all the familiar linguistic-turn reasons already offered by Rorty. More extreme and overtly foundationalist versions of this view make everything depend on the representational relation that supposedly holds between sentences and sentence-shaped entities, even if there has as yet been no adequate account of this relation. Similar problems continue to nag even the most subtle forms of experientialist epistemology. To make this point, we can parrot Rorty by referring to two of the most influential epistemologists of the late twentieth century. Donald Davidson argued that "no *thing* makes sentences and theories true: not experience, not surface irritations, not the world, can make a sentence true" (1974, 194). Wilfrid Sellars similarly showed that attributions of truth "do not assert relations between linguistic and extra-linguistic items" (1968, 82). The linguistic-turn philosophers thus made explicit the tight connection that holds between experiential givens and foundational representations. Sellars (1956, §22) in particular showed how experiential givens are perfectly suited to play a foundational role in our epistemologies in both of their standard forms: as immediate experiential wholes (as sometimes seems to be the case for Dewey and James) and as constituent elements in any unified experience (as often seems to be the case for Peirce). Rorty (1979, 155ff.) later reiterated in a pragmatist key Sellars's argument to the effect that it remains deeply puzzling how something of the order of wholly immediate percepts might be related in any justificatory sense to something of the order of wholly mediated beliefs. The point of these arguments is that experience is not related to language as ground is to representation or as quality is to symbol. These arguments thus show us that if we wish to endorse experiential givens at all, then we are obliged to see that they assume an entirely nonpernicious form that does not invite representationalist foundationalism. The best way of doing this is to deny that givens play any important epistemic role in our practices, if indeed they play any role at all there. This was precisely the strategy favored by Rorty when he drew a distinction between epistemic practices of justification (a wholly sociolinguistic matter) and nonepistemic events of causal sensation (a nonlinguistic but also nonepistemic matter). This distinction enables us to, as Rorty put it in an early essay on Dewey, "eliminat[e] the assumption that justification must repose on something other than social practices and human needs" (1977a, 81).[3] Givens would have a role to play in our epistemic practices only if we could find a way to linguistically represent them. But attempts to explicate such a form of representation always lead back to the same wicked problems of representationalism, foundationalism, and dualism.

Now whatever one happens to think of all these -isms, it is undeniable that one of the central aims of every variety of pragmatism is to rid philosophy of them. Although some philosophers remain foundationalists, representationalists, and dualists, pragmatism denies all of these for reasons that have been spelled out adequately elsewhere by pragmatists from Peirce to Putnam. It was Dewey and James who above all others helped us first see that representational foundationalism riddles our epistemic conceptions with intractable epistemological problems that we should seek to dissolve rather than resolve. But it really was not until Davidson and Sellars came along that we could see that experiential givenism issues an invitation to this very representationalist foundationalism in all its high-modern glory. This is my now familiar story, according to which the core problems of givenism in its relation to representationalism and foundationalism did not come into full view until long after the classical pragmatist intervention. It is notable for this story that subsequent recognition of these problems proceeded at least in part on the basis of these pragmatist interventions. Later, in rooting out some of the most perniciously subtle forms of these problematics, Sellars and Davidson were in fact building on classicopragmatist insights. Indeed, they did modestly acknowledge their debts to classicopragmatism even if they did not consider themselves pragmatists. It took Rorty to point out the implicit pragmatism in these later arguments. Thus it was Rorty who completed the assault on the modern epistemology industry initiated by James and Dewey. In the wake of Rorty today, it follows from the quintessentially pragmatist rejection of representationalism and foundationalism that we pragmatists ought to remain ever vigilant against givenism too. The lapses into givenism by the classical pragmatists were of course in a certain sense inevitable if we reflect on the intellectual problematics that furnished the material of their intellectual historical context. The conclusion to draw from all this is therefore not that we should dismiss the classical pragmatists as mistaken or antiquated but rather that we contemporary classicopragmatists are now fully obliged to avoid certain antiquated mistakes when we rewrite the epistemologies offered in those classic texts. Language does not represent experience, and knowledge does not express a relation between language-like beliefs and nonlinguistic objects.

Consider now the second option for explicating the relation between experience and language, namely neopragmatist linguisticism. This option may seem to have been given a new lease on life by the historicist perspective I am defending. This appearance is due to the not uncommon tendency to associate the historicization of experience with its linguistification. This clever but mistaken assimilation also happens to play a large role in the views of many other notable twentieth-century philosophers whose perspectives share much with Rorty's linguistic-turn neopragmatism. Take as one example Hans-Georg Gadamer, who took the linguistic or hermeneutic turn as a reaction against the foundationalist philosophy of experience offered by Edmund Husserl's phenomenology. Gadamer argued that the best way out of phenomenological foundationalism was to redescribe phenomenological experience as through and through historical. He further argued that such a redescription could be achieved only if experience is redescribed in terms of linguistic understanding. It is thus not at all incidental that Rorty made extensive use of Gadamer in the final chapters of *Philosophy and the Mirror of Nature*.[4] Nor is it incidental that

Rorty fondly quoted Gadamer's most quotable line: "Being that can be understood is language" (Gadamer 1960, 474). Gadamer and Rorty bear a striking resemblance to one another on these matters insofar as both claim that the linguistic turn is essential for turning away from foundationalism. Both, in other words, deny the claim for which I have argued here, namely that nonfoundationalism can be detached from linguisticism.

Gadamer's argument against foundationalist epistemology, like Rorty's, took its cue in part from Heidegger's radicalization of the basic hermeneutic situation.[5] This radicalization consisted in showing that all understanding is historically situated such that temporal finitude is taken as a basic context for human understanding. This perspective enables us to see that the foundationalist attempt to ground knowledge in something universal and unchanging is not only impossible but also unnecessary. Gadamer, also like Rorty, takes this Heideggerian radicalization as resulting in the idea that all understanding is linguistic. Critics have replied that there is much in human experience that seems manifestly nonlinguistic.[6] But Gadamer, again also like Rorty, never denied that there is such a thing as nonlinguistic experience. His point was just that all experience is in principle capable of being understood in language or potentially linguistic—insofar as experience can be meaningfully understood, it must be capable of being rendered into language.[7] Gadamer's argument at this point, once again like Rorty's, betrays a troubling ambiguity. If foundationalism is to be avoided by way of the strong claim that all understanding is *actually* linguistic, then it is not at all clear that the weaker claim that all experience is *potentially* linguistic gives us quite the foothold against foundationalism that the stronger claim does. Potentiality is cheap, but actuality is expensive, and it is not clear that we can use potentiality to buy our way out of foundationalism. Not only does linguisticism face internal problems regarding relations between linguistic and nonlinguistic contributions to our knowledge, but it also faces external problems regarding its ability to actually evade the snares of foundationalism.

Relating Experience and Language in Transitionalist Epistemology

Having canvassed both of the leading pragmatist proposals concerning the relation between experience and language, I can conclude that neither horn of the all-too-familiar dilemma should be grasped. It is at this point that we pragmatists should start casting about for some previously underdeveloped third-wave pragmatist epistemology. My favored approach of transitionalist epistemology enables a third pragmatist perspective according to which, employing Rorty's metaphors, experience is not necessarily vertical and horizontality is not necessarily linguistic. Transitionalism thus aims for something like the horizontality of experience or, better yet, the historicity of knowing. But we should note that there are at this juncture a number of other promising avenues that open up before us in addition to the way of transitionalism—a brief review will both help bring the motivating problems into clearer focus and help situate my proposal for a resolution.

One promising avenue for pragmatism increasingly traveled as of late is that of epistemological axiologies such as virtue-theoretic reliabilism and responsibilism.[8] In surveying the recent literature on epistemological axiology, Duncan Pritchard notes that contemporary work on knowledge is "undergoing a 'value-turn'" (2007, 85) that is already in full swing. This turn is particularly promising for the pragmatist because, as Guy Axtell has noted, both pragmatism and reliabilism "are deeply concerned with the complex ways in which factors of motivation and the quality of habits or methods of inquiry contribute to an agent's success or reliability" (2000, 26).[9] Brandom (2000c, 97–122) also points out that reliabilism helps us focus on ways in which even the simplest instances of knowledge are always the result of complex social learning processes that call for both philosophical and anthropological-sociological analysis. Despite the promises of reliabilism for a renewal of pragmatist epistemology, I will not here pursue this option. One defect common among the general types of epistemologies of which reliabilism is just one instance is that they are often technically elaborated in response to very precise philosophical problems that may not pose any difficulties in our real-world situations of inquiry. One way of making this point is to argue that these theories take as their starting point certain armchair intuitions that on closer inspection out to be little better than contentious philosophical assumptions rooted in ethnocentric or perhaps even idiosyncratic outlooks.[10] The general epistemological setting in which reliabilism operates tends to proceed with intuitions and assumptions about knowledge of which pragmatists should be wary. Particularly troublesome is the undefended, and indefensible, restriction of epistemic honorifics such as justification and knowledge to just those classes of entities resembling propositions, beliefs, and sentences. The pragmatist perspective opens up a broader conception of epistemic achievement according to which beliefs function alongside of skills, practices, bodily comportments, and habits in furnishing epistemic entitlements. Pragmatism finds no good reason for singling out beliefs and propositions as uniquely worthy of philosophical attention. Regarding knowing as a dynamic activity rids us of the motivations to thinking that knowledge is a property of only sentence-shaped entities. Pragmatist reliabilism, then, falls short of the philosophical requirements handed down to present pragmatist epistemology by the history of pragmatism itself. Despite departing from this program, I do however wish to underscore that it appears to be one of the most viable research projects for pragmatist epistemology announced in recent years and I very much hope that its proponents may yet find a way of expanding the variety of epistemological entities countenanced by pragmatist reliabilism.

Another promising avenue, much better traveled on the whole, is a semiotic or symbolic form of pragmatism. It is clear that there are many distinctive advantages of what might be called the "semiotic turn" in twentieth-century philosophy. For pragmatists, the best proponent of this view is Peirce, though the turn itself is not Peirce's alone. The general drift of argument anticipates on a number of points both Rorty's and Brandom's neopragmatism and a variety of hermeneutical positions including core aspects of both Gadamer's and Habermas's work. In the interim decades of the mid-twentieth century, similar approaches can be discerned in the work of a wide variety of different thinkers ranging from the neo-Kantian Ernst Cassirer to the psychoanalyst Jacques Lacan to the naturalist Suzanne Langer. Peirce, however, surely remains the greatest proponent of a semiotic theory of human practice, and for my pragmatist purposes he is also clearly the most important. If the linguistic turn amounts to repudiating foundationalism by insisting upon the irreducible linguisticality of all experience, then the semiotic turn attempts to repudiate foundationalism by more modestly insisting upon the irreducible meaningfulness of all experience. This route thus has much to recommend it for my transitionalist approach in that it seems properly positioned in relation to the crucial problems facing the pragmatist tradition in the present. In just being oriented to the correct problems, a semiotic pragmatism is already advanced beyond reliabilist pragmatism.

Particularly valuable in Peirce's semiotic pragmatism for my purposes is that he took the semiotic turn in large part by way of historicizing meaningfulness such that semiosis is conceptualized as a process. This led Peirce to a promising conception of knowledge or science as an ever-evolving historical process. In this way Peirce definitively anticipates the transitionalist themes I place at the center of pragmatist epistemology. I have already noted that his writings reveal a lifelong commitment to a conception of knowledge as through-and-through historical and temporal. Here is more evidence. In his late "Issues of Pragmaticism," he writes that "the Past is the sole storehouse of all our knowledge" and that "the conclusion of a Reasoning proper must refer to the Future" (1905a, 358). In his very early "Some Consequences of Four Incapacities" from the 1868 *JSP Cognition Series*, he similarly argued that "the mind is a sign developing according to the laws of inference" (1868b, 53).

Despite the obvious fact that Peirce's semiotic turn toward historicity and temporality has much to recommend it from my transitionalist perspective, certain problems beset both classical and contemporary conceptions of semiotic and symbolic philosophy. In short, these philosophies have always remained uncomfortably splayed between linguisticism on the one hand and givenism on the other. Some semioticians have explicitly relied on a primary category of self-evident awareness and in so doing have bought into something resembling givenism. This is, as discussed previously, motivated by Peirce himself in his discussions of immediate Quality, which do not sit well with the historicism that I take to be the kernel of insight in his semiotics. In the same 1905 essay just quoted he also writes: "There is no time in the Present for any inference at all. . . . Consequently the present object must be an external object" (1905a, 359). On the other hand, adherents of semiotics who recognize the dangers of givenism have yet to convincingly show just how it is that meaning might take us beyond self-evident experience without taking us all the way to language. Peirce motivates this problematic view too in writing, in the same 1868 essay, that "my language is the sum total of myself" (1868b, 54).[11] With this Peirce offers a beautiful metaphor but a reductive philosophy. These two passages (there are many others, of course) suggest that although Peirce exhibited a lifelong commitment to historicity, he remained always torn between givenism and linguisticism. In this he is in fact excellently representative of twentieth-century semiotic-symbolic philosophy on the whole.

I freely admit that there is much more intricacy in semiotics than I can feature in a brief review. An exhaustive consideration of this approach is beyond my intentions here. I only wish to explain why I provisionally accept that the typical tensions of pragmatism continue to plague the semiotic approach insofar as it pulls in one moment toward historicity but in other moments toward the bad alternative of either immediate experience or linguistic ubiquity. What this shows is that the semiotic approach is positioned quite correctly in relation to the pressing epistemological problems of the day even if it has yet to deliver a convincing solution to these problems. If future work in semiotics may yet yield a viable resolution of this tension, then it would seem prudent to regard the semiotic turn as a partner of the transitional turn I am urging. But I will leave it for another occasion to explore the complex connections between the third way of transitionalist epistemology and the third way of semiotics.[12]

At this point, it is time to start touring down yet another possible avenue for a contemporary pragmatist epistemology of the experience-language relation. I have said that pragmatist epistemology at present needs to develop a view that can countenance both experiential and linguistic knowledge without reducing one to the other by way of a subtly wicked foundationalism or a boldly overblown linguisticism. Pragmatist reliabilism does not even get this problem in proper focus. Pragmatist semiotics helps bring the issue into clear focus but intensifies the difficulties rather than resolves them. Transitionalist pragmatist epistemology is tailored expressly to this problem and so stands a better chance of working toward an adequate reconstruction of the difficulties we face. At the core of this approach is a reconceptualization of knowledge as a temporal process according to the description offered at the beginning of this chapter: knowledge is an essentially temporal relation in which a prior practical projection (for example, a belief or a skill) leads successfully to an anterior practical eventuality at which it aims (for example, the objects of beliefs or skilful performances).

This reconceptualization enables us to approach anew the crucial epistemological issue of the relation between language and experience. One fresh suggestion involves redescribing the relation between experience and language as analogous to that between a field and a type of action that occurs in that field, or as analogous to a stream and one kind of element composing that stream. The view here is that *language is just a kind of experience*, or, to put it more simply, that *speaking and listening and writing and reading are kinds of experience*. The crucial point is that language stands to experience not as its representative, proxy, or even as one of its many necessary conditions but rather as one of the many moments, elements, or forms in a diverse array that contribute to the field and flow of experience.

On this view, language is not different from other forms of experience in any deep and philosophically instructive way. The view holds that speaking and writing are not radically different from cooking. Or hammering. Or hiking. Or wild-orchid hunting. There are of course certain obvious important differences separating each of these forms of experience. But these are innocent piecemeal differences and not the sort of ponderous differences that philosophers have often supposed. Once such a view is up and running, it should never occur to us to ask either the foundationalist question of how language represents experience (because language is here part of the field of experience) or the linguisticist question of how language could ever hook up to anything other than more language (because there are all kinds of things in the field of experience that language hooks up with).

Why, we ought to ask, did philosophers ever think that language was so different from all other forms or moments of experience that it deserved philosophical analysis in its own right? Why not accord similar privilege to any other form or moment of experience basic to the human condition, such as eating, procreating, ambulating, building, or using an opposable thumb? We can get by without our language, I should think, better than we could get by without our hands. So what motivates the nearly exclusive concern so many philosophers have had with the truth of sentences? What presuppositions lurk behind this kind of talk? Foundationalists generally thought of epistemology as an attempt to explain the conditions under which our beliefs are true. This ultimate basis of belief, the truth-making conditions, could then serve as a foundation for human knowledge. This project, however, only makes sense if we stipulate in advance that the truth of beliefs, or propositions, or sentences is a unique form of practical success that stands in special need of explanation. Even after foundationalists had failed to deliver on their promises and gave them up, their linguisticist successors continued to think that truth was a unique form of practical success that deserves to be singled out as an item for special philosophical consideration. Those proffering linguisticism thus argued that they could fill in many of the gaps left behind from foundationalism by offering an account of truth that explicitly refused to ground beliefs in anything besides other beliefs.

Philosophers, be they foundationalist or linguisticist in disposition, can of course always stipulate that truth is a property of sentences, or propositions, or beliefs. But stipulations aside, why is it that the only thing we should care about is the truth of our sentences? What about the warmth of our dwellings, the nutrition of our meals, and the dexterousness of our fingers? What is so special about truth if we stipulate in advance that the only tools that it can apply to are sentences? Working with that stipulation we will of course end up with a deflationary theory of truth in which there is precious little for the philosopher to say about truth. Some philosophers will wish to defend the stipulation according to which truth is a unique form of good pertaining only to sentences by arguing that the truth of sentences is relevant to all other tools in a way that all other tools cannot be relevant to the tool of language. They will argue that we can construct sentences that are either true or false of all our other tools, while these tools cannot properly be about sentences. But this defense only repairs to the equally suspicious stipulation that there is a unique form of tool use called "reference" or "aboutness" that is particularly deserving of our attention. And what if only sentences can be "about" other tools? Why is this any more special than that only food can supply us with the nutritive energy to use all other tools? Why is "aboutness" any more deserving of special philosophical consideration than "nutritional"? And if there is something about philosophy that merits this extra attention, is there also something about living that merits this sort of narrowed philosophical perspective? If sentences are understood as one sort of tool among many other sorts and language is understood as one kind of experience among many other kinds, then it follows that the forms of success relevant to language use are not different in any philosophically significant way from the forms of success relevant to the use of other tools in other experiential contexts. Successful human practice most often requires the skilful use of a variety of tools at once (sentences, hammers, meals, and strategies for social cooperation). We need not single out any one of these tools as more philosophically worthy than any of the others because they are all, taken together, requisite for anything we would even vaguely count as practical success.

By working with the idea that knowledge is a process that develops within practical experience rather than a certain kind of state or episode either grounded in experiential givens or enabled by linguistic consensus, we pragmatists can affirm that valuable epistemic achievements invoke resources other than those that would be allowed by views that regard knowledge as a unique success that applies only to sentence-shaped entities. The broader field in which knowledge, like every other honorific name for practical success, shapes up depends not only on our sentences and our beliefs but also on our bodies, our skills, our tools, and a whole host of other accumulated practical material as well on the realities with which all of this material interacts. Knowledge, like every other form of practical success, consists in successful interexperiential leadings that draw on all these forms of experience and all their corollary kinds of tools. This is the value that knowledge has in our lives.

To begin summing up the advantages of this view, I wish to note that these important matters are not the province of pragmatism alone. The seemingly puzzling relation between experience and language has animated theoretical work across the disciplines over the past few decades. One of the most influential statements of this problem was Joan Scott's genealogy-inspired essay "The Evidence of Experience." Scott's influential claim in this essay was that "experience is at once always already an interpretation *and* something that needs to be interpreted" (1991, 797). Scott thus clarified the problem as one in which experience can no longer function as a foundation ("experience is not the origin of our explanation") yet at the same time cannot be reduced away as a mere epiphenomenon of discursive structures ("it seems futile to argue for its [experience's] expulsion"). The problem Scott ably brought into focus has reverberated throughout the disciplines over the past two or three decades. My argument is that transitionalist pragmatism offers the seeds of a solution to this crucial problem of the contemporary critical landscape. The key to this solution is in the fact that transitionalist pragmatism takes our conception of experience beyond both foundationalist givens and linguistic ubiquity.

The pragmatism I am urging is beyond foundationalism because it enables us to see that we need not ground our practical successes in any foundation of experience. We can, rather, understand successful inquiry as unfolding within experience and not on the basis of experience. Forms of epistemic success do not stand in need of any grounding above and beyond all those ordinary details we employ in our everyday inquiries: lab tables, notebooks, sophisticated technical equipment, peer-review mechanisms, subtle but crucial networks of affiliation, research journals, persuasive rhetoric, and, yes, even sentences. Knowledge requires no supertemporal support when it can get all the support it needs from the enormously dense temporal connections that tie past and future experiences together. Experience is like language in that it need not be purified of the contingent historical content that makes it up. We thus have no need for a concept of a primal experiential given-ness floating free of the actual historical stream of experience. An experience of experience, the kind of thing that a metaphysics of experience would supply to foundationalist epistemology, is simply not required. Just as the linguistic turn eventually resulted in the realization that we do not need a metalanguage that speaks the vocabulary of language itself, a new experiential turn can deliver the insight that we do not need any sort of metaexperiential experience of experience itself. The stream of experience itself is what supplies any experience with its coherence. Experiences gain their sense and force through their relations to other experiences. This means that we can regard experience as relevant to knowledge without insisting that experience is a foundation for knowledge.

The pragmatism I am urging is beyond linguisticism in that it enables us to understand language as just one part of an account of knowledge. On this view, we hash out our epistemic agreements and disagreements by employing bridges, paintings, sentences, and all the other little bits of our practical experience. Language on this view does not represent experience—it is just one more form of experience. Language, like any other tool we employ in hashing out what is true and what is false, is just one way in which we place ourselves in direct contact with the experiential field in which our lives, and all the successes and failures that make them up, unfold. Language is a way of getting in direct touch with reality in order to get something done. Like all tool use, language puts us in direct contact with the experiential reality in which we live. Now there are, of course, different uses of different tools. But there is nothing in general separating these various tools that a special discipline called metaphysics or semantics might give us an account of. Separations between different kinds of experience are due to contingent historical accretion rather than philosophic necessity. Why, for example, do we find the use of a hammer more like the use of a screwdriver than like the use of a paintbrush? Whatever the merits of this view, it is obviously the result of centuries of cultural contingencies and not that of the intrinsic properties of hammers, screwdrivers, and paintbrushes. The same, of course, goes for the thought that aesthetic uses of language have more in common with scientific uses of language than the former do with paintbrushes and the latter with microscopes. From another perspective, we might regard these different uses of language as less like one another and more like the other tools we use to accomplish the tasks that these uses of language are involved in. Perhaps aesthetic language has more to do with paintbrushes and painters than it does with scientific language, political language, or botanical language. Perhaps, after all, language is not nearly so special as some philosophers have thought. Perhaps we should no longer study our practices by carving them up into distinctive philosophical subfields but rather by carving them at the joints revealed in sociological, anthropological, and historical inquiries.

To sum up: Pragmatists who want to focus philosophical attention on the experiential field in which human action unfolds, hangs together, and then falls apart again would do good to remember that experience is a transition more complex than linguisticism could acknowledge and more flexible than foundationalism would allow.

Transitionalist Epistemology in Previous Pragmatism

There is a rich tradition of transitionalist themes found in all previous pragmatisms, most notably in the classicopragmatisms of Peirce, James, and Dewey and the neopragmatisms of Rorty, Brandom, and Putnam. Nevertheless, all of these previous pragmatisms have failed to define themselves in terms of these transitionalist themes of temporality and historicity. In every case, some other thematic focus, be it experiential qualitativeness or sociolinguistic consensus, has emerged as more central. In this chapter, I have offered an outline of an alternative transitionalist approach to pragmatist epistemology. This attempt should not be taken as an attempt to resolve the most pressing debates in contemporary philosophies of knowledge with some clever new solution nor as a showy claim that previous pragmatist interventions in these debates ought to be abandoned. My humbler intention has been to note that the specific advantages of the best pragmatist contributions to these debates most clearly emerge when brought into focus through transitionalism. So although transitionalism is *my* attempted improvement on the work of previous pragmatists, it is also my development of *their* work. To fully justify this claim for continuity, I would need to survey all of the pragmatists I have taken up over the course of my discussion, including James, Dewey, Rorty, and also Peirce. Instead of dwelling at length on this full range of pragmatist epistemology, however, I shall be content to take as representative the epistemological writings of the single pragmatist who I most often find closest to my own transitionalism, namely William James.

Transitionalist themes abound in James's work. But only a handful of commentators have keenly discerned the presence of these themes in Jamesian epistemology. Hilary Putnam notes well that for James "truth is a historical process" (1990a, 247) such that true ideas "come to agree with reality" (1997, 178) over the course of time.[13] Charlene Haddock Seigfried also rightly interprets James as holding that "all our understanding takes place over time" (1990, 385) such that "both reality and truth are processes" (1990, 296). Following the lead of Putnam and Seigfried, we can locate transitionalist themes throughout James's work.

"The fundamental fact about our experience," James once wrote, "is that it is a process of change" (1904c, 54). There you have an unequivocal statement by James for the importance of my favored transitionalism themes. Much earlier in the *Principles of Psychology*, James had noted that "Like a bird's life, [our thought] seems to be an alternation of flights and perchings" (1890, I.243). Later on in *Pragmatism* he offered a theory of truth centered around the idea that truth is a dynamic process rather than a static property. "The essential thing is the process of being guided" (1907, 102), said James, in specifying truth as that which qualifies "any idea upon which we can ride, so to speak" (1907, 34). But James's most famous transitionalist moment is surely his metaphor of the ever rushing "stream of experience." John McDermott notes well that James, in unpublished draft writings, once described experience as a "field" (1977, xlv). Metaphors of stream and field best capture the transitionalist sentiment ever at the heart of James's work on knowledge.

James's most precise statements of his transitionalist epistemology are featured in his *Essays in Radical Empiricism*, particularly in the essays "Does 'Consciousness' Exist?" and "A World of Pure Experience." James answers the titular question of the first essay with an argument showing that consciousness does not exist as a substantial entity but that it does exist as a functional process. James's argument here is that knowledge can be explained by considering solely those interexperiential relations that hold between different bits of experience strewn across a continuous field of experience. If one experience satisfactorily leads us to another, then that satisfactory relation between these two experiences sufficiently explains knowledge. We do not need some mysterious inexplicable relation between mind and world laid on top of this straightforward temporal relation. We need only focus on these experiences and "their relations—these relations themselves being experiences—to one another" (1904a,

170, 178). For James, experience itself has depth and breadth and reaches out beyond itself at its edges. This is because James understood experience as a temporal field in which different definite parts of experience may relate to one another. We can stay where we are, metaphysically speaking, by recognizing that we are always on the go, experientially speaking. Intellectual historian James Livingston rightly recognizes that "time is the key to [James's] argument" (1994, 268). The second James essay develops this argument of the first by explicating the cognitive relation not as a connection between a subjective knower and an objective known but rather as a connection between "two pieces of *actual* experience . . . with definite tracts of conjunctive transitional experience between them" (1904b, 200, 201). Here is the key line: "Knowledge of sensible realities thus comes to life inside the tissue of experience. It is *made*; and made by relations that unroll themselves in time" (1904b, 202). James accepts, with all other philosophers, that knowledge requires a relation to secure its stability. What he denies is that we need to get outside of experience to find that relation. The relation, he insists, can be found right there inside the field of experience itself insofar as experience is ever unrolling through time and history. Knowledge "consists in intermediary experiences" that carry us from, or relate, one experience to another. James concludes: "These relations of continuous transition experienced are what make our experiences cognitive. In the simplest and most complete cases the experiences are cognitive of one another" (1904b, 213). The cognitive relation holds between pluralities of experiences that develop out of one another within the temporal field of experience such that nothing within this field requires support from something outside of the experiences themselves.

None of this is to deny that James's epistemology was subject to all of the deficits and defects rehearsed above. Yet despite these persisting problems, it is undeniable that there is a transitionalist core featured in James's work on knowledge that, when developed, can be used to establish a more viable pragmatist epistemology. On more than one occasion, Dewey (1906, 1929, 1949) described James and himself as developing "the experimental theory of knowledge." In working out this experimental theory, James and Dewey distanced pragmatism from modern conceptions of experience as isolable mental states and recalled premodern views of experience as a test, a trial, or an experiment with temporal duration.[14] When early modern philosophers abandoned dynamic experimental conceptions of experience in favor of static atemporal conceptions, they invited a view of knowledge as a static property that could be anchored in a foundation of unmoving experiential awareness. That made for a pretty promise. But it was also something philosophy could never deliver on. Laboring under the burden of that entrenched pledge of epistemology, both James and Dewey sought out in much of their work a transitional conception of knowledge as a process. It was in one of his better moments that Dewey once wrote, in a clear invocation of James, that mind is "a moving stream, a constant change which nevertheless has axis and direction, linkages, associations, as well as initiations, hesitations, and conclusions" (1925, 282/LW1.215). I am afraid that my argument, in the end, is a relatively simple one: we should play up such emphatic invocations of temporality and historicity featured in the epistemology of these and other pragmatists so as to overcome some of the persisting deficits that continue to plague pragmatism in certain of its other moods.

Five

ETHICS AS PERFECTING

The Requirements of Modern Moral Philosophy

The central transitionalist themes of temporality and historicity help bring into focus quintessential pragmatist insights concerning some of the impasses at the heart of modern moral philosophy. The era of modern moral philosophy is usually told as the story of a contest between two dominant theoretical factions: teleology and deontology. This contest has left much of moral theory at something of an impasse. Bernard Williams has called our attention to this impasse in writing disparagingly of "the purity of morality" (1985, 195) as it has been conceived by the two major traditions of modern moral thought. What Williams recognized was the obvious one-sidedness of much teleological and deontological theory. The exclusive focus on pleasure by utilitarian teleologists and on will by Kantian deontologists has led both camps to deny the seemingly obvious fact that a moral life must concern itself with both outcomes and intentions, both pleasure and will. This general criticism of the leading traditions of modern moral philosophy is today widely accepted even by proponents of both views.

Today, the most common move—in fact almost the only move—made by those interested in overcoming the impasse between the modern moral philosophies of teleology and deontology is to turn toward the ancient moral philosophical tradition of virtue ethics.[1] One clear danger with this approach, however, is that it will not suitably answer to the unique requirements of a distinctively modern morality. Virtue ethics was originally developed in a cultural context vastly different from that in which Kant and Mill wrote, and few would deny that we are today much closer to the world of the moderns than to that of the ancients. Stanley Rosen notes well the problem in saying that "we cannot apply the classical doctrine of virtue as a standard for improving modern moral and political life except by transforming that life beyond recognition" (1989, 11). Proponents of contemporary virtue ethics have certainly not been ignorant of this danger, but it is not always clear that their reconstructions answer to the distinctive problems of a modern moral life that were first sharply formulated in utilitarian and deontological thought. One key requirement relevant to my project here is the severe stasis of ancient moral life in comparison with the fast flux of modern moral living.

In this chapter, I shall explore the impasse between teleology and deontology, which has for the past few decades led to the stalemate in contemporary moral philosophy that makes rival third theories such as virtue ethics seem so compelling today. In doing so, I will be particularly concerned to show what it is that these two traditions of modern moral thought they got right about the situation of morality in our modern world. What they got right is that they both brought into vivid focus the basic problems facing the modern moral life. These problems are simply not of primary concern for virtue ethics. I conclude that overcoming the frustrating impasse between teleological and deontological moral theories requires a different kind of third theory, namely one that is specifically formulated in response to the basic problems of modern moral life. A pragmatist moral philosophy suitably articulated under the heading of transitionalism offers a promising approach here.

I shall refer to the new third theory that I offer as pragmatist perfectionism. The innovation of pragmatist perfectionism in comparison to other alternative third theories is that pragmatist perfectionism explicitly acknowledges the benefits of both of the dominant modern moral theories and is thus consciously worked out as an attempt to integrate their better insights without succumbing to their failings. Pragmatist perfectionism, unlike much contemporary work in virtue ethics, is a characteristically modern moral theory pointed toward the basic problems to which teleology and deontology are responses. Pragmatist perfectionism as I shall here develop it flows out of two distinctively modern philosophical lineages: the moral perfectionism of

Stanley Cavell (a perfectionism he locates in the writings of Ralph Waldo Emerson) and the pragmatist ethics discernible in many of the writings of John Dewey and especially William James (both of whom were heavily influenced by Emerson). The proposal laid out in this chapter is offered in the same spirit as the argument of the last. I could not hope to definitively resolve the core impasses of modern moral philosophy in the space of a single chapter. My aim is rather to bring into focus the distinctive advantages of a pragmatist response to these impasses. I show that getting pragmatism's advantages into focus requires looking at pragmatism through the lens of transitionalism.

The Modern Moral Impasse Between Utilitarianism and Deontology

It will be helpful to begin with a quick summary of modern teleological and deontological moral theories. The paradigm of modern teleological theory is utilitarianism. The central concept for utilitarian moral theory is that of *pleasure*. At the beginning of *The Principles of Morals and Legislation*, Bentham boldly stated that we are "under the governance of two sovereign masters, pain and pleasure. It is for them alone to point out what we ought to do" (1789, 1). He goes on to explain that an act is right where we can reasonably expect that it will maximize the amount of pleasure enjoyed by those affected by the act. In utilitarianism, all that matters are future consequences. By contrast, deontology looks inward. Deontology is almost synonymous with the moral theory of Kant. The central concept of morality for Kant was that of *will*. At the beginning of *The Groundwork of the Metaphysics of Morals*, Kant boldly claimed that the only thing "which can be regarded as good without qualification" is a good will itself (1785, 393). The resulting moral theory tells us that acts are right which are done only out of a good will itself. This implies that all that matters for the deontologist are intentions. Outcomes count for nothing so long as your will was good.

Under the banners of utilitarianism and deontology, pleasure and will have been the two grand forces of modern moral thought. Pleasure takes people as they are; will demands them to be otherwise. But it is important to note the way in which each side grants absolute priority to just one of these moral concepts so as to exclude the theoretical concerns voiced from the other side. The danger of both of these elements when isolated from the other is severe—accepting persons as they are runs the risk of complacency whereas demanding them to be otherwise runs the risk of revolutionary transformation. Cavell offers a way of understanding these two theories in terms of their responsiveness to only one of these risks: "For Mill, in *On Liberty*, the reality of morality is discovered in the overcoming of conformity by inclination or desire. For Kant, the reality of morality is discovered in the overcoming of inclination by duty" (2004, 119). In accepting persons as they are, utilitarians skirt conformism. In demanding persons to transform themselves, deontologists skirt the passions of romantic hedonism.

The two major modern moral theories thus form an odd inverse pair. Each pours all of its focus into just one of the major concepts of modern moral thought, takes as its project rectifying the dangers of doing just this, and in the course of this rectification passes by the other theoretical construct in attempting to flee to the other pole. A singular focal range obliges both traditions to run back and forth between opposite extremes. Allow me to explain. First utilitarianism. Fearing the complacency of a conformist socialization of the moral life, utilitarian thought insists that we unlock the power of our pleasures and in so doing cultivates a powerful individualism. Though it begins with sociality and universality, utilitarianism attempts to develop a way of doing justice to individuality and particularity. Now deontology. Fearing an absolute anarchy of self-determined individuals, deontological thought insists that we must chain the will to the duty of a universal reason and in so doing seeks to cultivate a powerful socializing force. Beginning with individuality and particularity, deontology finds that it needs to develop conceptions of sociality and universality. What Cavell's observation helps us recognize is that utilitarianism tries to pass from social conformism to individual inclination while deontology tries to pass from individual inclination to socialized duty.

According to most critics, both projects have failed, though by no means miserably. Among critics of modern moral philosophy, Williams has best captured their signature failings: "if Kantianism abstracts in moral thought from the identity of persons, Utilitarianism strikingly abstracts from their separateness" (1976, 3). There you have a fairly compact statement of what has been wrong with modern moral philosophy for well over a hundred years now. Deontology remains mired in conceptions of personal individuality and separateness; utilitarianism is bogged down in the fact that persons are associated and in some respects identical. Williams is not alone in pressing such criticisms. In the case of utilitarians, critics have pointed out that this theory has never made it clear how the individual can be preserved in a moral order in which it is ultimately permissible to sacrifice the life of one human for the pleasures of one million others. John Rawls forcefully put this point in arguing that "Utilitarianism does not take seriously the distinction between persons" (1971, 27). Those skeptical of the compatibility of utilitarianism with individual human rights are still waiting for a convincing reply to this line of criticism.[2] On the other hand, deontologists have still not made it clear how sociality can be preserved in a moral universe ultimately grounded on the autonomous exercise of an individual's reason. If autonomous individuals must will the moral law for themselves, it is unclear how they are to universalize their wills so as to include a moral concern for other humans whose supposed exercise of reason is by definition inaccessible to us. For Kant, reason is a faculty of the mind that we must exercise in complete autonomy. Thus, that which makes us moral is also that which makes us individual. Kant's great invention in the history of moral philosophy was, as J. B. Schneewind (1998) has excellently recounted, that of autonomy. This resulted in a moral theory decidedly tilted toward the autonomous individual in their separateness from other persons. Hannah Arendt thus noted that "in Kant the question 'What ought I to do?' concerns the conduct of the self in its independence of others" (1970, 19).[3]

I am not attempting to offer here damaging refutations of both utilitarianism and deontology in the space of a single paragraph. Rather, I simply want to call attention to the continuing lack of consensus among moral theorists regarding the success of each tradition. If there is any consensus in contemporary moral theory it is just this: we are still very much split between utilitarianism and deontology. Yet despite the problems facing both traditions, most reflective persons hold that both of these moral theories nevertheless capture something of decisive importance. We keep returning to teleological and deontological moral philosophies not because we are convinced that one or the other must be finally and completely right. Our interest in both theories abides because we feel that each must be right in certain moral moments. This suggests that the most promising line of inquiry for contemporary moral philosophy is to explore more fully why it is that these two leading moral theories have been continuously and conjointly embraced throughout the modern age despite their stark opposition to each other.

My view is that our appreciation of these two theories abides due to their success in stating the basic problem of moral life in modernity. The context in which this problem first becomes recognizable is one in which individuality and sociality are understood as constituting the core elements of the modern moral life. On this view, modern morality is in large part a response to those features of modern life in which individuality and sociality form a tension. The basic problem for modern moral theory is thus to show how the individual and the social can coexist. As I argued above, utilitarianism starts with the social and has never been able to successfully recuperate the individual, while Kantianism has never been able to fully integrate sociality into its primarily individualistic morality. It is notable in this regard that when Kant turned his hand in his later writings (1784, 1795) to the problem of human sociality, he employed not a deontological but a teleological theory of human history. This suggests that Kant himself may have understood there to be mutually exclusive fits between individuality and deontology on the one hand and sociality and teleology on the other. This view is further made plausible by a broad construal of Kant's larger critical project as an attempt to cleanly bifurcate the two standpoints of theoretical reason and practical reason. A similar claim could also be issued about Mill, insofar as one of his most central projects was that of a careful separation of two spheres of public and private activity. If plausible, then these interpretations of Mill and Kant in very broad brushstrokes suggest that both of these giants of modern moral philosophy were rightly focused on the basic problem of modernity in terms of the relationship between sociality (the public sphere of theoretical reason) and individuality (the private sphere of practical reason).

Unfortunately, neither utilitarian nor deontological thought has been able to achieve the sort of integral relationship between individuality and sociality that they have assumed as their central problematic. This is perhaps because both deontology and utilitarianism begin their theoretical reflection with the assumption of the very gulf between individuality and sociality that they will later seek to overcome. Deontology and utilitarianism make sense (and the solutions they formulate are intelligible) only if seen as a response to the idea that individuality and sociality are not simply two different tendencies within modern moral life but rather two separate spheres in which this life simultaneously takes place. In Kant, this is most clearly signaled in his conception of immorality as making an exception of oneself.[4] On his view, the core contradiction that is immorality is one between an individual private act of will and a universal social law of willing. In utilitarian thought, there is an overriding requirement that individual happiness not contradict the greater happiness of the community. The basis common to both the deontological grounding of morality in noncontradiction and the utilitarian moral calculus is that of a gulf between the two spheres of individuality and sociality.

Thus utilitarians and deontologists both approach moral theory as an attempt to overcome a gulf between individuality and sociality. Both are led to this problem because they postulate this gulf as a seemingly impenetrable reality. It thus makes a great deal of sense that both theories have met with continual frustration. In order to accept the solutions that these moral theories offer, one must first adopt a philosophical framework that is very likely to preclude the very solutions aimed at. This type of failure is a quite familiar story in the history of modern philosophy. Perhaps its most prominent recent instance is that of Cartesian dualism. The myriad solutions to the gulf between mind and body are bound to fail, given the rigid distinction in terms of which the problem itself is formulated. Philosophical impasses are often not failures to formulate solutions but rather failures in setting up problems. Why begin with the assumption that we are attempting to bridge the gap between two separate spheres of existence? If we start in this way, then we are going to locate ourselves on one side or the other of that gap such that we will find it almost impossibly difficult to get to the other side. Think of the Cartesian mind trying to think itself into the body, the Kantian individual trying to will itself into a social relationship, or the utilitarian society trying to justify the existence of unhappy individuals. Why not assume instead that we are attempting to bring together two contingently separable but not necessarily separate tendencies that make themselves manifest in our lives? If we start in this way, then we may find ways of kindling a relationship between these two tendencies such that they reconcile themselves to one another.

So perhaps a different approach is in order. Perhaps the real problem with these two dominant modern moral theories is that each one denies the relevance of the concerns articulated by the other. Teleologists and deontologists both want to be able to tell the whole story about our moral lives. Both want a monopoly on moral theory. Both express too much system. Such systematicity, however, make little sense given the basic problem of modern moral philosophy as formulated by both bodies of theory. If the basic problem is that of harmonizing the relation between individuality and sociality, then it is entirely counterproductive for each tradition to deny the relevance of the other. Greater social happiness and freer individuality will hardly seem valuable when divorced from each other. The basic problem confronting modern life is to come to terms with the requirements of both sociality and individuality, both outcomes and intentions, both pleasure and will. The basic problem confronting modern moral theory is thus to come to terms with both utilitarianism and deontology as more integral.

Only philosophers aiming at absolute systematic consistency would ever deny the kinds of things that utilitarians and deontologists readily deny. This is what Bernard Williams was referring to in his criticisms of the "purity of morality" (1985, 195). The result of this purifying impulse, Williams claimed, was that "the resources of most modern moral philosophy are not well adjusted to the modern world" (1985, 197). This disappointment in modern moral philosophy was first voiced in its recent vintage by Elisabeth Anscombe (1958). Following Anscombe's claim for the basic failures of modern moral theory, similar criticisms have been sounded time again and again by a variety of thinkers working across a range of quite different philosophical traditions. Stuart Hampshire resolutely claimed that "moral theory cannot be rounded off and made complete and tidy" (1983, 125), which of course is exactly what most modern moral theorists following Bentham and Kant have hoped for. Amartya Sen (1981) argued that we need an alternative to modern moral theories insofar as these have typically been one-sided. Charles Taylor (1989) criticized the narrow range of vision expressed in much of modern moral theory. Michel Foucault (1984a) elaborated a critique of modern rule-based moralities in his late work on ancient ethical practice. Richard Rorty conveniently summarized this wide swath of discontent when he advised, in characteristic pragmatist fashion, that we ought to get over "the obsession with the opposition between consequentialism and non-consequentialism which still dominates elementary courses in ethics" (2004a, 202).[5]

The unfortunate result of most of these critiques of modern moral philosophy has been to abandon the basic problem of modern moral philosophy and look instead to a revival of ancient virtue ethics. But what is really needed now is a new solution for the problem first worked out under the auspices of modern utilitarianism and deontology. The problem that needs addressing is that of reconciling the two profoundly powerful tendencies of individuation and association. Ancient virtue traditions are not well attuned to this problem. Samuel Scheffler, yet another moral philosopher who suggests the need for a hybrid theory integrating elements of consequentialism and deontology, nicely frames this requirement:

> When we hear longings expressed for the kind of moral coherence that is said to have characterized traditional, hierarchically ordered societies with clearly defined systems of social roles, we would do well to remember that the inclusiveness of modern morality, along with many of the other values it expresses, and that we rightly cherish, had no place whatsoever in those societies. . . . The important question is how to effect the necessary changes while preserving those portions of the Enlightenment legacy that matter most to us (1992, 10).[6]

Taking my cue from Scheffler's suggestion for simultaneous change and preservation, what I called "renewal" in a previous chapter, I want to argue that a more promising approach for contemporary moral philosophy involves taking seriously the usual skepticism toward the modern moral philosophies of utilitarianism and deontology but without thereby applying that skepticism to the very possibility of modern moral philosophy itself. What we need is skepticism toward utilitarian and deontological solutions coupled with a healthy respect for the problematics that originally motivated these proposed solutions.

The best way to take this approach is to follow up on Rorty's pragmatist suggestion that the usual efforts to purify the two currents of utilitarianism and deontology need to now give way to attempts to integrate them. The pragmatist perfectionism I sketch below seeks just such an integration. A central element of this shift of theoretical perspective from purity to integrity is, I shall show, a transitional sensibility. It is by taking time and history seriously as contexts in which moral living occurs that we can develop an integrated moral theory that serves both the socializing impulse of utilitarian pleasure and the individualizing impulse of the deontological will.

Convergences Between Perfectionism and Pragmatism

As a first approximation to pragmatist perfectionist ethics, it will be helpful to come to terms with the very proposal itself. For it is not immediately clear that moral perfectionism as it has been developed by Cavell is compatible with pragmatist ethics as developed by my two elected representative pragmatists for this chapter, James and Dewey.[7] Indeed, Cavell has always shied away from applying the pragmatist label to *his* Emerson, and he explicitly denies attempts to associate *his* perfectionism with pragmatism in such essays as "What's the Use of Calling Emerson a Pragmatist?" I find that Cavell's doubts about pragmatist ethics rely on a mistaken interpretation of pragmatism. But although it is mistaken, this interpretation is both sufficiently popular among critics and adequately rooted in textual warrant to deserve our serious attention. The fairly typical criticisms that Cavell offers of pragmatism are thus not wholly off the mark even if they are largely wide of the mark. His criticisms, I would like to suggest, are rooted in what might be thought of as forgivable misinterpretations. These are misinterpretations of pragmatism indeed, but we pragmatists ought to admit that certain prominent pragmatist formulations have served to court these particular misinterpretations. Showing how pragmatism actually avoids these forgivable misinterpretations requires, at least in this case, moving some way toward pragmatism's transitionalist wing.

Drawing on a passage in which Dewey rather nonpragmatically gives too much play to the phrase "the only authentic means,"[8] Cavell holds that pragmatists spend too much time focusing on how we can make our knowledge "better than it is" when they would better turn their attention to the fact that sometimes even the best knowledge "fails to make us better than we are, or provide us with peace" (2004, 5). Cavell's criticisms here and elsewhere restate the familiar concerns that pragmatism, especially Dewey's pragmatism, lacks a sense of the tragic and is excessively enamored of scientific technical rationality. I will return to these concerns about certain formulations of classicopragmatism in my final chapter.[9] There I suggest that pragmatism must further involve itself with other transitionalist traditions of thought (I propose Foucaultian genealogy, but one could also imagine different collaborators playing the part) to better clarify how it can answer these familiar twin criticisms. For now, though, I will persist in the thought that these criticisms are misguided even if rooted in forgivable misinterpretations. Pragmatism is not naïvely doe-eyed about tragedy and scientism.

The best way of dispelling these criticisms is to focus upon the meliorism that is at the heart of pragmatist philosophy. More central for pragmatism than methodic intelligence is a meliorism that resonates with perfectionism's central focus on processes of perfecting. I have been arguing throughout this book that pragmatists are above all concerned with melioration—with how we can make our lives better than they presently are. What Dewey called scientific method is simply one tool among many we have at our disposal for ameliorating our imperfections. It is certainly not the only such tool, nor is it even the most important, nor is it always capable of improving our lives or providing us with peace. But Cavell's criticism, even if ultimately misguided, does help us recognize that Dewey's writings do not often enough encourage us to see pragmatism in the appropriate melioristic light. In order to understand pragmatism in broadly melioristic rather than strictly scientistic terms, we ought to focus our attention on a thread that indeed runs through all brands of pragmatism but is perhaps more conspicuous in the pragmatism of James than that of Dewey. Encouraging for this thought is an explicit acknowledgment by Cavell (2004, 17) of a perfectionism in James that may prove capable of enabling the right perspective on tragedy and scientism.[10] Indeed, Cavell is not the only commentator to suggest that James provides a surer route than Dewey for articulating a pragmatism not subject to these forgivable misinterpretations.[11] I would suggest that the increasingly common move of favoring James over Dewey on these matters is explained by the fact that it is in James and not in Dewey that we find the boldest statements of pragmatist moral meliorism. Resonances between this moral meliorism and moral perfectionism provide a point of view for exploring the possibility of a pragmatist perfectionist ethics that is Cavellian (and Emersonian) as much as it is Jamesian (and Deweyan). This ethical confluence affirms the distinctive values of both teleology and deontology without succumbing to the oppositional perspective typical of these two great traditions of modern moral thought.

Perfectionist Ethics

Cavell says that he does not "conceive of [perfectionism] as an alternative to Kantianism or Utilitarianism" (2004, 11). Rather, perfectionism makes room for, and stimulates us to, both teleology and deontology, but without insisting that one of these approaches exclude the other. It is precisely this demand that each crowd the other out—the urge for purity—that weakens the most typical forms of both teleology and deontology. "All moral theories," says Cavell, "have to treat both the good and the right, both consequences and motives" (2004, 84).[12] The idea is simply that teleology and deontology do not by themselves capture everything of ethical importance. The claim is not that they are wrong but that they are incomplete—they are wrong only insofar as they insist on their own completion. Moral perfectionism is thus to be understood as conceptually prior to both utilitarianism and deontology.

Perfectionism integrates, rather than simply aggregates, teleology and deontology—and it thus yields a new direction in ethics. Cavell writes that "perfectionism is the province not of those who oppose justice and benevolent calculation, but of those who feel left out of their sway, who feel indeed that most people have been left, or leave themselves out, of their sway" (2004, 25).[13] Perfectionism, in answering to the underlying concerns that motivate both utilitarianism and deontology, generates ethical resources that neither calculations nor rights can yield on their own. By integrating the most valuable aspects of utilitarian and deontological thought, perfectionism engenders a new conception of the ethical life that is particularly suited to moments of morality where traditional normative theory typically fails.

The moments where teleological and deontological theories are most useful are those where we find ourselves demanding moral judgment, where we feel the need to stand above the complexity of a moral situation and pronounce actions as blameworthy or praiseworthy. The moments where perfectionism is most useful are precisely those where traditional moral judgment is recognized as ineffective, impotent, and perhaps even inimical to ethical action. These are situations where moral energies may be mounted in service of a better life despite the failures of moral theories to enforce obligations upon us. These are moral moments that utilitarianism and deontology, in catering to lower common denominators, do not aspire to. Cavell writes that "this aspect or moment of morality—in which a crisis forces an examination of one's life that calls for a transformation or reorienting of it—is the province of what I emphasize as moral perfectionism" (2004, 11). The essential idea of perfectionism is that of transformative growth: perfectionism pushes us to forge moral possibilities yet actual. Everything hinges on our efforts in creating new moral actualities. Cavell's idea here echoes James's claim that "the *highest* ethical life . . . consists at all times in the breaking of rules which have grown too narrow for the actual case" (1891, 625). The focus for Cavell is upon acts of "liberation from a present state, to a further or next state" (2005, 121). This thought, essential for Cavell's perfectionism, indicates that perfectionism is not so much about attaining a perfect ideal as it is about a process of perfecting, or improving, the present situation in which we find ourselves.[14]

Cavell's central idea of ethical transformation achieves a simultaneous focus on the two aspects of morality central for modern moral reflection: the tendencies of individuation and association. This can be seen in Cavell's claim for "two dominating themes of moral perfectionism" (2004, 26ff.). The first is that of the self as transitive and always aspiring simultaneously away from and toward itself. The second is that of the other, or the friend, as the figure through which these transformations are made possible and given meaning. Cavell explicates these in considering Emerson's concept of self-reliance, which is commonly but wrongly understood as naïvely individualistic. Self-reliance for Cavell is a process of differentiation *with* others. Cavell writes that "what is wrong with [the common] picture is that it seems, in combating conformity, to detach one's self from the rock of others only to attach itself to another fixity, this time within." Instead, the point of "the liberation of the self is precisely to let it become unsettled, to let what is thought to be great and important 'dance before your eyes'" (2004, 298). Do not rely on anything other than your capacity for transformation—and at the same time realize that this capacity is not properly your own but rather that which you create with others insofar as you live through them. According to the perfectionist concept of self-transformation, morality takes place where we transform ourselves with and through others. It ends, or rather dissipates, where we are no longer involved with others in co-creative projects of self-transformation. Cavell summarizes his view as follows: "Perfectionism proposes confrontation and conversation as the means of determining whether we can live together, accept one another into the aspirations of our lives" (2004, 24, cf. 173).

In envisioning moral perfecting in a way that invokes both the moral other and the moral self, Cavell clarifies the value of a moral theory that answers to both the utilitarian emphasis on socializing pleasures and the deontological emphasis on individualizing wills. For Cavell, morality consists in putting pleasure and will into fluid interaction with each other. This fluidity can be grasped by understanding will as referring to the formation and criticism of values and pleasure as referring to the fulfillment and consummation of values. The moral life involves both the active formation of values (will) and their passive consummation (pleasure). Without an interactivity in which these aspects are inseparably intertwined, action will tend to degrade into either the hedonism of pure pleasure or the austerity of pure will. To more fully elucidate this approach, it will be useful to put perfectionist ethics in conversation with pragmatist ethics.

Pragmatist Ethics

Like perfectionism, the pragmatist moral vision is developed as an integration of otherwise disparate poles represented by teleological and deontological assumptions. I will argue that the characteristic pragmatist strategy of integrating the vital elements of the two traditions of modern moral thought without succumbing to their urges for reductive moral purity is best understood in light of what I take to be the central conceptual thrust of pragmatist philosophy as a whole: transitionalism. In reconstructing pragmatist ethics in light of transitionalism, it is natural to turn to meliorism as the central feature of pragmatist ethics insofar as the melioristic emphasis on improvement and growth connotes precisely the temporality and historicity at the heart of pragmatist transitionalism. The idea of meliorism can help inflect the strengths of a pragmatist moral philosophy in ways that recent work in pragmatist moral theory has not often brought into sharp focus.[15]

Meliorism is a single idea with two sides: the first side is that we humans really can improve the world in which we live; the second side is that the only way our world is going to be improved is through our actions. Meliorism thus offers our efforts a leading role in the very drama of reality itself. Seen in such terms of meliorism, pragmatist ethics strikingly resembles perfectionist ethics. At the center of Cavell's perfectionist ethic of transformation is the idea I also find at the center of pragmatist ethics: ethical effort or moral energy. Perfectionist ethics is, in good Emersonian fashion, an ethics of striving. And ethical striving, I suggest, implies both of the central aspects of teleological and deontological thought: pleasure and will. It involves both of these aspects of morality by seeing them as integrated with each other, as implying each other, as synergistic with and therefore necessary for the good functioning of each other.

Ethics for James and Dewey, as for Emerson and Cavell, is not so much about determining what is right or wrong in advance of action (the theoretical programs of principle-based moral philosophies such as Kant's and Bentham's) as it is about the effort to live better lives where there are no rules guiding us in advance. The point of a pragmatist moral theory is not to develop rules of morality that must be followed in practice but rather to develop tools for inquiry that we can employ within experience in order to improve it. This is widely acknowledged by scholars of pragmatist ethics. "The subject matter of moral philosophy is the moral life itself," writes James Gouinlock (1993b, 80); Gregory Pappas concurs that "moral philosophy is thus a function of the moral life" (1998, 103); and Steven Fesmire claims that pragmatism returns ethics to "ordinary life-experiences" (2003, 58).[16] But we need to be careful here lest we make moral life itself (under the description of immediate moral experience) into something that might function as a moral foundation. Indeed, each of these commentators just quoted emphasizes a conception of "morality as experience" that perhaps too readily plays into subtle forms of moral givenism. Experiential foundationalism indeed remains a very real risk in pragmatist ethics in many of the very same ways that it continues to represent a risk in pragmatist epistemology.

The question that pragmatist moral philosophers ought to consider at this juncture is the following: what makes a *life* moral? Central for pragmatist ethics is not a traditional demand for a moral judgment encapsulated in questions such as "What is good?" and "What is right?" but rather the demand for moral efforts captured in questions such as "What can I do?" and "How can I do it?" On this view, moral achievement is contingent above all on our efforts. Pragmatism answers the questions of ethics by encouraging us to focus attention on those acts that actually improve our moral living. As Pappas (2008) rightly argues in his recent book on Dewey's ethics, this requires a moral theory simultaneously attuned to both the scientific and aesthetic dimensions of moral experience.[17] Dewey suggested, though he was never sufficiently explicit on this point, that pragmatist ethics should be seen as an attempt to integrate the concerns of scientistic utilitarians and romantic deontologists by way of shifting focus to the melioristic capacities of our moral practices.[18] Moral reconstruction for Dewey was thus first and foremost a meliorating process such that "if it cannot be told by qualities belonging to the moment of transition it can never be judged" (1922, MW14.195). Yet Dewey too often cashed out this transitionalist ethics in experience-centric terms and thus misled numerous subsequent pragmatists down the garden path of an experiential morality when he really meant to lead us instead down the path of moral meliorism. The task before us now is to play up transitionalist meliorism so as to play down any residual foundationalist emphasis on experience (not to mention the rare but real attempts to reduce morality to linguistic usage, a tendency that has fortunately never been seriously proffered in pragmatist circles). Since the meliorism underlying this proposed integration often remains largely implicit in Dewey's moral theory, it may be helpful to turn for these purposes to James's more explicitly melioristic ethics.

James was acutely aware that in those moral moments where we must create for ourselves the right act, which are also those moments where the most stringent ethical challenges face us, what we most need most is the simple yet tremendous phenomenon of ethical effort: "In what does a moral act consist?. . . . It consists in the effort of attention by which we hold fast to an idea" (1899a, 126).[19] Effort is central wherever one finds oneself in the midst of severe uncertainty. Hence meliorism, which philosophically focuses effort by holding that actually improving our moral realities depends above all on the efforts we put forth in the attempt. Focusing ethics in terms of the effort of attention is, of course, consistent with a variety of conflicting moral positions—James's approach thus does not aim to theoretically resolve ethical conflicts so much as it suggests what form possible resolutions might look like in practice. This clarifies why meliorism will be central for any ethics that takes seriously, as does pragmatism, the ideas that "uncertainty and conflict are inherent in morals" (Dewey 1930c, LW5.280) and that "some part of the ideal must be butchered" (James 1891, 622). In a world where morality requires of us that we face up to irresolvable conflicts, moral achievement depends above all on our uncertain efforts.

James's detailed psychological analyses of the experience of effort offer a helpful starting point for understanding the significant advantages of his meliorist ethics:

> The maximum of attention may then be said to be found whenever we have a systematic harmony or unification between the novel and the old. It is an odd circumstance that neither the old nor the new, by itself, is interesting; the absolutely old is insipid; the absolutely new makes no appeal at all. The old *in* the new is what claims the attention,—the old with a slightly new turn (1899a, 82).

Combining this description of attentive effort with the claim that moral action consists in such effort of attention yields the transitionalist result that the central moral category in James's thought is that of continuity of growth—or melioration. In this way, James historicizes and temporalizes ethics by situating it in the context of a transformation from old into new. Such transitionalist moral progressivism starkly contrasts with the static moral fixity urged by both utilitarians and deontologists. Yet at the same time James's approach also acknowledges the better aspects of each tradition. But before explaining exactly how James's view integrates the utilitarian emphasis on pleasure with the deontological emphasis on will, it will be necessary to consider how he envisioned moral progress as a temporal-historical integration of old and new.

A transitionalist interpretation of James's ethics fits quite well with the work widely acknowledged to be his fullest contribution to moral theory: "The Moral Philosopher and the Moral Life." In this essay, James weighs in for a morality of increasing inclusiveness. What this involves is the forging of moral ideals that achieve two things: first, they do not completely depart from extant ideals; second, they create new actual ways of harmonizing old ideals. The central moral problem for James is the real conflict between the very ideals that make our lives significant: "Every end of desire that presents itself appears exclusive of some other end of desire" (1891, 622). It is within this problematic context that James understands the melioristic victory of increased inclusiveness as the core of moral living: "See everywhere the struggle and the squeeze; and everlastingly the problem how to make them less" (1891, 624). James's conclusion is that "the victory to be philosophically prayed for is that of the more inclusive side" (1891, 623). Not just a typical liberal claim for tolerance, James here offers a claim for a more radical and strenuous increase of inclusiveness. The crucial point is that of the *more* inclusive side. Ruth Anna Putnam excellently captures James's view: "For James, moral progress occurs when more and more human beings in their demands and in their actions realize ideals that encompass greater and greater numbers of lesser ideals. . . . That is why one must begin with the ideals one finds existing in one's society, but it is also why that can only be a starting point" (1990, 86). This is an irreducibly transitionalist perspective. Moral melioration is an achievement that occurs in the form of time and is realized through actual historical specifics. We start from where we are and develop the resources within our situation in order to improve it. This does not solve all our problems once and for all. But it does improve the situation, open up new problems, and enable us to progressively struggle for a better world.

This melioristic integration of old and new is the central thrust of James's pragmatist perfectionist ethics even if commentators have not generally emphasized the central place in pragmatist moral thought of dialectics of old and new, recurrence and variance, repetition and difference, banality and originality.[20] This melioristic vision of morality as historicist was however central for all the classical pragmatists including Dewey, who wrote in his *Ethics* that "at each point there is a distinction between an old, an accomplished self, and a new and moving self, between the static and the dynamic self" (1932, LW7.306). This moral insight common to both James and Dewey was in their work already itself a repetition with a difference (or what I call a "renewal," hearing both the "re-" and the "new" in that word) of Emerson: "Old and new make the warp and woof of every moment. There is not a thread that is not a twist of these two strands" (1868, 1028).

Pragmatist Perfectionism as Integrating Teleology and Deontology

By focusing on ethics in terms of the effort of attention, and by describing attention in transitionalist terms of the warp and woof of old and new, James temporally integrated the moral concerns that utilitarianism and deontology are best seen as responses to. Hilary and Ruth Anna Putnam are thus correct to note that "if there is a strong Utilitarian strain in James's ethics, there are also some striking similarities to Kantianism" (1989, 218).[21] The result of this, for James then and for us now, is the need within pragmatism for an integration of revolutionary rationalist approaches (deontology, intuitionism) and conservative empiricist approaches (utilitarianism, hedonism).

One way of developing these interpretations is to focus on James's view of the relation between attention and transition, according to which the central moral act of attention consists in the actual transitions that carry us from old to new. This strategy involves recognizing that the analogues of old and new in modern moral philosophy are our inherited pleasures, as focused by utilitarianism, and our restless willings, as focused by deontology. Pragmatist morality gives due attention to both the pleasures we find given to us and the acts of will through which we transform these pleasures. Moral action challenges conformity to our extant pleasures but without fully abandoning them in favor of an unattainable ideal—morality is willful but not just willful. Moral agents thus take seriously their extant pleasures but without ever fully indulging them—morality is thus pleasurable but not just pleasurable. These are the terms of James's transitionalist proposal for addressing the basic problem of modern moral philosophy.

Of course, it must be admitted that all this appears a little too neat and tidy. Utilitarianism is certainly not *always* about accepting things as they are. I am rather urging that the central point of much utilitarian doctrine is that the pleasures actually enjoyed by actual persons are the best measure we have of moral acceptance. Things must be changed, but only so that they better conform to what we already take pleasure in and desire. The point of utilitarianism is never to reform our pleasures but only to augment them. Deontology is also not *always* committed to making things otherwise than they already are. So I urge that its central point is that how things presently stand empirically cannot serve as a ground for morality. We need a new measure of right that does not conform to our extant desires. That is why the idea of right, for Kant, was so intimate with the idea of immortality. Morality is always drawn toward the future and the new. So while utilitarianism is not always about repetition and deontology is not always about revolution, utilitarianism clearly *tends toward* the old (conformity to our extant pleasures) and deontology clearly *tends toward* the new (the transformations associated with our willing). Pragmatist perfectionism integrates these tendencies, which teleology and deontology otherwise leave helpless in their separation.

Here, then, is how pragmatist perfectionists propose to integrate the valuable aspects of teleological and deontological theories. On the one hand, pragmatist perfectionists take from Kant the important idea that volitional effort is a necessary condition for moral action. Kant's insight here was that morality requires an employment of the will in order that our sometimes weaker impulses of duty may overcome our sometimes stronger impulses of pleasure. Thus moral willing is a necessary condition of actual moral progress. On the other hand, pragmatist perfectionists take from Bentham and Mill the important idea that satisfaction is essential to any well-lived life. The insight here was that morality requires some amount of conformity to extant human desires in order that our moral deliberations retain a connection to the actual moral agents performing them—otherwise we risk imposing on these moral agents demands so stringent that they begin to feel completely alienated from moral utopias so abstract that they have no chance of survival in the real world. Thus moral pleasure is a necessary condition of actual moral progress. Together these two moves show why the moral growth central to pragmatist perfectionism requires both will and pleasure: because each is a necessary condition of real moral progress.

Cavell well captures the aim sighted by the pragmatists when he writes the following: "What I call Emersonian perfectionism I understand to propose that one's quarrel with the world need not be settled, nor cynically set aside as unsettlable. It is a condition in which you can at once want the world and want it to change" (2004, 18). Cavell here echoes Ruth Anna Putnam's (1990, 86) view, quoted above, to the effect that we must both begin with the conditions in which we find ourselves situated and at the same time take those conditions as only a starting point. Their mutual perfectionist pragmatism is already an echo of that quintessential vision of transitionalist critique exemplified in its American context by those meliorist cultural critics discussed in chapter 1. Among those critics I counted James Baldwin who, anticipating both Cavell and Putnam, wrote: "I love America more than any other country in the world, and, exactly for this reason, I insist on the right to criticize her perpetually" (1955, 9). The meliorist vision, stated here by Baldwin with as much inspiration and insight as by anyone else, proffers a twofold modality of critique according to which we shall accept the world as we find it and also work to change that world. We shall be party to both the old forms already existent and to the new forms we must make manifest.

In the context of ethics, this meliorist vision is ably translated by James's idea that moral effort consists in the integration of the lingering past in which we find ourselves present and the impending future toward which that present ever rushes. Moral effort, as such, integrates the temporal and historical stream of moral practice. And it is through such integrations that we actually improve the moral realities we inhabit. Dewey succinctly stated the core of this pragmatist perfectionism when he wrote that a moral life seeks "not perfection as a final goal, but the ever-enduring process of perfecting" (1920, 177/MW12.181). Both major alternatives to such a transitionally situated meliorism are unacceptable: a complacent acceptance of what is given us and a cynical abandonment of the present in flight toward unattainable utopias. In the context of politics, this vision similarly expresses an irreducibly valuable insight, as I show in the next chapter.

Pragmatist perfectionists from Emerson and Baldwin to Cavell and James embody a conception of ethics that would turn us away from traditional preoccupations with monopolizing moral principles and toward the energetic efforts sustaining actual moral achievements. This turn is invited in part by the thought that ethical life is better approached as taking place under conditions of contingency and uncertainty than under conditions of necessity and certainty. Dewey was explicit about this idea in always turning attention toward "the element of uncertainty . . . in any situation which can properly be called moral" (1930c, LW5.279). In the modern moral life characterized by uncertainty, we must draw our resources for moral living not from some fixed constant but out of the stream of moral life itself. This conception of the ethical life as uncertain will be crucial for moral theory if it is to remain resonant with the exigencies of modern moral life. The hope and confidence of pragmatism is, I am urging, the best response to the widespread skepticism about modern moral theory characteristic of the second half of the twentieth century. It is in this sense that, in the face of the deep emptiness of much modern moral theory, pragmatism and perfectionism can together provide an important renewal of modern ethics. At the center of this renewal is a vision of ethics as centered primarily around ethical effort. Once we finally motivate ourselves to ask about it, it begins to seem thoroughly surprising that effort is a concept so widely neglected by modern moral philosophy. The reason for this neglect is that modern philosophy always assumed that the moral life would necessarily flow from the correct moral principles. So it was to these principles, be they empiricist or rationalist in origin, that modern moral philosophy devoted itself. But the great unexplored assumption behind this approach was that ethical living is better served by demonstrations of necessity than by affirmations of contingency and provocations to perfectibility. It is that assumption which pragmatist perfectionism finally and firmly rejects. It was Emerson who inaugurated this rejection when he wrote, "it is not instruction, but provocation, that I can receive from another soul" (1838, 66). Pragmatist perfectionism is accordingly an ethics of provocation and as such it offers a much needed alternative to the current theoretical dominance of moralities of purity, whose most lasting effect seems to be not the achievement of moral living but rather the increasing apathy characterizing contemporary moral life.

Six

POLITICS AS PROGRESSING

Utopianism, Dystopianism, Conservatism, and Meliorism

A melioristic ethics can be usefully described by way of contrast to the purified forms of utilitarian and deontological theory that have dominated modern moral philosophy. Similarly, a melioristic politics can be described by way of contrast to a familiar trinity of genres in modern political philosophy: utopianism, dystopianism, and conservatism. But whereas in discussing pragmatist ethics I sought to describe meliorism as integrating the best insights of the two leading traditions of modern moral philosophy, in discussing pragmatist politics I shall here prefer to emphasize more heavily pragmatism's departure from the leading traditions of modern political theory. This is not to say that pragmatism does not share much with these traditions. To be sure, it does and I would vigorously insist that pragmatists have much to learn from theorists in other leading traditions. Nevertheless, if we neglect to emphasize the remaining differences, it is unlikely that pragmatist political philosophy will ever become melioristic in the sense of contributing to already existing political transitions. For contemporary political philosophy's lack of engagement with concrete political realities is precisely the point on which its leading traditions need to be severely contested. I thus prefer to make the case in this chapter for pragmatism's departures from, rather than reconstructions of, the mainstream. This has consequences not only for pragmatism's contributions to political philosophy but also for how we ought to approach the very project of political philosophy as pragmatists. After making my case for meliorism as against other genres more prominent in contemporary political philosophy, I will turn in the final sections of this chapter to recent pragmatist work in political philosophy so as to show the value of taking meliorism as central to the tradition. Meliorism, I will argue, reorients pragmatism away from the dangers of a narrow overemphasis on linguistic deliberation or experiential community as the founts of democracy. I will be particularly eager throughout this chapter to point out resonances with political philosophers who do not describe themselves as pragmatist but who can help pragmatism better describe itself: I focus at greatest length on Bernard Williams, but I also consider Iris Marion Young, Axel Honneth, Amartya Sen, and Michel Foucault.

Since the primary aim of this chapter is to show how pragmatist meliorism offers a viable alternative to the leading modes of utopianism, dystopianism, and conservatism found in contemporary political thought, it will help to begin by specifying these other modes. Although I differentiate pragmatist meliorism from all three of these modes, only two of them are taken quite seriously today among academic political philosophers: namely the utopian and the dystopian. The conservative tradition has lost its footing in the academic establishment, though it has gained a surer stability in the political realities propping up our ivory towers. This is a symptom of the severe disconnection between contemporary political theory and contemporary political reality. Meanwhile utopian and dystopian conceptions of political philosophy have risen to the fore in the academy. This is distressing, as both of these conceptions can be rightly described as ahistoricist insofar as they conceive the work of political philosophy as in some essential way abstracting from the exigencies of actual political reality.

I will begin with approaches that are more rationalistic and utopian in orientation. These political philosophies take as their explicit goal the formulation of an ideal theory of political association that all really existing polities ought to measure themselves by. This mode of presentation is concerned almost exclusively with accurately conceptualizing the best of all possible political worlds, and it is only tangentially concerned, if at all, with how we may begin to approximate this ideal on the basis of the real possibilities present in actual political reality. The paradigm, and still the best possible sketch of, this sort of rationalistic utopian political philosophy is to be found in Plato's *Repub-*

lic, where the political association described is tautologically identified as the best insofar as it will be ruled by philosopher-kings who, it is stipulated, know what the best possible form of political association in any situation would be. If Plato's stipulations are simply too fanciful for modern sensibilities, then we would do better to look for an exemplar of rationalism nearer to our own time.

The later work of John Rawls offers a nice test case for differentiating the pragmatist's melioristic approach to political philosophy from other approaches now prominent. If it can be shown that Rawls's later work is relatively rationalistic and utopian in comparison to Dewey's and James's work, then this should signal something important about the pragmatist approach to political philosophy, insofar as Rawls is often understood as having sufficiently departed from the rationalist and utopian models of political philosophy in his later work. Samuel Scheffler nicely captures the standard interpretation of the later Rawls: "Rawls's work as he now presents it is addressed to modern democratic societies at a certain historical moment. His political liberalism seeks to establish a liberal conception of justice on the basis of ideas that are implicit in the public political culture of such societies" (1994, 146). Rawls came to describe his later view in these very terms, writing of it as "realistically utopian" (1999, 11; 2001, 4). According to one of his descriptions of that view, "By showing how the social world may realize the features of a realistic utopia, political philosophy provides a long-term goal of political endeavor, and in working toward it gives meaning to what we can do today" (1999, 128). Rawls (2001a, 2007) recognized at least three other roles for political philosophy in addition to realistic utopianism (namely reconciliation, orientation, and working for social order). But it is clear that he presents his own theory of justice as first and foremost assuming the role of realistic utopianism. In assuming this role, Rawls presents his view as probing "the limits of practical political possibility" (2001a, 4). Clearly this view is intended to be one that is distanced from classical utopianisms such as Plato's, insofar as it aims to be both realistic and practical. But I worry that Rawls does not succeed on his own terms. I agree with Rawls that this is the right goal to have, but I am not sure he ever attains that goal in his own work.

My worry is that despite his better intentions, Rawls remained much too much the rationalist utopian. Rawls may have wanted to historically locate his later political philosophy in the context of twentieth-century liberal democratic practices, but he did not succeed in doing so insofar as the rationalist utopianism of the old ahistorical model of political philosophy continued to determine both the concepts that Rawls worked with and the way in which he worked with these concepts. While Rawls's later work is clearly not as straightforwardly ahistoricist as was Plato's, Hobbes's, Rousseau's, or even Rawls's early work, there is nevertheless a lingering rationalist utopianism in his late work, which renders it a relatively ahistorical enterprise.

The realism in Rawls's realistic utopianism is supposed to be that "justice as fairness starts within a certain political tradition" (1993, 14) and addresses itself to that tradition, namely the tradition of modern industrial liberal democracy. But, for Rawls, "starting" within and "addressing" himself to this tradition seems to reach no further than adopting certain "fundamental" ideas that will orient his presentation of an ideal theory of justice. These fundamental ideas include social cooperation, free and equal citizens, and a well-ordered society (2001, 5). But these ideas seem to be so general as to clearly have come not from historical inquiry into the actual so much as from philosophical abstraction from the actual. An inquiry into actually existing liberal democracy should yield more specific ideas, such as ideas of, say, corporate capitalism, global media networks, digital technoculture, environmental catastrophe, industrial agriculture, failing nationalism, and deep (rather than merely reasonable) pluralism. These ideas name specific realities we might be able to work with in contrast to the heady abstraction of "a well-ordered society." There is, of course, room for heady abstractions in even the most engaged practice of political philosophy, but if we never descend from this abstract realm in order to carefully engage our actual political realities then our political philosophies inevitably turn out utopian and not realistic. In defending a utopianism that Rawls framed throughout his career in terms of what he called "ideal theory" or "strict compliance theory," he insures that the conceptual material forming the major part of his theory of justice will consist entirely of idealizations that are explicitly disarticulated from the concrete political realities out of which they are abstracted.[1]

One may reply that Rawls does take at least one such concrete political reality very seriously indeed, namely the fact of pluralism, and that this reality is crucial for determining how the theory and practice of liberal democracy must transform itself today. Rawls's ideas of overlapping consensus and public reason were introduced in his later work to accommodate precisely this reality of pluralism. Rawls is unequivocal about his intentions: "The idea of an overlapping consensus is introduced to make the idea of a well-ordered society more realistic and to adjust it to the historical and social conditions of democratic societies, which include the fact of reasonable pluralism" (2001, 32). But if we look at how overlapping consensus and its companion idea of public reason actually function, we note that they are clearly not intended to tailor a theory of justice out of the fabric of our actually existing political reality. Rather, they are intended to adjust the fabric of a rational and utopian theory of justice to certain pressing exigencies of any actual politics. Rawls is clearly not ambivalent about the workableness of his theory of justice in contemporary liberal democracies. But he is not especially concerned to determine how we might get from our contemporary realities to his ideal theory. Overlapping consensus and public reason show *that* this ideal could get traction in any actual political reality, but they do not show *how* this traction is to be gained in our actually existing politics.

Those of Rawls's ideas that are oriented toward the fact of reasonable pluralism should not be understood as making theoretical concessions to actual political realities. Considering the possibility that Rawls conceded to the pressures of political reality in developing those of his ideas oriented toward pluralism, Joshua Cohen explicitly argues against such an interpretation. Accommodating realities in this way would be a defect, Cohen argues, because it would amount to compromising ideals of justice to the burdens of reality in such a way as to deprive those ideals of their normative force: "We are accommodating basic principles not to the reality of power but, rather, to the way that social reality reveals the powers of practical reason" (1993, 288). Cohen here well captures Rawls's view concerning the role played by abstraction in his theory of justice. Rawls holds that we perform abstractions to get ourselves clear of the clutter of political reality: "We should be prepared to find that the deeper the conflict, the higher the level of abstraction to which we must ascend to get a clear and uncluttered view of its roots" (1993, 46). This suggests a way of thinking about Rawls's later political philosophy in terms of a picture in which overlapping consensus and public reason are one level of abstraction up from the cluttered roots of political reality and the original position is up at an even higher level of abstraction. Overlapping consensus and public reason do not force those in the original position to concede anything to political reality. They help us specify the way in which any political reality might orient itself toward an ideal theory of justice that can be worked out from within the original position. These lower-level abstractions do not compromise ideal justice for the sake of real society. They help that reality see its shortcomings to that ideality. Rawls's project is to formulate general principles of justice that can help us explain not just why we contingently happen to endorse this or that conception of the basic structure of society but why this or that conception is the most reasonable and therefore the most just conception available. Lower-level abstractions would detract from this project if they offered explanations of justice in terms of the contingent exigencies of actual political reality. This is why Rawls sees abstractions rather as helping us understand how general principles can be articulated alongside of particular judgments without compromising the former for the sake of the latter.[2]

So even when he does attempt to tune his ideal theory to the actual political reality in which he finds himself, Rawls works from the ideal back to the real rather than from reality toward ideality. This is moving in the wrong direction. Political progress gets made when we start from where we are and then lift ourselves up to some vaguely specified ideal. Philosophers can spend their whole lives dreaming up the most beautiful utopias, but if nobody can ever get there then it is not clear that this sort of work is worthwhile. The risk of focusing all our energies on specifying ideals is that our realities will never get improved if we do not work out ways of leveling up the real world to the daydreams of the philosophers. A better bet for improvement is to leave our ideals vague in order to focus our energies on improving our realities.

Turning now from utopianism to a second and seemingly quite different form of ahistoricist political philosophy, we can discern similar errors in works of a more irrationalist and dystopian temper. If the rationalist abstracts from political realities in order to formulate a rational ideal, then the irrationalist does so in order to show that politics is beyond the ken of reason. The point of political philosophy practiced in this mode is not so much to show what our political associations should look like as it is to show the danger of any rationalist pretense to anticipate future political orders. That is what characterizes these political philosophies is irrationalist. In attempting to show that the political exceeds the rational, philosophers of this persuasion conclude that we ought to let the best possible political future arrive unblocked by the tortures of reason. This is a humble politics of a silent passivity that calmly awaits the unforeseeable crash of the eschaton, the real, the messiah, the other, and the event into the expected rhythms of the rational world. One can find such a politics in the work of Walter Benjamin, Martin Heidegger, Emmanuel Levinas, and Jacques Derrida, and perhaps even more pointedly in many very prominent interpretations of their work. But the most vocal contemporary proponent of this view is the provocative social critic Slavoj Žižek.

What is ultimately so defeating about messianic politics in any form is the passivity they engender. Žižek's political philosophy is best seen as a brief against the dangers of purposive and activist politics: "The threat today is not passivity but pseudo-activity, the urge to 'be active,' to 'participate'" (2006, 334). Beginning with this perhaps useful caution about the dangers of over-zealous activisms, Žižek goes on to infer that we should never be active. Žižek advocates what he calls "Bartleby politics," in reference to the Herman Melville character whose entire literary vocation is to calmly reply to any and every question that he is asked, "I would prefer not to." I find Žižek's reading of this story very much out of touch with the sense of American experimentalism that pervades Melville's major works such as *Moby-Dick* and *The Confidence Man*, but the nascent pragmatism I detect in Melville is not really the issue here. The issue rather is Žižek's claim for a politics that "is not merely the first, preparatory, stage for the second, more 'constructive,' work of forming a new alternative order" but is rather "the very source and background of this order, its permanent foundation" (2006, 382). The political passivity for which Bartleby is Žižek's paradigm offers a seemingly profound "gesture of subtraction at its purest" (2006, 382), which is supposed to be the only way of counterweighing the maniacal politics of an Ahab. Passivity would not prepare the way for the construction of a new political practice but would rather seek to unbalance existing practices without itself risking a constructive move. The big assumption resting behind Žižek's approach is that one can effectively engage in what we might call purely negative criticism, a criticism that does not pose alternatives by critiquing the existing order from the vantage of some newer and better order. A purely negative criticism just denounces what exists and rejects it in the name of, well, nothing at all. It is not clear that politics requires any such practice as its "permanent foundation" even if politics surely does require that from time to time we tentatively reject certain political activities before we have landed on better alternatives. There is a crucial difference between a restless and active negative politics and a slumbering and passive negative politics enacted through the semicomatose figure of

Bartleby. But there is a difficult paradox facing any argument against purposive activity, be it Žižek's, Heidegger's, or anyone else's. How can one go about just letting things be? How, in other words, do we get out of the active mode and into the passive mode of Bartleby or *Gelassenheit*? Is the abandonment of activity some final last act before we slip into passivity? The argument is that we should let go of our active, technological, and rational approach to the world. But those who make this argument need to more carefully specify how one can go about doing this without perpetuating the purposive activity that is supposedly the source of all of our problems.

The meliorist conception of political philosophy made available in pragmatism is easily distinguished from the sorts of rationalisms and irrationalisms I have been considering. Pragmatists hold that political reason is always situated within a context but in such a way as to provide the resources for its own improvement. Reason cannot transcend its situation (as the utopian hopes), but it certainly can purposively engage with it in order to improve (as the dystopian denies). In urging these views, however, pragmatists must be careful that they do not become identified with certain strains of conservative political thought, an important but neglected tradition in contemporary political philosophy. Certainly pragmatism has much in common with some central assumptions made by most conservatives. Against the ahistoricism of both the rationalists and the irrationalists, pragmatists tend to side with those conservatives who articulate evolutionary, developmental, and situated conceptions of political practice.[3] Pragmatists thus share with conservatives a faith in reformism against revolutionism. But this is as far as the comparison to the conservatives can really go. The pragmatist and the conservative draw two quite different lessons in their respective affirmations of reformism as potentially radical and necessarily conservative. The conservative urges that we ought not to engage in too much purposive political change (in the name of ethical ideals, for instance) lest we interfere with the invisible hand set into motion by the transparent cunning of reason. The pragmatist urges by contrast that an evolutionist conception of political reason shows us precisely the terrain on which ethical interventions into political realities ought to be situated: within the domain of political reality itself. We ought not flee from political reality in order to engage an ethical perspective, as both the rationalist and the dystopian do. Political reality itself affords us the very perspective from within which we might engage in the ethical work of political melioration.

It is, of course, quite an easy game to poke holes in the great paper tigers of political philosophy. The real challenge for a pragmatist political philosophy today is to develop viable alternatives to utopianism, dystopianism, and conservatism once defanged. I now turn to pragmatism's meliorist alternative.

Meliorism in Pragmatist Thought

A useful first approximation of this pragmatist practice of transitionalist political criticism can be discerned in the writings of two energetic young pragmatists who were at the height of their critical powers in the era of American Progressivism. Randolph Bourne, who learned no small portion of his pragmatism from John Dewey at Columbia, possessed one of the most brilliant critical minds of his time. The core commitment of that mind was precisely the melioristic orientation. Bourne offers us a memorable image of this orientation in his essay "The Life of Irony." Here Bourne paints the portrait of an adjacent and connected critic. The crucial idea is this one: "if he is critical, it is his own world that he is criticizing" (1913, 143). Criticism, for Bourne, was surely an attempt to change the world, perhaps even dramatically. But it is crucial, Bourne was arguing, that the critic must occupy some place within the world he is criticizing. Only then can he position himself in that delicate space of adjacency: right up beside that which he criticizes yet ever so subtly distant from it such that the criticism can be effective.

Walter Lippmann, who learned no small part of his pragmatism from William James at Harvard, offered a similar conception of criticism in his beautifully written *A Preface to Politics*. Lippmann's book revolves around a contrast between the energy of "inventiveness" and the slumber of "routine." Lippmann's argument was that the value that democratic self-government in his day stood in greatest need of was precisely that of inventiveness: "We have hoped for machine regularity when we needed human initiative and leadership, when life was crying that its inventive abilities should be freed" (1913, 23). Democracy is the politics that can cultivate this inventiveness, argued Lippmann. For him, such democracy would be a function of our effort: "Effort moves it, intelligence directs it; its fate is in human hands" (1913, 222). It follows that democracy is experimental: "There is no such thing as Democracy; there are a number of more or less democratic experiments" (1913, 220). On

Lippmann's view, the most important thing about democratic politics is inventive experimentation. Experimentation is at its best where inventive persons break free of the routine crusts of consensus in order to generate dynamic new possibilities of democratic individuation and association. We do this, Lippmann argued, by building up the political and ethical resources already available to us in the situations in which we already find ourselves. We self-governing inventors can thus improve actually existing political and ethical realities, which is a quite different project from thinking about how political and ethical reality ought ideally to look.

Pragmatist meliorism thus articulates that mode of temporal adjacency and critical connectedness that dwells somewhere in the middle of that vast space between the conservative clinging to the past and the revolutionary embrace of the future. Meliorism enables an experimental time that cannot be determined in advance either by conservative convention nor radical rationality. Meliorism is experimental in regarding moral and political life as something we must work out in actual practice rather than pronounce judgments upon in advance. How, though, are we to occupy this experimental terrain? Or, better yet, how might we experimentally construct the as yet nonexistent edges upon which we meliorists ever push outward from present to future reality? Or, recalling my description of the engaged cultural critic in chapter 1, how can the melioristic critic situate themselves as connected and adjacent? Dewey, James, and Rorty are here quite helpful.

The melioristic sensibility colors almost every aspect of John Dewey's philosophical engagements. In a journal article summarizing the lectures that would later be published as *Reconstruction in Philosophy*, Dewey describes rationality as "the power of using past experience to shape and transform future experience" (1919, MW11.346). This is about as transitionalist a statement as you can get. It is particularly in the context of his contributions to democratic theory that Dewey's reconstructive meliorism really shines. Dewey refused to indulge in typical political philosophical speculations about universalist principles of justice, right, and good. He rather engaged himself in an attempt to improve the democratic experiment as it was already underway in the context of early twentieth-century America. This explains why all of Dewey's most important political writings—*The Public and Its Problems* (1927), *Individualism Old and New* (1930), *Liberalism and Social Action* (1935), and *Freedom and Culture* (1939a)—do not resemble the standard form of political philosophical treatises to which we are today, perhaps unfortunately, all too accustomed. These books do not offer systematic theories of justice, of democracy, or of the state. They are better read as philosophical engagements with the actual political conditions defining the cultural conditions within which Dewey and his contemporaries found themselves. The most striking thing about these books is their concrete orientation toward very specific cultural configurations such as corporate capitalism, heavy industrialism, mass communications, cultural pluralism, economic consumerism, credit economies, the age of surplus, and a whole host of other historically specific conceptions. The result of such an orientation cannot be an idealized theory of democracy, of justice, or of the state. It can only be an experimental proposal about how we might leverage our existing political conditions in such a way as to improve these conditions.

Dewey's experimental approach to political philosophy offers the basis for a working definition of political meliorism as the improvement of political realities on the basis of resources already available within the very realities on which we are working. Dewey's engagement with the actual exigencies of his cultural situation suggests that he sought to understand how existing situations could be improved without having to specify what the best possible situation might be. He sought political betterment without a foundation of political perfection. Improvement is not measured against the perfection of an unrealizable ideal but against the development and growth of those already extant capacities we hold to be valuable. Improvement does not answer a call from some ideal on high but answers the calls of the situations in which we already find ourselves. This reconstructive approach is exemplified in some of Dewey's best passages on the function of ideals in politics and ethics. In *Individualism Old and New*: "Ideals, including that of a new and effective individuality, must themselves be framed out of the possibilities of existing conditions. . . . The ideals take shape and gain a content as they operate in remaking conditions" (1930a, LW5.122). In *Human Nature and Conduct*: "Men have constructed a strange dream-world when they have supposed that without a fixed ideal of a remote good to inspire them, they have no enticement to get relief from present troubles, no desires for liberation from what oppresses and for clearing-up what confuses present action" (1922, MW14.195). Dewey's central vision of democracy as a way of life is all about improving the situations in which we already find ourselves in the present on the basis of the resources afforded to us within those situations. We need not, nor could we ever hope to, transcend the present situations in which we find ourselves in order to locate the resources we need for meliorating that situation. Democratic melioration thus enables the energy of a reliance on what is available to us.

Dewey's political criticism was built on William James's model of political critique as a connected and adjacent practice. Dewey more precisely specified the core of pragmatist meliorism as it was initially envisioned by James. We should accordingly look to James for vivid examples of pragmatist political meliorism just as we should look to Dewey for more precise conceptions of how pragmatist political meliorism is to function.

For a vivid portrait of James's meliorism, we can hardly do better than to look to one of his topical essays that, as a piece of political criticism, still remains one of the most relevant contributions of the entire Progressive Era: "The Moral Equivalent of War" (1910). The crux of this essay is James's formulation of a new political ideal of moral militarism, which he offers as reconciling the previously incompatible ideals of moral pacifism and immoral militarism. James's elaboration of a moral equivalent of war is meant to provide us with the means for getting from here to there. In other words, it is meant to provide a transitional link between some untenable present reality and some improved future possibility. James is clear that in the old dispute between the pacifists and the militarists he is on the side of peace. But he recognizes that the peace party has thus far remained unconvincing. Pacifism has been mistaken for passivism. Passivism is then regarded as incoherent with, and disconnected from, the more militaristic forms of aggressivism found in the real world today. While passivism is thus an alternative to aggressivism, its proponents offer no concrete terms by which we might actually transition from one to the other. They look not toward political improvements but toward political utopias. In all their chanting in service of what would be best, they forsake the opportunity to make things better and thus end up with a situation that is actually worse.

All of the most forceful statements in James's essay focus on the importance of this melioristic attitude toward political criticism. Distinguishing his view from the disconnected ideal of the pacifists, he writes: "So long as anti-militarists propose no substitute for war's disciplinary function, no *moral equivalent of war*, analogous, as one might say, to the mechanical equivalent of heat, so long they fail to realize the full inwardness of the situation" (1910, 666).

And setting forth the outlines of his own connected conception of moral militarism, he writes: "We must make new energies and hardihoods continue the manliness to which the military mind so faithfully clings" (1910, 668). What James is proposing in this essay is the experimental fashioning of a new ideal, one more inclusive than the old oppositional ideals of moral pacifism and immoral militarism. This is, by the way, an application not only of meliorism but also of the vision of moral inclusivism that James had previously urged in one of his most important pieces of moral and political criticism, "The Moral Philosopher and the Moral Life" (1891). The new, more inclusive ideal James proposed was indeed relevant to its times such that it was, in somewhat altered form of course, put into widespread practice during the thirties as Franklin Roosevelt's Civilian Conservation Corps. The broader outlines of this ideal are continued in many governmental and nongovernmental projects taking place even today.

The ideal that James proposed was "a conscription of the whole youthful population to form for a certain number of years a part of the army enlisted against *Nature*." Some self-appointed critics have been quick to pounce on James's proposal in that it seems to have the ring of a rabid industrialism bent on desiccating the natural environment. But this criticism, of course, relies on a distinction between nature and artifice, which James did not countenance for good philosophical reasons. James was not proposing military assaults on the "wilderness" (a term available to him that he consciously did not use) nor on the "environment" (a term whose modern connotations were not yet available). If one goes on to actually read James's specification of his proposal, rather than some previous commentator's unhelpful gloss of it, it is clear that he is proposing a war against those untamed human realities that human energies can meliorate by building sustainable artifactual environments. There is no reason not to construe this war as aiming toward the construction of vast hybrid networks consisting of such diverse elements as railroads, skyscrapers, levees, national parks, ecology boards, and solar-energy farms. "War has been the only force that can discipline a whole community," wrote James, "and until an equivalent discipline is organized, I believe that war must have its way" (1910, 669). If there is anything disconcerting in James's proposal, it is not his ambiguous references to "nature" but rather his loose invocation of an ideal of "discipline" that from a later perspective informed by the work of Michel Foucault we ought to approach with serious caution.

We can best appreciate James's prescient insights not by focusing on possible equivocations that may only appear ambiguous in hindsight but by focusing rather on the broader contours of his melioristic approach to political criticism. The crux of that meliorism can be schematically summarized as advocating the triadic relation of transitionality (from *ab* to *bc* by way of *b*) as an alternative to the binary relation of opposition (from *a* to *z* without the assistance of any mediating terms). James's own practice of political criticism manifests this melioristic conception of the function of ideals. This conception, later developed in detail by Dewey, was clearly anticipated by James in his political writings. It was anticipated even more clearly in a remark, though perhaps a casual one as it is excavated from his correspondence, that cuts to the heart of the transitionalist perspective: "Ideals ought to aim at the *transformation of reality*—no less!" (James to Charles A. Strong, April 9, 1907, in James 1920, II.270).

The pragmatist meliorism developed by James and Dewey remains a central component of the political criticism of the most important and influential of contemporary pragmatist philosophers, namely Richard Rorty. Fortunately, it is sufficient to be brief here because of the quality of Rorty's prose in capturing the sense of pragmatist political meliorism. Take, for instance, this bold pronouncement: "My candidate for the most distinctive and praiseworthy human capacity is our ability to trust and to cooperate with other people, and in particular to work together so as to improve the future" (1999, xiii). It would be difficult to find in the whole of pragmatist literature a more compressed and fecund statement of both the essential qualities of meliorism and its centrality to the pragmatist vision.

The most careful readers will note, however, that Rorty (1989a, 44ff.) has written generously of the function of "utopian" thought in politics. Is this at cross purposes with my interpretation of meliorism as distinct from both dystopian and utopian politics? A detailed analysis would show that Rorty's embrace of romantic utopianism is not offered in the same key as Rawls's assumption of a more rationalist utopianism. Rorty's utopianism is actually better understood in terms of a meliorist hope for a better future than as a call for ideal political blueprints or model theories of justice. Rorty has always been clear that theoretical blueprints in politics are noxious and that flexible hope serves our purposes much better. This is, to cite just one example, exactly how Rorty invokes "utopia" in the last paragraph of *Achieving Our Country*: "Whitman and Dewey tried to substitute hope for knowledge. They wanted to put shared utopian dreams—dreams of an ideally decent and civilized society—in the place of knowledge of God's Will, Moral Law, the Laws of History, or the Facts of Science" (1998b, 106).[4]

Other contemporary pragmatists similarly carry forth the meliorist banner. Particularly impressive is Vincent Colapietro's energetic work on pragmatism's irreducibly historicist tendencies. Colapietro's expositions of a historicist pragmatism usefully focuses attention on the way in which the transitionalist sensibility I have here been attributing to pragmatism lends itself quite naturally to the melioristic forms of criticism I have just located in James, Dewey, and others. Colapietro forcefully states the crucial meliorist point: "The defining mark of the pragmatic outlook is preoccupation with the present, critical engagement in the here and now, self-conscious reconstruction of what are in this place and time the culturally authorized forms of authority, expertise, practice, and so on, of what are in this place and time the personally recognizable forms of experience, desire, work, and so on" (1998b, 118). Pragmatism's preoccupation, in other words, is with the way in which we can critically improve our situations on the basis of resources available in the here and now. And, in an important moment, Colapietro specifically connects this melioristic preoccupation with a historicist sensibility: "going *beyond* is possible, if at all, only by going *through*—where that which is to be gone and worked through are the complex histories inscribed in our institutions and in our very habits" (1998b, 127). This precisely captures the connection between meliorism and transitionalism that I propose as a model for a third-wave pragmatist political criticism.

The meliorist who works within, and through, our political situations does so on the basis of the specific historical trajectories defined within those situations. This is the basic upshot of the meliorisms that range from the classical pragmatisms of James and Dewey (and Lippmann and Bourne) to the contemporary pragmatisms of Rorty and Colapietro (and others). This meliorism ought to be understood as the result of inflecting political philosophy with the core pragmatist sensibility of transitionalism. To summarize the core of this transitionalist meliorism, allow me to conclude with a distinction. Consider that the facts of our present political situation, say the current state of debates on heteronormative sexuality, can be interpreted in at least two ways. Taken purely logically, we might find current cultural opinion both intractable and difficult to work with insofar as it is difficult to understand on a purely logical basis how we might persuade those who enforce heteronormativity to adopt some other perspective on modern sexual practice. But taken historically, as a situation with a precise historical trajectory that both comes from somewhere and is going in some definite direction, we might be both more hopeful about the possible future of modern sexuality and more aware of ways in which we might engage in these debates in order to nudge them along in the directions in which most everyone is already going.

The point I am making is that for political realities it matters not only where we stand but how we got to where we are. Or, to subtly alter the metaphor, in political reality we are never standing still but always constituted according to some inertia bearing upon us. In politics, inertia goes a long way: it can mark the ever important difference between a condition of strife in which a settlement is about to be achieved and another condition of strife in which a settlement has just broken down. It matters not only where we are but how we got here and where we are going. Politics, ever unstilled, is a moving sort of thing. Lose sight of its direction, and you lose sight of just about everything that makes it work well.

Meliorism in Contemporary Political Philosophy

The meliorist form of cultural criticism I take to be the core of pragmatism's engagement with the many cultural, political, and ethical situations in which we ever find ourselves importantly resonates with the work of other contemporary political philosophers. Indeed, the impress of meliorism is increasingly wide in contemporary political philosophy such that fewer and fewer intellectuals are comfortable explicitly assuming a utopian model for their work. Even Rawls, as we saw, hedges about utopianism, though it must be admitted that his theory of justice does very little to deliver on its promise of realism. Other contemporary political philosophers fare much better in articulating the requirements for meliorism. One philosopher in particular stands out: Bernard Williams.

Perhaps the most crucial contribution made by Williams in the context of his widely ranging work in philosophy over the past half-century was his claim for the necessity of bringing a sensibility for history into the practice of philosophy. By seeking out an integration of philosophy with history, Williams showed one possible way in which we might overcome some of the more pressing deficits internal to philosophy (and presumably history too) as currently practiced. By bringing philosophy and history together, Williams developed a conception of intellectual practice that is highly complementary to the pragmatist meliorism I have here elaborated. Indeed, just as it is impossible to understand the work of James, Dewey, and Rorty without understanding their meliorism, I would also argue that Williams is simply incomprehensible if not understood as a meliorist. Williams is best read as a hopeful philosopher whose hope was tuned to the possibilities of the problematic situations in which he found himself. He was hopeful that we may find ways of improving our condition by reconstructing certain practices and ideas already found in that condition. Explicating Williams in light of the pragmatist spirit of meliorism both helps us better understand the way in which his captivating intellectual projects ought to be understood and helps us appreciate the way in which pragmatism remains crucially relevant to some of the most important intellectual work taking place today.

I begin by noting that in the final years of his life Williams was working on a book whose subject was to be political and moral philosophy with a specific focus on liberalism. While Williams was never able to finish this book, he did leave behind a number of published and unpublished essays thought to form much of the argumentation of the proposed work. These have been collected together, along with a few of Williams's other political writings, in the posthumous *In the Beginning Was the Deed*, surely a pragmatist-sounding title if ever there was one. The editors of this volume note an important fact about the approach Williams had hoped to take in his book. Williams intended to frame his exposition with a leading autobiographical piece on "the ways in which his thinking about politics had been affected by his experiences in the political, intellectual, and artistic life of post-war Europe and America" (Hawthorn 2005, xix). This suggests that Williams held that reflection on the political and ethical life of our liberal culture can take place only by involving itself in the actual political and ethical practices found in that culture. Understanding liberalism involves understanding the way in which liberalism is actually lived and experienced. The essays composing the posthumous publication of Williams's planned book can in this respect be fairly read as making good on Williams's much earlier claim, offered in one of his first essays on political philosophy, that "genuine historical understanding is of the first importance in the understanding of politics and political thought" (1980, 165).

Williams's clearest account of this melioristic conception of political philosophy is developed in the volume's titular essay. Williams there describes the advantages of liberalism and the way in which these advantages must be conceived: Liberalism "will have a chance of being [better off] only if it accepts that like any other outlook it cannot escape starting from what is at hand, from the kinds of life among which it finds itself. Like everyone else, it must accept the truth that in the beginning was the deed" (1999, 24). Williams wants to defend a certain conception of liberalism in this book, but he wants to do so in a manner that is obviously different from the typical defenses of liberalism we find in other branches of contemporary political philosophy. Whereas liberalism is typically developed and defended from a perspective that is more or less ahistorical, Williams argues that liberalism must be understood and evaluated from a perspective that explicitly starts from where we find ourselves. A political philosophy, Williams explains, "will seem to make sense, and will to some degree reorganize political thought and action, only by virtue of the historical situation in which it is presented" (1999, 25).

This involves not merely a passing acknowledgment that one's work is intended for an audience somewhere within one's culture, the position that Rawls finally came to in his later work, but a deeper connection in which the political conceptions offered by the philosopher are explicated in conversation with the real political practices arising out of actual political history. Against more utopian approaches, Williams's view holds that it will be unhelpful to criticize conceptions rooted in the distant past from our own point of view and for our own purposes. Williams writes: "Political moralism, particularly in its Kantian forms, has a universalistic tendency which encourages it to inform past societies about their failings. It is not that these judgments are, exactly, meaningless—one can imagine oneself as Kant at the court of King Arthur if one wants—but they are useless and do not help one to understand anything" (2005c, 10). Williams argues in Collingwoodian fashion that nonliberal politics needs to be seen as answers to problems presented in differing historical circumstances.[5] It is not all that helpful to inform ourselves of the obvious failings of these cultures when judged by our standards, because these cultures are bound to fail by our standards, as our standards are responses to our problems and not to theirs. Normatively criticizing our standards, on the other hand, is both useful and important insofar as it is the only way to inform ourselves about how well we are responding to the problems posed by our historical situation. But, as in the case with past cultures, we should critique our own culture not so much by reference to some utopian ideal as by reference to the possibilities inherent in our own historical situation.

This is the crucial point on which the meliorist diverges from the utopian. The utopian thinks that cultural critique must ground itself in something much deeper, something far closer to the transcendental or the ideal, than the ordinary political realities in which we find ourselves already located. The meliorist thinks that we can muster all the force that we can mount for cultural critique by focusing on the differences between better and worse aspects of our political realities. These realities, the actual practices constitutive of them as well as the potential practices latent within them, are the only wellsprings of critical force. Williams is led to the meliorist conception of critique above all by his view that "political projects are essentially conditioned, not just in their background intellectual conditions but as a matter of empirical realism, by their historical circumstances" (1999, 25). Instead of entering the pure mode of ideal philosophical evaluation, Williams urges that we evaluate practices in terms of the actual historical situations out of which they arose. And instead of entering the pure mode of empirical description, he further urges that we describe the actual empirical development of practices in terms that enable us to evaluate them.

The crucial point repeatedly emphasized in Williams's late work is that "political philosophy requires history" (2005b, 53).[6] Williams's justification of this view is that history alone can provide philosophy with traction in the cultural realities in which we find ourselves and that philosophy can contribute to our understanding of ourselves only insofar as it has some such traction. Philosophers can dream up the grandest ideals, but if these ideals bear no definite connection to existing realities, then this only goes to show the limits of the philosophy in question. History provides the kind of self-understanding and self-explanation that philosophy needs if it is to make any definite contribution to the actual situations in which we find ourselves. This is why, for Williams at least, historical understanding is internal to the philosophical work of justification. Williams's claim for the importance of history for philosophy represents an important new direction for future work in political philosophy. Beneath this claim lies a complex body of work in which Williams makes the case for a combination of philosophy and history in his signature exquisite detail. Delving into the complexity of his argumentation for this point would require a lengthy excursus that I cannot here present. For the present purposes, I must remain content to simply point out that Williams's arguments here suggest an internal connection between history and justification.[7]

This internal connection between history and justification is the crucial feature of Williams's late attempts to revise the practice of analytic philosophy. For example, in his genealogy of truth and truthfulness, in the book of that name, Williams (2002) suggests that the philosophical appreciation of the value of truth requires the historical appreciation of the development of truth. And in his various writings on liberalism, Williams takes precisely the same approach. He concludes an essay on Isaiah Berlin and Judith Shklar with the thought that liberalism, as he would like to see it developed and defended, "regards the discovery of what rights people have as a political and historical one, not a philosophical one" (2005b, 61). He means that it will not be a purely philosophical discovery: the question of liberal rights must involve itself in the history of liberal rights as much as in the philosophy of liberal rights. To take another example, consider the approach suggested by Williams in the context of his defending the quintessential liberal value of toleration: "the case of toleration is, unsurprisingly, a central one for distinguishing between a strongly moralized conception of liberalism as based on ideals of individual autonomy, and a more skeptical, historically alert, political direct conception of it as the best hope for humanly acceptable legitimate government under modern conditions" (1996, 138). In all of these projects, Williams the meliorist affirms that our existing historical and social realities contain all the resources we require for effective normative critique: "Once the resultant picture of ethical thought without foundationalism is made historically and socially realistic, in particular by registering it in the categories of modernity, it provides a possibility of deploying some parts of it against others, and of reinterpreting what is ethically significant, so as to give a critique of existing institutions, conceptions, prejudices, and powers" (1992, 37).[8]

The gist of Williams's more skeptical and more historical approach is summarized in his discussion of his own "political realist" position: "liberal political theory should shape its account of itself more realistically to what is platitudinously politics" (2005c, 13). This sounds remarkably similar to claims advanced by pragmatist thinkers on behalf of liberal democracy. In Williams's case, the most instructive comparisons are to his contemporary Richard Rorty. Despite all his effort to distance himself from Rorty, Williams time and time again offered formulations that are strikingly Rortyan in character. Here is Williams: "Instead of trying to reach the politics of liberalism from a moral assumption that concerns toleration, we should rather consider first the politics of liberalism, including its practices of toleration, and then ask what, if any, kinds of moral assumption are related to that" (1996, 135). One would be hard pressed to find in all of contemporary political philosophy a better expression of Rorty's (1988) central idea of the priority of democracy to philosophy. Rorty and Williams long stood together in arguing that the best way of defending and deepening our democracy is to situate our philosophical theories about what democracy should be in the terms offered by the actual historical practice of democracy as we find it. The philosophy of democracy follows from democracy itself, not the other way around.

That Williams was often at such pains to distance himself from Rorty on these and other matters is in many respects a reflection of deep differences over what philosophy may achieve.[9] But in other respects, it was merely a reflection of Williams's recognition that he had gradually migrated to a conception of moral and political critique that is virtually indistinguishable from Rorty's meliorist cultural criticism.[10] One point on which Rorty and Williams were in noticeable agreement concerns their shared emphasis on hope and confidence.[11] Rorty and Williams stood together in holding that democratic progress depends on what we can do with the resources we have at hand within our actually existing liberal democracies. Their view was that we should begin with these resources and see how we might further them, rather than beginning with a philosophical ideal and only afterward considering how existing situations might be transformed so as to match that ideal. It is hope and confidence that model the appropriate attitude of energetically putting our resources to work for the sake of melioration. On their views, progressive melioration is achieved by taking what is best from within the confines of our historical situation and developing it in such a way as to both extend and deepen it. What else, they asked, could progress look like?

Williams and Rorty are not alone in affirming the importance that hope and confidence may play in the progressive improvement of our liberal democracies. The past few decades have been witness to an increasing number of influential political philosophers who share these melioristic sentiments.

Among these we can count Michael Walzer, Alasdair MacIntyre, Charles Taylor, Amartya Sen, and Michel Foucault. Meliorism has been on the rise in recent decades.

In some of his most recent work, Sen has defended a "comparative" approach to political philosophy in opposition to a "transcendental" approach. For Sen, a comparative theory of justice is "linked to inquiries about advancing justice, or reducing justice" and can thus safely ignore seemingly transcendental questions about "perfectly just social arrangements." Sen's conclusion is that "it is not frivolous to seek a framework for a theory of justice that concentrates on advancement, not transcendence" (2006, 236, 216, 237). Sen's notion of comparative advancement without a transcendental frame of reference against which such advancement is measured is an excellent illustration of the sort of melioristic politics featured in Williams and Rorty.

Foucault perhaps seems an unlikely ally here. However, Foucault's political criticism belongs alongside the pragmatists insofar as he understands the role of the political and cultural critic to be that of temporal and historical engagement with the present. His widely cited distinction (1977a) between the specific and the universal intellectual illustrates such a conception of critique.[12] If the universal intellectual strives to develop a systematic conception of political critique, the specific intellectual takes a quite different approach, which involves the theoretical and practical melioration of actually existing political realities: "The role for theory today seems to me to be just this: not to formulate the global systematic theory which holds everything in place, but to analyze the specificity of mechanisms of power, to locate the connections and extensions, to build little by little a strategic knowledge." From this description of the intellectual's practice of critical inquiry it was but a small step for Foucault to invoke pragmatism in his widely cited reference to theory as a toolkit: "The notion of theory as a toolkit means: (i) The theory to be constructed is not a system but an instrument.... (ii) That this investigation can only be carried out step by step on the basis of reflection (which will necessarily be historical in some of its aspects) on given situations" (1977b, 145). Like the pragmatists, Foucault held that the path of radical reform is paved with stepwise success. In a discussion with Gilles Deleuze a few years prior to these remarks, Foucault offered another pragmatist characterization of critical inquiry. He urged the view that "theory does not express, translate, or serve to apply practice: it is practice. But it is local and regional and not totalizing. . . . It is an activity conducted alongside those who struggle for power, and not their illumination from a safe distance. A 'theory' is the regional system of this struggle." To which Deleuze replied, "Precisely. A theory is exactly like a box of tools" (1972, 208). Here is the famous pragmatism shared by Foucault and Deleuze.[13]

The engaged orientation endorsed by all of these theorists is one rooted in a certain conception of the basis for political critique. Can we mount political criticisms from within the realities we are criticizing, or can normative criteria only be fashioned by transcending the actual political contexts in which we find ourselves? The meliorist affirms that our existing political realities contain all the resources we require, or indeed can ever muster, for effective normative critique. For Williams, this means that history plays an important role both in the justification of a liberal culture and in the progressive development of that culture once we take it to be justified. Critique, Williams urged, must come from some point internal to the cultural situation of which we find ourselves critical. We cannot jump outside of our historical and social realities in order to judge them against a nonexistent ideal. Judgment comes from inside of the situations judged, insofar as these situations are sufficiently complex as to enable us to deploy their better parts against their worse parts and to do so with effectiveness. In this way, the situations in which we find ourselves already contain the resources for their own improvement.

Democracy, Deliberation, and Experience

Having surveyed the import of pragmatism's transitionalist and meliorist core in the wider context of contemporary political philosophy, I now turn to the narrower context of recent work in pragmatist political philosophy so as to show how a transitionalist approach departs from other versions of pragmatist democratic theory now on offer. To do so, I will return to the general theme that informed my earlier intellectual-historical review of the three waves of pragmatism. According to this review, transitionalist pragmatism can renew pragmatism by playing itself off of the two competing concepts of experience-centric and language-centric philosophy. Transitionalist pragmatism moves beyond both linguistic pragmatism and experiential pragmatism in a way that preserves the best insights of each. This shift of emphasis has important consequences for pragmatism not only in epistemology and ethics but also in politics.

Recent work in pragmatist democratic theory exhibits the same two problematic tendencies of past pragmatisms that transitionalism helps us guard against. On the one hand, we have a number of political philosophers who have taken up pragmatism for the purposes of enriching contemporary deliberative democratic theory. Although it is not my intention here to understate the value of deliberative democratic theory, I do wish to note that a tendency to construe democratic practice as exclusively deliberative is very much out of step with political practices that cannot be entirely captured in accounts of deliberation, reason exchange, and linguistic interaction. A transitionalist pragmatism helps ward off certain extreme versions of deliberative democratic theory that suggest that deliberation is all that matters for democratic practice. Deliberation matters to democracy, but democracy invokes far more than mere deliberation can muster. On the other hand, there are a number of political philosophers who continue to hew quite closely to political-theoretical conceptions derived from Dewey's classical pragmatism in their claim that a democratic politics must focus above all on the immediate lived experiences of those who would constitute a democratic community among themselves. Again, it is not my intention to suggest that the experience of democratic community is of little value for a theory of democratic politics. I only wish to suggest that a requirement that democracy be conceptualized in terms of experiences that are immediate and direct is grossly out of tune with contemporary political realities, in which our experiences are often thickly mediated by all manners of technologies and practices intervening between disparate and yet tightly connected persons. Experience matters for democracy, of course, but it also matters how we conceptualize experience, if we are to avoid an endless clash of appeals to conflicting experiential accounts.

Consider first the recent spate of work in pragmatist deliberative democracy. The pragmatist versions of deliberativism developed by Cheryl Misak (2000, 2004a) and Robert Talisse (2005, 2007a, 2007b) take as their primary source of inspiration the classical pragmatism of Charles Santiago Peirce. But immediately noteworthy is the way in which their conception of pragmatism remains thoroughly invested in core assumptions of the linguistic turn. Pragmatist deliberativism serves to conceptualize practice in terms of epistemic states over which participants in practice exchange reasons in an attempt to justify their practices to one another. "Political decision-making must be responsive to *reasons*," is how Misak (2004a, 12) puts it. Politics on this model is primarily a practice of giving and asking for reasons and as such is primarily a linguistic practice insofar as reasons are construed in terms of propositional attitudes, sentential utterances, or some other linguistic medium. Misak and Talisse rarely, if indeed ever, seriously consider the ways in which we interact with one another through media other than beliefs, propositions, and utterances. Such theories of deliberating are, I would like to suggest, politically debilitating.

Note that we need not find anything wrong with the Peircean approach to deliberative democracy offered by Misak and Talisse in order to recognize that there may be something wrong with the amount of work they expect their accounts to be able to perform. Although I have my worries about using a thin Peircean theory of true belief as a model for democratic deliberation (recall that not only did Peirce never write anything important about democracy but he also never wrote anything important about politics), I want to focus for now on the limits of any model of democratic deliberation, be it pragmatist or nonpragmatist in basic orientation. For even if we can develop a viable model of the epistemic virtues of deliberative democratic practice, we will continue to run up against the problem of the limits of deliberation itself for the purposes of a democratic politics. Transitionalist pragmatism helps reveal these limits.

The problem, in short, is that democratic deliberation cannot function by itself as an independent element in a full theory of democratic politics. This is because deliberative democratic theory tends to treat deliberation as if it can be abstracted from the other political conditions that contribute to successful democratic practice. But if we divorce our model of deliberative practice from those other conditions of democracy in order to put forth a swollen conception of deliberation as the central core of democratic practice itself, then we risk losing sight of two things: first, those nondeliberative elements of politics that are equally as important for successful democratic practice as the deliberative elements, and second, the way in which those nondeliberative elements are often crucial for deliberation itself.

Talisse beckons us "toward a deliberative culture" (2005, 123). But we should be cautious about such invitations, given their enormous faith in the power and promise of deliberation. This is a faith clearly expressed by Talisse when he urges that "a viable account of deliberative democracy must be a political theory in its own right" (2005, 95), by which he means that deliberative theory must stand on its own as a full-fledged political theory that does not lean on liberalism, communitarianism, or any other political philosophy in order to do its work. There are two possible interpretations of this view. One is that democracy is for the sake of deliberation and the other is that democracy can be fully theorized in terms of a conception of successful deliberation. Considering each in turn, we can see how on either interpretation this version of deliberativism wrongly takes deliberation as theorizable or practicable apart from other enabling conditions of democracy.

According to the first interpretation, democratic politics is taken as valuable insofar as it enables us to realize successful deliberation. Talisse urges along these lines that "the Peircean endorses a specific model of democracy and citizenship *for the sake of* proper epistemic practice" (2007a, 73). Misak is more cautious in this respect but nonetheless describes her argument in similar terms: "the requirements of genuine belief show that we must, broadly speaking, be democratic inquirers" (2000, 106). The disadvantage of this view is that it reduces democracy to the realization of proper epistemic practice cashed out in terms of a Peircean story about belief and truth. Once we organize our political institutions in such a way as to achieve "proper epistemic practice," we need not bother with organizing any of the other political institutions traditionally associated with democracy but not requisite for "genuine belief." In adopting such a view, the Peirceans burden themselves with the enormous task of showing that all of the most important political institutions at the core of democracy as we know it (including not only liberty of thought and discussion but also rights of suffrage, rights in property, and rights against search and seizure) really are necessary for proper epistemic practices realizing genuine belief. But do we really need property rights to exhibit epistemic virtue? Indeed, do we even need suffrage rights? Some of our epistemic practices—think of the early modern isolatoe scientist, the late modern corporate research lab, and perhaps even the courtly world of the contemporary academy—suggest that perhaps this is not the case. Peircean deliberativists risk a dangerous move in endorsing a view that implies that democracy can be legitimately abandoned if it can be shown that it is not necessary for our appropriate epistemic achievements.

On the first interpretation, then, this view is a nonstarter. Turning to the second interpretation, the core idea is now that democracy can be fully and adequately theorized in terms of deliberative practice. I find this claim for the completeness of deliberative democratic theory rather overblown. Where are the nondeliberative elements that we have traditionally taken to be crucial for viable democratic organization? What about marching, demonstrating, boycotting, hunger striking, and even voting? Of course, such acts can become subjects of democratic deliberation and must themselves be taken up in conjunction with deliberation to be effective, but the question concerns how far deliberation can proceed without them. My point is not that deliberation is not relevant for democracy but that deliberation is not often relevant all by itself. As Deweyan political theorist Melvin Rogers notes, "Tying the practice of reason-giving to Dewey's larger concern with managing power entails that we look beyond the extent to which citizens are committed to, and institutional structures embodying, the epistemic virtues of democracy" (2008, 218).[14] Although the epistemic virtues of reason giving and justification offering are indeed important for democratic practice, there are indeed other virtues of democratic practice. A viable pragmatist philosophy of democracy must take account of the complex constitution of democratic practice and affirm the multiple intersections between deliberation and other political practices.

Other conceptions of pragmatist deliberativism, those drawing more on Dewey than on Peirce, fare much better in these matters. I am thinking of recent work on Deweyan deliberative democracy by Elizabeth Anderson (2006), James Bohman (2007), Alison Kadlec (2007), Hilary Putnam (1990c), and Jeffrey Stout (2004).[15] All of these theorists offer rich versions of democratic deliberation that could benefit enormously from further consideration of ways in which deliberation intersects with other aspects of political practice so as to maintain and expand democratic political organization. This would counterbalance the common deliberative tendency, also unfortunately expressed by the Deweyan deliberativists, of granting too much priority to deliberative procedures. Bohman, for example, overprioritizes deliberation in writing of "the fundamental power to initiate deliberation" (2007, 36) and in describing deliberation as "the most basic" (2007, 5) of our normative powers. But why should deliberation be more basic than any other normative power also necessary for democratic organization? The version of deliberative democracy Bohman develops is a thoroughly Deweyan one in which deliberation is envisaged as a "decentered" form of political practice. As such it could benefit, in a way that Peircean views could not or at least not without making very major concessions, from further explicating ways in which a diverse array of deliberative forms intersect with other elements equally crucial for viable democratic organization. Bohman indeed already explicitly acknowledges that his posited "democratic minimum" (2007, 188) of deliberative powers is meant to describe "necessary but not sufficient conditions for democratic arrangements to be a means of realizing justice" (2007, 176). Kadlec's (2007, 115ff.) recent work similarly points in the right direction in attempting to develop a conception of Deweyan "critical pragmatism" that would bring together core democratic rubrics of deliberation and power without theorizing either in isolation from the other. I am merely urging that Deweyans now put at the fore of their agenda these already proposed projects of theorizing and experimentally testing how deliberation intersects with the full array of other conditions necessary for successful democratic practice. One way of doing this would be to regard democratic deliberation as a crucial but not founding aspect of a core political project of democratic transitions.

To the extent that deliberation can be and actually is integrated with nondeliberative elements of democratic practice, deliberative theory will be valuable for democratic theory. But without such integrated conceptions of deliberative and nondeliberative practice, deliberative theory will remain crippled. A major obstacle standing in the way of such an integration is a call for thinking about democratic politics as exclusively a project of reason exchanging and justification making. While this calls is more likely to develop in the context of a Peircean idiom than in a Deweyan idiom, I am happy to concede that Talisse's and Misak's deliberativisms could be revised so as to outflank the criticisms I am putting forth. Misak already seems well on her way when she notes that her version of pragmatism "does not [entail] that deliberation is always appropriate" (2000, 107; c.f. 150ff.). I welcome that thought insofar as my goal here is not to undermine the various conceptions of deliberative democracy now being developed by pragmatists but is rather to suggest some steps that should be taken to save these theories from irrelevance.

Of course, my arguments against theorizing deliberation in isolation from other elements constitutive of democracy are not new. I am following on many points standard criticisms of deliberativism offered by Michael Walzer (1999) and others.[16] The most insightful of these criticisms for my purposes is Iris Marion Young's "Activist Challenges to Deliberative Democracy," where it is argued that deliberativism fails to adequately theorize nondeliberative conditions that may enable or disable democratic deliberation. Of the disabling conditions, Young observes that "the theory and practice of deliberative democracy have no tools for raising the possibility that deliberations may be [systematically] closed and distorted" (2001, 686).[17] Deliberative democrats have yet to convincingly answer the tough challenges put forth by Young and others, but not for not having tried. David Estlund (2001) has responded to Young's (and Walzer's) concerns about deliberative democracy by arguing that we should expand our conception of deliberative procedure in cases where normal deliberative constraints break down in the manner described by Young.[18] Estlund emphasizes the value of "wider standards of civility in order to restore to public political expression some missing epistemic dimensions" (2001, 61). These wider standards would accommodate "disruptive and impolite political expression, especially when it is legal, nonviolent, and does not suppress the speech of others" (2001, 64). As I see it, Estlund's argument fails to address Young's worries in two related ways.

First, Estlund is clear that wider deliberative standards are to be endorsed as only temporary means for restoring democracy to its narrowed deliberative condition. This fosters an image of deliberation as primarily about what goes on where those tighter standards function well. Estlund does not embrace Young's activist challengers as crucial for democracy so much as he merely tolerates them as occasionally helpful for steering democracy back into a deliberative but nonactivist track. Second, given that Estlund understands democracy as primarily deliberative in this way, he is only able to accommodate the activist in a very limited sense, which he might regard as capacious but which activists can only experience as quite limiting. Whether the limits on deliberation are tight or loose, deliberation for Estlund is about "political behavior that is essentially expressive" (2001, 61). But this fails to address ways in which Young's activist challengers may sometimes seek to engage in nonexpressive but prodemocratic political action. Activism is sometimes about expressing political beliefs that do not get a normal hearing, and here Estlund's wider standards of civility may be helpful. But activism is at other times about manifesting and developing new forms of political practice, and Estlund's wider standards do little to accommodate this sort of activity.

Deliberative democratic theory will remain incomplete as a model of democracy so long as it continues to theorize political expression apart from theorizing political action. Democratic practice suggests that deliberation is essentially intertwined with other aspects of democracy. Treating deliberation as separate skews our standards for democracy. Walzer says that "deliberation does have a place, in fact an important place in democratic politics, but I don't think it has an independent place—a place, so to speak, of its own" (1999, 67). The larger lesson to draw from this discussion is that deliberative democratic theory must not trod the garden path of a politicized linguistic turn, which has led to so many dead ends elsewhere in philosophy. For the purposes of a democratic theory as much as for the purposes of an epistemology or an ethics, there is little to be gained by isolating practices of language-centric reason exchange from the broader political context in which such exchanges always occur.

Although the linguistic turn leads to many of the same incautious views in political philosophy that it does elsewhere, there are nonetheless obvious philosophical lessons about politics that we simply could not have reached without the linguistic turn. In the context of epistemology, we learn from the linguistic turn that we ought to be severely cautious of the high-modern triumvirate of givenism, representationalism, and foundationalism. In the context of political and moral philosophy, we should use the insights of the similarly situated deliberative turn to encourage similar cautions against overblown appeals that would seek to legitimate claims for justice in the indisputable experiences of either individual moral agents or social groups. These insights for political philosophy are of particular value insofar as many pragmatists continue to conceptualize democracy by way of Deweyan appeals to immediate, lived, primary, or direct experience. Such appeals expose pragmatism to the charge of being tethered to a kind of foundationalism insofar as experience on these views can be too easily relied upon to provide a foundation when the going gets tough. Such a conceptualization readily lapses into the politics of certainty, whose requiem has long been sung by pragmatists.

The unfortunate tendency on the part of some contemporary pragmatists to conceptualize democracy in terms of immediate experience can be traced back to some of Dewey's more blinkered claims about democratic experience. Dewey frequently described democracy in terms of intimate relations in lived experience, such as when he wrote, "In its deepest and richest sense a community must always remain a matter of face-to-face intercourse" (1927, 211/LW2.367). This passage highlights a certain communitarian strain in Dewey's thought, which was perhaps appropriate for the nineteenth-century political environments in which he intellectually matured but which is hardly useful for the thickly mediated political realities of the twenty-first century. It is time to admit that Dewey too often conceptualized democracy in terms of what be might be called the old village morality of the communitarian democrat: "The heart and final guarantee of democracy is in free gatherings of neighbors on the street corner . . . and in gatherings of friends in the living rooms of houses and apartments." The quote is from Dewey's *The Public and Its Problems* (1939b, LW14.227), but its quaint evocations suggest that it could just as well have been a caption to a Norman Rockwell frontispiece for *The Saturday Evening Post.* Over the course of the twentieth century, our political experience exploded out of the village and disseminated across the entire planet. The old village morality is now unwarranted, indeed perhaps even undesirable, in light of the expansive political networks in which we are all implicated in our everyday living. Think of the huge array of commodity chains implicated in something so ordinary as your morning cup of coffee (the plantations, the trade networks, the transportation infrastructure, the immense marketing apparatus, and the expansive heavy manufacturing industries invoked in turn by each of these). Think of the enormous complexity of the political and social institutions necessary for curbing our global environmental degradation (not just commitments on the part of a whole legion of governments but also the changes that will be required of corporations and of consumers). Clearly the democratization of these immense political gargantua cannot be achieved by converting these distributed and decentered publics into relations of "face-to-face" intercourse and interaction. Yet if anything today requires the cure of more democracy in virtue of triggering requirements for justice, it is these dense networks of interaction extending over vast distances with increasing impact on the lives of the global rich and the global poor.

There are other strains in Dewey's political and moral writings that furnish better resources for our projects in reconstructing democracy today. Chief among these is his melioristic metaphilosophy of social and political philosophy reviewed above. Other useful conceptions featured in Dewey include his emphasis on the full depth of pluralism in the modern world, a sensitivity to the crucial importance of more inclusive political relations, and a conception of democracy as an ethical way of life in which an entire culture must be suffused, a conception that continues to provide an enormously useful counterweight to state-centric conceptions of democracy as being only a matter of suffrage or of deliberation. My argument is simply that those pressing Dewey forward today for the purposes of developing a political philosophy relevant to contemporary political conditions ought to play up these aspects of his thought and play down the outdated village morality within which Dewey sometimes framed his thinking about politics.

Unfortunately, a number of political and moral philosophers writing in Dewey's wake continue to adhere to those strains of his thought that would style the democratic experience as a village phenomenon. John Smith writes that "the most important and, at the same time, the most comprehensive function of community and shared experience in Dewey's view is that of serving as a foundation for democracy as a mode of life" (1974, 145). James Gouinlock similarly writes of Dewey that "it would be hard to find a philosopher . . . who identified a more profound value in the experience of intimately associated life" (1993a, 55). Even the very best work in contemporary pragmatist democratic theory continues to perpetuate this view. Gregory Pappas proffers a Deweyan theory of "democracy as experience" (2008, 218) according to which "democracy strives to have certain enriching and meaningful experiences" (2008, 230) such that democracy "must grow out of but continue to return to what is local" (2008, 263). Democracy on this view is regarded as "grounded" in experience so that we "justify democracy by the quality of lived present experience" (2008, 287). Judith Green, in her earlier compelling presentation of a pragmatist conception of "deep democracy," at times lapses into this view in issuing a Deweyan call for "revitalizing the face-to-face local community" (1999, 57).[19] These views all lead us back to Dewey's village conception of local political relations taken as ultimate and hence capable of serving as a normative foundation for an ostensibly democratic community.

But surely the deservedly most influential contemporary pragmatist who continues to employ the classical pragmatists' concept of experience for the purposes of an elaboration of the American democratic experience is John McDermott. McDermott holds in high regard this grand concept of American philosophy, whose importance for this tradition he summarizes with characteristic verve: "From the Puritans to Dewey, one is offered a series of efforts, alternating in stresses and varying in success, to account for man's most profound difficulties and concerns within the context of ordinary experience" (1965, 86). McDermott explores in fascinating ways this conception of ordinary experience as a theme at once pragmatist and existentialist. McDermott's writings provocatively suggest that the revitalization of American democratic culture depends upon our reconstructing our experience. I find his offerings in this vein incredibly illuminating. So I want to be clear here about the modality of my criticism: the point I wish to press is that the immensely valuable resources provided by McDermott and many other contemporary pragmatist democrats are too often hindered by their refusal to reconstruct the core of pragmatism such that democracy is no longer rendered a quality of immediate experience. The valuable contributions of all these pragmatists are not best focused through the lens of experience-centric conceptions that myopically reduce pragmatist conceptions to existentialist and communitarian optics. Identifying democracy with experience, particularly in terms of something like immediate or lived experience, results in a conception of democracy that is severely disabled for many of the purposes for which we might need a democratic theory and practice in our contemporary world. A better model for democratic practice today than the old face-to-face community morality of the village is the highly mediated moral atmosphere of city life.

Here again I find Iris Marion Young's critical social theory quite instructive for pragmatism. Young criticizes the communitarian conception of democracy in favor of an ideal of "city life" understood as "an openness to unassimilated otherness" and "the being together of strangers" (1990, 227). Perhaps the strongest thought in favor of Young's proposal is simply the fact that city life is today ubiquitous while community life is increasingly rare or, as Young puts it, "urbanity is the horizon of the modern, not to mention the postmodern, condition" (1990, 237).[20] Dewey and others may, however, be construed as warning us against the dangers of the onrushing tide of urbanity as it washes away the dissipating foam of the old village morality. To this, Young's response is not only that city life is here to stay but that this is a good. City life, says Young, enables social differentiation, variety, pleasure, and pluralized publicity in a way that the old village never did. These are remarkable accomplishments on behalf of democracy and we ought to work with them while fully acknowledging their dangers and doing what we can to overcome their persisting failures.

What we require is a political philosophy that enables us to grasp the myriad ways in which our political practices are producing political problems that demand amelioration and reconstruction. What we need to focus on, in other words, are the possibilities for transforming our political practices. Transition-alist pragmatism takes just this as its focus. In the context of transitional reconstructions we may indeed find a conception of democratic lived experi-ence useful at times, but there is no reason to think that a conception of face-to-face experiential relations could function as the stable core of our trans-formative efforts in the horizon of our modern urbanity. The experience of democracy that we should strive to achieve is an experience that grows at its edges by transforming itself at its furthest reaches. It is an experience of im-provement, melioration, and reconstruction. And this will not always mean more intimate relationships, because in some contexts what we require is the democratization of relationships that shall never and need never achieve the old intimacy of the village. An experience-centric democratic theory, to sum up, too readily lends itself to substantive metaphors and concepts reminiscent of a communitarianism not sufficiently impressed with liberal proceduralism. A pragmatic emphasis on democracy as local could be useful, but it is better cashed out in terms of transitionalist processes than communitarian concerns. We should be all for localism if it means pluralistically working outward from where we find ourselves without resorting to utopianism or giving in to dysto-pianism. But if localism means instead focusing our attention on the experien-tial immediacies of community life, then it is better avoided. The point should not be to develop a democratic community in which we all feel like neighbors to one another. The point should be to develop a plurality of polities in which we lessen relations of oppression and increase relations of inclusion day by day, whether we be next-door neighbors or distant strangers whose eyes shall never meet. Transitionalism supplies the terms needed for this reconstruction of pragmatist political theory.

It is thus notable that all of the contemporary-experience pragmatists I have criticized indeed exhibit transitionalist tendencies in their writings.[21] McDermott furnishes the best examples insofar as his writings abound with the transitionalist sensibility I am here urging. He writes, for instance, about reconstruction as a process "in which we are constantly obligated to fuse the critique of previous forms with an attempt to create new forms" (1968, 27). I am urging that we pragmatists can do much with these transitionalist themes in our tradition by reconstructing them such that they no longer rely on a conception of experiential immediacy as their support. Acts of transitional melioration need not lean on anything other than their own flow through history and over time. This brings me back to the core of the melioristic political philosophy of the pragmatist: betterment can be achieved without a basis in what is supposedly best. McDermott catches the core of this transitionalism in a line I have always found memorable: "Salvation may be illusory, but salving experiences can occur day by day" (1976, xv; 2007, 12).

Democracy, Commitment, and Procedure

I offer my renewed third version of pragmatism as a philosophy of transitions in part as a means of emphasizing caution against both linguistic turn and immediate experience democratic theories and in part as a means of drawing on the valuable lessons enabled by both. Pragmatist political philosophy has in recent decades been too often tempted by these obviously alluring formulations of democratic politics. I am suggesting that we have good reason to be wary of giving so much of our attention to either language or experience in the context of developing our democratic theories and practices. Too great a focus on experience leads to the errors of political conceptions that are too substantive for modern conditions of pluralism—the cautions of the deliberative democratic emphasis on proceduralism provides a useful counterweight against substantive foundations. Too great a focus on deliberation leads to the errors of reducing democratic politics to pure procedures of exchanging reasons—the conception of democracy as experience helps us recognize that there are crucial substantive issues that democratic theory cannot afford to ignore. Transitionalist pragmatism thus offers an alternative in which the focus is on melioristic improvement first and language and experience only second.

The transitionalist alternative to deliberative and experiential formulations of pragmatist democratic theory can be extended in ways that demonstrate its relevance to other central debates in contemporary democratic theory. One way of doing this would be, as I have just intimated, to place the deliberative model in its proper context of liberal proceduralism and the experiential model in its proper context of substantive republicanism-communitarianism. Situating the theories in this way would enable us to regard the transitionalist pragmatist alternative as a contribution to contemporary debates between liberals and republicans. This strategy would also carry the added advantage of articulating connections to the moral philosophical interventions of the last chapter according to which pragmatist perfectionism is an alternative to both pure deontological and pure teleological normative theory.

The thought that pragmatist democratic theory can be fruitfully developed as an alternative to these two currently dominant strains in contemporary political philosophy has already been argued by others, including most notably Axel Honneth. Honneth interprets Deweyan democracy as offering a crucial third way out of the longstanding impasses between liberal and republican theory in offering a model of democracy as "reflexive cooperation" (1998a, 765). Honneth's reinterpretation of Dewey has the dual advantage of both working toward a conceptual resolution to the longstanding liberal-versus-republican impasse and as locating this resolution in terms of a general conception of politics as a pluralistic struggle. We ought to pay more attention to Honneth's unfortunately neglected contribution to pragmatist democratic theory. This is so even if, as I am arguing we should, we locate the core of a pluralistic democracy in a conception of melioristic growth rather than reflexive cooperation and thus diverge from Honneth on this matter. It is notable in this respect that Honneth (1998b, 706) explicitly considers the Deweyan concept of growth (albeit in the slightly different context of moral theory rather than political theory) and rejects it as a substantive ethical orientation in its own right. But Honneth's rejection is based on a misinterpretation. Growth is not a substantive conception of the good so much as it is the condition of moral and political practice when those are taken as temporal and historical processes. Melioristic growth, in other words, is the upshot of a deidealizing reconstruction of moral and political practice undertaken from the perspective of transitionalist pragmatism. When Honneth endorses the process of "forming an overlapping good out of the conflicting ends in life by preserving as extensively as possible both the moral obligations and the other goals aspired to" (1998b, 707) as the core of a pragmatist moral-political theory, he is endorsing nothing other than melioristic growth itself when properly interpreted.

Understanding democracy as a transitional project of melioration enables us to affirm the value of achieving critical connectedness and adjacency to our democratic practices in a way that involves both being attentive to how they have emerged and firmly focusing on what they may yet become. The energies and efforts forming a connected and adjacent democratic critique require a philosophical perspective that is far broader than either a language-centric or experience-centric moral-political theory can muster. We ought to be transition-centric and in so being free ourselves to invoke language and experience and much else besides as is required for our ever expanding project of growing democracy along its edges.

I want to conclude these reflections by reiterating that the critical reinterpretation of the pragmatist theory of democracy I have here offered is itself a reconstruction of the tradition. This means that taking up transitionalism as the core of pragmatism should enable us to continue to deploy the valuable theoretical tools developed by previous pragmatist political philosophers, including the work of those I have here criticized. There is much in their work that is of immense value. A reconstruction of the tradition aims not to debunk previous pragmatisms but rather to provide a vantage from which we can gain a new focus on what is valuable in previous work. A pragmatism invested by temporality and historicity right from the start provides the best vantage for sighting the values of a pragmatist philosophy of democratic transitions. In taking democracy as a transitional practice, we will be better equipped to refine, sharpen, and deploy the valuable tools of democratic deliberation and democratic experience already featured in existing works of pragmatist political philosophy.

Yet there is no good reason to think that pragmatism need envisage these democratic vistas on its own. The democratic experiment in all its richness and complexity can be achieved through generous efforts drawing on a multitude of philosophical traditions. In the final chapter of this book on pragmatism, I end with a call for being the kinds of pragmatists who go beyond our pragmatism. We transitionalist pragmatists would do well to take up our critiques of and inquiries into democracy in conjunction with the philosophical tools made available by other traditions of thought equally inflected with a sense of the historical and temporal rhythms of critique and inquiry. On a pragmatist view, the point of philosophical thought is to equip us with forms of reflection, inquiry, and critique that enable us to improve the situations in which we find ourselves. Why should we, as pragmatists, expect our pragmatism to do everything that we would want of philosophy, critique, and inquiry? Philosophies need not offer systems if they can offer concepts, strategies, and tools. With this in mind, I turn in the next chapter to developing a conception of critical inquiry that takes seriously the transitionalist commitment to the thoroughly temporal and historical qualities of our ever growing fields of experience. I conceptualize critique and inquiry in transitionalist terms by suggesting the combination of the forward-looking reconstructive practice of the pragmatist with the backward-looking problematizing practice of the genealogist. The result is a broad-based conception of critical inquiry that is thoroughly in tune with the full breadth of the temporality and historicity of our practices.

Seven

CRITICAL INQUIRY AS
GENEALOGICAL PRAGMATISM

Integrating Pragmatism and Genealogy

Since pragmatism understands epistemic, ethical, political, and cultural practices as historical processes, there is already contained in pragmatism an implied commitment to historical inquiry as a central aspect of pragmatist reconstruction. On this view, history ought to supply philosophy with materials it
works with, and philosophy ought to devote itself to work firmly rooted in the
historical details of the problems under consideration. By deeply involving itself
in historical inquiry (including historically minded inquiries in nearby disciplines such as sociology, anthropology, economics, and psychology), pragmatist
philosophy can make good on the promises of transitionalism laid out in previous chapters. If the central promise of a transitionalism about knowledge, ethics, and politics is that the pragmatist is concerned with helping us find our way
from some present situation to some improved future situation, then it follows
that historical inquiry is a crucial component of pragmatist thought just insofar
as the task of transitioning from present to future depends on the possibilities of
the present as constituted by its historical trajectory. The present in which we
find ourselves, since it is temporal in its structure, is shaped by its inertia. A history of our achievements, then, offers invaluable guidance in thinking about the
possibilities of our futures.

In thus turning toward history, it ought to be noted that pragmatists cannot make use of just any old form of history. Pragmatism must be attuned to the right sort of historiography. Many errors await pragmatism here. Pragmatism's practicality suggests to many a results-oriented and problem-solving approach. But the critical edge of history is not to be found in its record of successes. History helps us understand the specific contingencies out of which we have formed ourselves. And in this sense, history usefully counterweighs the pragmatist tendency to focus on consequences. The pragmatist ought to weigh anticipated consequences against historical contingencies. History, or at least some forms of history, can help pragmatists do just this.

In this chapter, I conclude the broad-based reinterpretation of pragmatism I have developed throughout this book by focusing on potential difficulties that ensue from previous pragmatism's overemphasis on a purely results-oriented approach to inquiry. Pragmatism, I will argue, must orient itself toward both the development of solutions and the development of problems. After describing how this potential problem surfaces in certain formulations of pragmatism, most notably in Dewey's, I turn to a consideration of the historiographical resources already available in pragmatism, including Dewey's, which we might use to repair this deficit. This will pave the way to a discussion of the importance for pragmatism of more fully engaging with the right sort of historiography as a means of circumventing the potential difficulties of a forward-looking but backward-blind style of thinking.

I am above all eager to stress the value for pragmatism of the historiographical model for critique and inquiry offered in the work of the genealogical philosopher-historian Michel Foucault.[1] Foucault enables pragmatists to turn toward a conception of history as a critical tool for problematization. Foucault's conception of genealogy as problematization nicely complements Dewey's conception of pragmatism as reconstruction. The proposal I thus put forth is for a historical-philosophical perspective that integrates pragmatism and genealogy. This perspective allows us to practice critique and inquiry in a stepwise motion that shuttles between problematization and reconstruction.

Dewey and Pragmatist Reconstruction

John Dewey understood thought or intelligence on the model of what he referred to as reconstruction. The central idea of reconstruction is meliorative transitioning, or the purposive remediation of a problematic situation. Dewey's view of thought as purposive transformation can be characterized at a general level in terms of a directed transition from a problematic situation into a situation that is relatively more determinate. As Dewey put it, "thinking is the actual transition from the problematic to the secure" (1929, LW4.181). Dewey conceptualized knowledge according to this very model: "knowledge is the fruit of the undertakings that transform a problematic situation into a resolved one" (1929, LW4.194). And when Dewey turned in his later years to a precise specification of the work of thought or intelligence, which he referred to in technical terms as inquiry, he wrote: "Inquiry is the controlled or directed transformation of an indeterminate situation into one that is so determinate in its constituent distinctions and relations as to convert the elements of the original situation into a unified whole" (1938a, LW12.108).[2]

The discussion over the course of the previous chapters has revealed three crucial themes in Dewey's conception of reconstruction that I would like to make explicit by way of summary of how pragmatism can continue to be deployed for theoretical and critical inquiry today. First is the metaphilosophical theme that reconstruction must occur organically within a problematic situation rather than being developed from some external position occupied by the detached theorist. This suggests that we philosophers would be wise to deepen our existing collaborations with practitioners and the other social scientists and humanists who are generally more close to the ground of practice than we theoretical speculators. The role of the philosopher in reconstruction is thus not to think up potential solutions to perplexing problems but is rather to help clarify and develop reconstructions that are already underway in practice. A second crucial theme of reconstruction is that the melioration of problematic situations must be fashioned on the basis of resources already furnished in that situation. While it would be nice to bring resources not extant in our situations into those situations, this is rarely possible. We must fashion what improvements we can out of the materials, ideals, and human energies available to us. A third crucial theme of reconstruction goes to the heart of my argument throughout this book. Reconstruction is at its core a meliorative transitioning. The purposive remediation of a problematic situation is essentially temporal and historical in quality. Reconstruction takes time and is in history. The reconstructive dimension of the pragmatist conception of thought betrays that irreducibly transitionalist aspect of pragmatist philosophy that Dewey precisely underscored in one of his many articulations of his conception of intelligence or thought: "this remaking of the old through union with the new is precisely what intelligence is" (1935, 50/LW11.37). The point is not merely that reconstruction is historically and temporally contextual, though that is certainly true. The point is rather that reconstruction is historical and temporal in its very occurrence. Reconstruction begins with a problematic past situation and fashions transitions to a reconstructed future situation. The dynamic movement from past to future, where it is meliorative, is the heart of reconstruction.

To better specify these three crucial aspects of reconstruction, it will be helpful to contrast reconstruction with traditional philosophical conceptions of inquiry. On traditional conceptions, be they idealist or realist in character, the work of thought is often seen in terms of the precise specification of an ideality or reality in virtue of which we can make appropriate judgments. In this way, ideal and real thought have a standing that is in some ways external to the situations they can be used to judge. Dewey, however, was interested in reconstruction specifically as it is already internal to the situations with which it engages. Dewey did not want to adopt a purely theoretical stance that would allow him to judge a situation as if from outside. Rather, he wanted to adopt a practical theoretical stance from within a given situation, which would enable him to urge ways in which the situation itself might be reconstructed on the basis of resources already featured in the situation. In contrast to the optimist or pessimist who would urge upon us that a situation must assume such and such an outcome (be it the best or the worst conceivable outcome), Dewey the meliorist urges us to look within the situations in which we find ourselves in order to do what we can to improve them. Dewey's concept of reconstruction excellently captures this hopeful tone of meliorism.

The basic structure of Dewey's reconstructive meliorism is, to put the point rather simplistically, problem solving. But this metaphor can be misleading if not qualified in two ways. Reconstruction is not mere problem solving just insofar as the solutions that emerge in response to the problem are not made immediately available by the problematic situation itself. In a reconstruction there emerges a distinct solutional element not analytically decomposable into the elements made available by the original problem situation. Second, while solutions are seemingly situated on the same level as their problems, reconstructions should be seen as second-order (or, better, critical) interventions into the conditions of possibility constitutive of a problematic situation. With these important qualifications, it is helpful to think of reconstruction as working with the materials found within a problematic situation and transforming their conditions toward their resolution into a secure situation.

Dewey devoted an enormous number of pages to explicating his conception of the complex patterns which reconstruction can assume.[3] At the core of each of his accounts is a rather technical conception of inquiry that can be schematically summarized as follows: indeterminacy → problematicity → determinacy. This scheme suggests that inquiry is a process whereby we transition out of those indeterminate situations we face toward relatively more determinate situations. In Dewey's vocabulary, situational indeterminacies are *had* or *felt* in primary experience and determinate solutions are *known* in reflective experience.[4] According to this jargon, problems fall somewhere between having and knowing and can be described as immediate havings on the way to mediated knowings. Although Dewey's terminology varied throughout his career, this three-place structure of inquiry as the movement from felt indeterminacies to midway problems to known determinacies pervades all of his work.

There are some major shortcomings in Dewey's conception of the pattern of reconstruction that I think pragmatists should be more honest about airing. These concern the incompleteness of Dewey's overall account of practical problematization (that is, his overall account of the first two technical stages of inquiry). Dewey's focus was always on the third moment of inquiry, in which inquiry terminates in a determinate outcome. Dewey was thus consistently led away from an attempt to sufficiently articulate the first two stages of inquiry. We pragmatists ought to more readily admit that although Dewey devoted hundreds of pages to the genesis of solutions, he hardly ever wrote about the genesis of problems. Dewey simply had too little to say about how we might fashion forms of inquiry that help us bring the right kinds of problems into focus. He did on occasion (1934, 1930d) describe aesthetic experience as exemplifying that phase of inquiry that takes us from indeterminacy to problematicity. But even these accounts remain tremendously underdeveloped and thus stand in need of resources that can be supplied by more rigorous conceptions of problematization furnished in philosophical work outside of the usual ambit of pragmatism. Useful for these purposes will be the kinds of critiques mounted by genealogists, critical theorists, psychoanalysts, hermeneuticists, phenomenologists, feminist theorists, race theorists, and queer theorists, not to mention the invaluable work of muckraking journalists and social-protest novelists. What the practices of critique instantiated in these critical traditions can help us see, and what pragmatism is relatively unprepared to help us understand wherever it stands by itself, is how we might effectively engage with complex cultural, social, and psychological difficulties engendered in our all-too-familiar habits of self-deception, reflexive ignorance, and cognitive dissonance.

The problem is that Dewey's theory of inquiry as he developed it makes it quite difficult to say where problems come from, how they are generated, and what contribution inquiry itself makes to the recognition of a situation as indeterminate and then problematic. This theoretical shortfall manifests most clearly in Dewey's work in two related but distinct ways, corresponding to the first two stages of his technical theory of inquiry. One difficulty concerns Dewey's insufficient account of the basis or origin of felt indeterminacies. On Dewey's theory, we simply cannot specify where indeterminacies come from insofar as they are the material of raw primary experience. Indeterminacies are, on his view, simply given to us. But if they are just given as raw perception or awareness, then it is not at all clear how they might play any substantial role in the epistemic process of knowledge without playing the classically foundationalist role played by the raw awarenesses countenanced by representationalist epistemologies. This is a difficulty in Dewey's theory of inquiry that he was never able to fully overcome, even if he did at times see his way partly clear of givenism. The second and related difficulty is that Dewey does not have a clear account of how inquiry can lead us out of our raw experience of indeterminate givens into a formulation of a problem as a statement of work to be performed. Dewey was simply too confident in thinking that "problems will abundantly present themselves" (1917, 41). Not only is this not always true, but very often it is the wrong problems that present themselves.

This argument against Dewey's two-pronged account of problematization can be seen as building on previous work by sympathetic critics of pragmatism, including H. S. Thayer (1952) and John Stuhr (2002), who anticipate my claim

that Dewey's theory of reconstructive problem solving does not contain a sufficient theory of the genesis of problems. For the sake of technical accuracy, we
should point out that these arguments indicate two shortcomings in Dewey
rather than just one (namely Dewey's inattention to the emergence of indeterminacies and his insufficient account of the ways in which inquiry delivers us
from indeterminacy to problematicity). But I also believe that it is helpful for
expository purposes to focus on this twain shortcoming in terms of a single
overarching difficulty, which can be concisely stated in terms of the insuffi-
ciency of Dewey's account of the genesis of problems. By bringing this single
overarching difficulty into proper focus, we can begin to see how it might be
redressed from within a perspective congenial to pragmatism itself. In furthering the criticisms offered by critics from Thayer to Stuhr, I aim to assist in the
reparation of certain problems currently, and persistently, plaguing pragmatism. Of particular note is that my efforts here are relevant to addressing two of
the longest-running criticisms of pragmatism.

The first of these standard criticisms is that pragmatism lacks a sensibility
for the tragic—call this the Pangloss or Pollyanna critique.[5] The second standard criticism is that pragmatism exhibits a fetish for instrumental rationality and scientific method—call this the Prometheus or technocracy critique.[6]
These are two of the most damaging criticisms that have been leveled at pragmatism throughout its history. Each has been voiced for well over one hundred
years now. Pragmatists have yet to effectively answer these criticisms. Despite
many attempted replies, these concerns have been reissued by each new generation. I agree with previous pragmatist respondents that these related criticisms evince misunderstandings of pragmatism. But unlike most previous respondents, I see no reason for arguing that these criticisms are entirely off the
mark. I find these misinterpretations, while rooted in misinterpretations of
pragmatism, somewhat forgivable. This is to say that I can see how certain formulations of pragmatism may give rise to these misunderstandings. Rather
than insisting that our critics have got us all wrong, we pragmatists ought to
work to improve our pragmatism so that it is not as easily exposed to these
plausible objections. Rather than insisting that pragmatism has no weaknesses
on these related fronts, we ought to acknowledge these as real deficits in the
pragmatist sensibility as thus far articulated. Doing this does not require accepting these criticisms as refutations. It might involve rather accepting these

criticisms as not easily blocked by a philosophical perspective wholly rooted in pragmatism as we know it. In this way we might accept these criticisms as describing limitations (that is, we can take them as critiques in Kant's sense). The pragmatist conception of inquiry as reconstruction has its limitations insofar as inquirers sometimes require other modes of inquiry, such as inquiry in the mode of problematization. This is to note a limitation in pragmatism but not a failing. By affirming this limit, we can make room for more effective practices of pragmatist inquiry. By affirming this limit, we enable ourselves to draw on resources found in other philosophical traditions in order not to shore up our pragmatism but rather to strengthen our uses of it.

Turning back now to my argument against Dewey, my intention is to further this line of criticism in order to ultimately resolve it in a way that strengthens pragmatism against the longstanding charges of Panglossian and Promethean sensibilities. To get a better sense of this criticism of Dewey's conception of problems, it will be useful to consider why Dewey may have been motivated to adopt the view that he did and why he was not otherwise motivated to look deeper into the genesis of problems.

Dewey's lack of clarity about problematicity was I think motivated at least in part by certain of his metaphysical-sounding formulations that have proven quite perplexing for a number of critics. My worry is not that these formulations are unhelpful because they sound metaphysical but is rather that they are unhelpful in that they imply a particular kind of metaphysics that runs afoul of pragmatism.[7] For example, Dewey at one point describes "the intrinsic troublesome and uncertain quality of situations" (1929, LW4.178). It is not clear why Dewey thought that the problematicity of a situation might somehow be intrinsic to it. I would have thought that it followed from Dewey's evolutionary theory of thought as an interaction between organism and environment that there is not much to be gained from the dichotomy between intrinsic and extrinsic qualities. If problems are intrinsic to situations, then do problems exist in environments even if organisms are not there to feel their impress? Are problems simply given to us by external reality? Clearly we are here in philosophically very precarious terrain. And yet time and time again, Dewey described problems in such a way that they assumed the form of given features of situations: "Thinking takes its departure from specific conflicts in experience that occasion perplexity and trouble" (1920, 138/MW12.159). "All reflective inquiry starts from a problematic situation" (1929, LW4.151). "Objects in their first mode of experience are perplexing, obscure, fragmentary; in some way they fail to answer a need" (1929, LW4.99). "We are doubtful because the situation is inherently doubtful" (1938a, LW12.109). But how does a situation get characterized as conflicting or problematic or perplexing or obscure or doubtful? "The indeterminate situation comes into existence from existential causes," Dewey (1938a, LW12.111) once urged. But this just sounds like a fancy way of saying that indeterminacy is, like "the imbalance of hunger" Dewey employed as his analogy here, a brute fact simply confronting us. Brute facts, and so raw indeterminacies too, are just fancy ways of construing what is just given in a situation. It is not clear what role such givens can play in an account of human practice. Whatever role we do assign to them, we must be wary to steer clear of the difficulties of givenism discussed in previous chapters. The shortest way of summarizing those difficulties is to say that nothing in our experience carries with it its own rules for interpretation and justification—even the seemingly obvious feeling of hunger requires some interpretation, in order that we might learn to take it up in our practices and intelligibly deal with it, as is evidenced by those surprising occasions in which we misinterpret even the seemingly most obvious experience.

Dewey's fullest attempt to respond to these sorts of worries is in his *Logic.* His work there suggests that if he had devoted more attention to the genesis of problems he very well may have gone in the right direction: "The indeterminate situation becomes problematic in the very process of being subjected to inquiry" (1938a, LW12.111). Dewey certainly saw the dangers of the most obvious forms of givenism even if he did not always see his way clear of some of its most subtle formulations. His rejection of the philosophical dualism between ratiocination and observation suggests that he took the object as knowledge to be an outcome of inquiry rather than an item that precedes it.[8] In the context of his theory of inquiry, Dewey's technical distinction between indeterminacy and problematicity further suggests that problems strictly speaking are not so much given to us as they are clarifications of indeterminacies that are given.[9] Yet despite this, Dewey's account of inquiry still relies on a deficient characterization of indeterminacies as given. This deficiency concerning the impetus to problematization spills over into Dewey's account of forms of inquiry that we might characterize as problematizations insofar as he can only account for such inquiries in terms of the clarification of already existing indeterminacies. But what about inquiries in which the work of problematization reflectively provokes instability in situations that we previously took as fully determinate? Concerning this mode of inquiry Dewey offers very little in the way of guidance, explication, and orientation.

It may be useful to discern how Dewey's theory of inquiry can be seen as inheriting many of these difficulties from the pragmatism of Charles Santiago Peirce.[10] (This inheritance cannot, however, be traced to William James, who knew much more than Dewey did about what is involved in cultivating living doubts in oneself. Some commentators would interpret Peirce as closer to James than to Dewey on this score. For my purposes here I can accept that interpretation if it is pressed in the right way. I aim not for a definitive interpretation of Peirce but only a plausible one that helps illuminate difficulties in Dewey's pragmatism, which is my real target.) In one of the founding texts of pragmatism, "The Fixation of Belief," Peirce develops an account of thought as the "passage" from doubt to belief. Peirce wrote: "The irritation of doubt causes a struggle to attain a state of belief. I shall term this struggle *Inquiry*" (1877, 113, 114). Dewey inherited Peirce's official theory of inquiry more or less intact along with the unquestioned assumption that only beliefs but not doubts are born of the struggle of inquiring thought. For Peirce, at least in his major published writings, doubt is always the beginning and belief always the terminus of inquiry. In short, inquiry is a struggle to rid ourselves of doubt and achieve belief. You need only glance at the title of Peirce's essay to understand that though he is very much interested in how beliefs get fixed, he is scarcely concerned with the quite different process of unsettling beliefs. Peirce once wrote along these lines that "the first step toward *finding out* is to acknowledge you do not satisfactorily know already" (1897, CP 1.13). His view seems to have been that we already possess a dim awareness of error or incapacity which we merely need to liven up in order to set inquiry going. There is no sensibility in this view for producing or generating doubt rather than merely acknowledging it as already dimly available. There is accordingly nothing in this view that will help us understand how we might actually undertake inquiries whose terminus is not belief but doubt. Peirce (1905a, 348) in one place even goes so far as to deny that we can intellectually court doubt. Such a view makes sense only if doubt has already been totally identified with surprise such that one cannot intelligibly assess other means by which real doubts might be produced.[11] Peirce's unwillingness to take seriously modalities of doubting that are both reflective (*pace* Peircean inquiry) and engaged (*pace* Cartesian doubt) perhaps explains why he only ever conceived of inquiry as running in just one direction. Peirce and Dewey both would have benefited from recognizing that inquiry profitably runs both ways: sometimes we need to find ways of unsettling ourselves and on other occasions we need ways of getting resettled.

Recent neopragmatists reap a better harvest in these fields left fallow by their classicopragmatist predecessors. Hilary Putnam notes that an important feature of the pragmatist model of inquiry is its entailment of antiskepticism such that "doubt requires justification just as much as belief" (1992, 20). If Putnam is right, then pragmatists are obliged to provide accounts of doubting that can help determine when and when not to take skeptical challenges seriously. Dewey and Peirce unfortunately shirked this obligation when they identified doubt with qualities of precariousness, surprise, or danger, which are figured as simple givens that do not stand in need of explication, justification, interpretation, or inferential articulation. Against this view we must affirm that doubts are not just given to the mind. Doubts are results of challenging intellectual inquiry. One way to see this is to note that two beliefs forming a contradiction do not always suffice to generate a doubt. We live with contradictions regularly. It is only when a challenging intellectual inquiry serves to problematize our practices that doubts begin to arise. Such challenges are themselves processes of inquiry, forms of thought, and labors of the intellect. Pragmatism will do little to help us understand what forms such a process of inquiry might take if it remains exclusively focused on the other side of inquiry, which works to resolve doubts once they are already going. Recent interventions by certain neopragmatists who, now fully clear of the nuanced givenism still lingering in classicopragmatist accounts of doubt, emphasize the need for inquiries into our expressions of doubt. On this newer view, doubts constitute challenges to beliefs only when accompanied by some well-worked-out conception of how a belief is going wrong. As developed by Robert Brandom and Michael Williams (both of whom count philosophically as neopragmatists in core aspects of their philosophical views and sociologically as former students of Rorty's), doubt is not default, which is to say that it is not some unanalyzable given state of mind. On their view, doubt is rather an achievement of challenges issued in the context of inquiry.[12]

This point is instructive in helping us understand that the philosophical errors of givenism do not apply to just one type of psychological item but rather apply much more widely to any psychological items (perceptions, beliefs, doubts) that are purported to play some important practical role in our knowings, doings, and sharings. Pragmatists ought to be committed to avoiding givens of every variety—this includes givens in the form of immediate perceptual qualia as well as givens in the form of immediate experiences of danger or doubt. Experiences of danger and doubt are learned habits just as much mediated by our accumulated histories of practice as are our most complex concepts. The view that situations are simply given to us as either perilous or secure betrays the observation, which I take to be at the core of all forms of pragmatism, that situations themselves can be specified only relative to an interaction between an organism and its environment. Change the organism, and the situational qualities of peril and safety are subject to change as well. Compare the different ways in which a grizzly bear and a Chihuahua might experience what we take to be the same environment. Or change the example by varying the organisms not in respect of biology, size, or shape but only in respect of their historical accumulation of practical engagement in the world. An abused Chihuahua has learned one sort of way about the world whereas a loved and confident Chihuahua has learned another. Or, to take an example more to the point of my thinking on these matters, consider that what an aristocratic matriarch in high Victorian society experienced as a secure situation may be precisely the paradigm of a perilous situation for a feminist activist in America one hundred and fifty years later.

One way of summarizing the limits of the pragmatist model of reconstructive inquiry I have been describing is in terms of that model's attempt to provide a general explanation of the origin of all our problems: they all come from the felt experience of doubt or the indeterminacy of a situation. Any general explanation of something as complex and diverse as problematicity is likely to be so abstract as to be obfuscating. Such explanations usually just propel us to ask for further explanations: what explains doubt or indeterminacy? Here the pragmatist model breaks down insofar as doubt and indeterminacy are treated as given. The infinite regress triggered by the attempt to offer a general explanation is halted only by throwing up some supposedly unassailable feature of experience that is simply asserted as unquestionable and incorrigible. The result of this attempt can only be that problems are ultimately accepted as givens themselves, in precisely the manner I described in my above discussions of Dewey and Peirce. But what if we go back and ask why problems ought to be treated in the first place as something in need of a general explanation? A better approach for pragmatists would be to claim that problems are the product of a diverse set of inquiries that do not stand in need of a general unifying explanation. If pressed for such an explanation, we could perhaps vaguely suggest that all problems are the result of something like curiosity and are as diverse, protean, and remarkable as curiosity itself.[13] But the important point that we should emphasize is that we do not need a general explanation that shows us some common origin of all our problems when we would be better served by a diverse set of specific explanations of specific problems. Think again of the diverse kinds of explanations that historians, sociologists, and anthropologists will offer. Rather than a unifying explanatory origin, what we really need are diverse accounts of the emergence and descent of our diverse sets of problems. Problems, like their solutions, are the product of various forms of inquiry. As for inquiry, it is something to be performed and perfected rather than something to be explained or even explained away.

In order to move toward a more constructive approach to these deficiencies, that is, to explore the ways in which pragmatism may in fact be in a good position to improve its model of problems, I would like to turn now to a consideration of the different ways in which a situation might come to be characterized as problematic. I suspect that many of the difficulties in Dewey's account of problems stem from the fact that when he was thinking of problems, his attention was often focused on homegrown examples like a small fire on the kitchen stove, a discrepancy in a bookkeeping account, or trying to figure out how to get uptown in the quickest way possible. But these innocent sorts of surprises, which also interested Peirce, are clearly not the only kinds of problems we face. It has been repeatedly pointed out by critics that Dewey's conception of reconstructive pragmatism leaves little room for coming to terms with problems of tragic proportion. This is the first of the two standard criticisms of pragmatism I mentioned above, namely that pragmatism lacks a sense of the tragic. One particularly convincing statement of this worry was penned by Ella Lyman Cabot, an early classicopragmatist and a student of both Dewey and Royce:

> Dewey perhaps understates what Royce dwells on too much—the storm-stress aspects of life. Dewey's attitude is tremendously healthy. . . . A healthy scorn for all things abstract and spiritual is a bracing tonic, but passion and pathos

and the tragedy and mystery of life are real and sometimes so life-giving as to be the only world we can see and they must be met with understanding criticism not mere condemnation (Cabot 1892, cited in Kaag 2008, 137).[14]

Unlike the numerous critics who are eager to insist that pragmatism should have an enhanced capacity for the tragic, I want to urge that we pragmatists should take as our foci for reconstruction yet another third class of problems falling somewhere between the tragic and the innocent ends of the spectrum. This third class of problems is not quite tragic in dimension but neither does it yield mere difficulties as easily resolved as Dewey's rather pithy examples of problematicity. This third class is best illustrated by those deep ethical and intellectual problems of modern culture that we democrats are increasingly intimate with. These are, for most cultural critics and critical inquirers, the most important types of problems. Consider ways in which groups of peoples sometimes come to recognize their political practices as somehow terribly wrong or unjust. Think here of racism or feminism. Consider how cultures sometimes come to regard their highest intellectual treasures as containing the seeds of their own destruction. Think here of colonialism or many of the motivations to secularism. Consider also how we often come to recognize even our relations to ourselves as premised on practices in which we discern forms of self-deceit or self-loathing that we may consider problematic. Think here of ideals of body and beauty or many of the social roles we force ourselves to act out. Problems falling into this crucial third class are not just given, as irresolvable tragedies and innocent difficulties might conceivably be construed to be, but are rather the work of the difficult and patient labor of engaged critics who fearlessly ask of their societies and their selves whether or not they are living well enough.

Focusing on this third class of problems brings into relief the positive upshot of my discussion of the deficiencies of a givenist conception of problems. The positive lesson to be learned is that the work of reconstructive problem solving can be usefully integrated with the work of ironic problem generating. The lesson is that Dewey's problematic account of problems can be remedied by synthesizing the pragmatist practice of instrumental reconstruction with the genealogical practice of ironic problematization. This is precisely the relevance that Foucault's problem-generating genealogy holds for Dewey's problem-solving pragmatism. Before we get to Foucault, it will be helpful to first approximate this complex point at a more general level, where we can note the relevance that inquiries aiming to uncover previously unrecognized problems have for philosophical approaches like pragmatism, which are easily misinterpreted as technocratic and Panglossian. Consider a similar point urged by Habermas in the context of his contributions to political theory, where he argues that the official procedures of democratic "justification" by which we deal with our political problems are legitimate only if they are in close dialogue with unofficial public procedures of "discovery" by which we specify new problems we take to be politically salient.[15] This argument in political theory can be generalized to show that historical inquiry, which aims to render determinate situations problematic, can easily be the natural ally of reconstructive inquiry, which aims to render problematic situations determinate. In other words, we seem to need both problematization and reconstruction, and we seem to need them both together.[16] I will show in the next section how Foucault can be interpreted so as to provide an exemplary model of the way in which the critic can work to generate crucial problems that would otherwise remain neglected by the regular activity of solving problems. While Habermas would of course hesitate to regard Foucault as such an exemplar,[17] others, including Nancy Fraser, Richard Bernstein, Thomas McCarthy, and Amy Allen, have convincingly argued (in terms Habermas should find mostly amicable) that Foucaultian genealogy could usefully play such a role within a practice of critical theory informed by pragmatism.[18] The implicit claim of all these commentators, which I find ripe for development, is that Foucault's genealogical mode of problematization contains resources that could fill in crucial gaps in pragmatist and critical theoretical projects of reconstruction.

Toward a Pragmatist Historiography

I can now round out my discussion of pragmatism by considering just how ripe this tradition is for an importation of genealogical accounts of the development of problems. History has an important role to play in a pragmatist philosophy by supplying a practice of problematization that anticipates and informs the quintessential pragmatist project of reconstruction. Historical inquiries supply problems to philosophical inquiries oriented toward solving these problems. If pragmatist philosophy must think in terms of historically situated practices, and if pragmatist philosophy is further oriented toward solving problems, then it is natural to expect that pragmatism should at times require a historiography that would be oriented toward producing the problems that pragmatist philosophy might solve.[19]

It is this approach that will best enable pragmatism to overcome the two standard critiques it has thus far failed to shake off despite well over a hundred years of trying: that pragmatism is Panglossian in lacking a tragic sensibility and that pragmatism is Promethean in its blind pursuit of means without concern for ends. These two criticisms are tightly knit together: if either of these criticisms holds then the other is helped along quite nicely. Although I find both of these criticisms rooted in misinterpretations of the tradition, I also concede that there has been a definite orientation toward solutions on the part of pragmatists and that this orientation will appear to many as both technocratic-scientistic (overly instrumentalist) and Pollyannaish (under-tragic). The persistence of these criticisms is best explained by their unfortunate plausibility, not by the obtuseness of those who proffer them. To answer these criticisms, we should not merely reply with more of the same pragmatism: we should rather work to reinterpret the tradition itself. My proposal for a reinterpretation is that of a transitionalist pragmatism informed by a transitionalist genealogy. Bringing pragmatism into closer dialogue with other philosophical traditions that have emphasized the valuable role of problematization, especially problematization through the practice of historical inquiry as emphasized by genealogy, will yield a more robust form of pragmatism that is not as susceptible to these critiques. This cross-tradition and counterdisciplinary conception of inquiry has much to recommend it. But it also has many hurdles to overcome. I want to consider just two.

One potential concern some may have about this bidirectional commitment to a counterdisciplinary form of inquiry is that it may seem at first glance too complex to effectively coordinate. But that it is complex and therefore difficult to achieve in practice says less about the viability of this conception of critical inquiry itself and more about the shortcomings of contemporary formations of thought. That we find it difficult to integrate philosophy and history together into a synthesized practice of critical inquiry speaks against, not for, the disciplinary matrices that too much of our thought currently inhabits. As our thought inhabits the disciplines, the disciplines inhibit our thought. What we need instead are innovative and experimental conceptions of critique and inquiry that weld together formerly disparate patterns of thinking.

A second potential concern with my argument may be that it simply sounds at first quite strange to suggest that we genealogical historians ought to go around kicking up the dirt. Skeptical philosophers will ask how historians might even produce problems. And embattled historians will demand that we give them a good reason for doing so. Both disciplines will ask if we do not already have enough problems hanging over us such that we have no need for philosopher-historians going around muddying things up even more. My reply is that the pragmatist commitment to uncertainty in all of its forms, from which there follows thoroughgoing epistemic and political fallibilism, suggests that pragmatists ought to be on the lookout for ways in which our own best practices are already rife with problems that we hardly suspect. This orientation toward uncertainty, which historian James Kloppenberg rightly explicates as at the heart of the genesis of pragmatism, is usefully glossed by Richard Rorty in his description of pragmatists as ironists.[20]

The pragmatist ironist is someone who takes seriously the possibility that they just might be wrong about even their most cherished beliefs. As Rorty describes this figure: "The ironist spends her time worrying about the possibility that she has been initiated into the wrong tribe, taught to play the wrong language game. She worries that the process of socialization which turned her into a human being by giving her a language may have given her the wrong language, and so turned her into the wrong kind of human being" (1989a, 75). The Rortyan attitude of irony follows quite naturally from pragmatism's orientation toward the general cultural implications of uncertainty and contingency. Ironists are, says Rorty, "always aware of the contingency and fragility of their final vocabularies, and thus of their selves" (1989a, 74). Because the ironic attitude is one that is oriented by contingency and uncertainty, I find that this attitude fits quite naturally into the pragmatist tradition even if the tradition before Rorty did not always do well to emphasize it.

We can also, to be sure, glimpse the ironist in both Dewey and James. James urged ironism in his "On a Certain Blindness in Human Beings," where he described our common human failure to regard the values and beliefs of others where they do not intersect with our own. James's essay recounts an instance of his own former blindness to the ways of life of mountain settlers in an Appalachian cove. Noticing that his former judgments against their ways of life were rooted in blindnesses to these ways of life, James recalls a conversion where "I instantly felt that I had been losing the whole inward significance of the situation." What had previously been to him "a mere ugly picture on the retina" was always for these cove-clearers "a symbol redolent with moral memories." James reflects, "I had been blind to the peculiar ideality of their conditions as they certainly would also have been to the ideality of mine, had they had a peep at my strange indoor academic ways of life at Cambridge." By immersing ourselves in the ways of others, we achieve ironic detachment from our own ways such that, says James, "our self is riven and its narrow interests fly to pieces" (1899c, 631, 634). By gaining insight into the inmost depths of one another, James is saying, we thereby gain insight into our own full contingency.

The pragmatist ironist is best seen as a figure for critical engagement with one's self and one's culture in the mode of problematization. I am suggesting that historical inquiry helps us adopt this sort of ironic attitude and hence enables us to recognize certain blindnesses in our views of both ourselves and others. History reveals the contingency of our beliefs and values in such a way that we can see these beliefs and values as no longer necessary features of ourselves. This in turn enables us to explore these beliefs and values with a degree of ironic detachment to find out whether or not they employ assumptions or entail consequences that we find problematic. History in the sense in which I am describing it is neither a celebratory mode of inquiry in which we prove to ourselves that we have historically evolved in the right kind of way nor a denigrating mode of inquiry in which we discover that our inheritance is full of injustice—in other words, we need not be a Hegel or a Nietzsche boldly flaunting some form of genetic fallacy. A history oriented by pragmatism can instead furnish us with problems that provoke the difficult work of reconstructive thought. History neither vindicates nor invalidates our practices. History enables us to reflectively problematize our practices and thereby shows us where to focus our attention so that we might ameliorate them. I find such a use of history in keeping with the best historiographical work in the pragmatist tradition.[21] As I have focused much energy here on describing why Dewey's philosophical reconstruction so badly needs a perspective that can be supplied by historical problematization, I turn now to a discussion of some of the ways in which such a historical perspective is already featured in Dewey's pragmatism, even if Dewey himself did not sufficiently explicate this aspect of his work.

I mentioned above that when Dewey did discuss problems, he sometimes did so in ways that would lead us to expect him to develop them through genealogical inquiry. And although I have here argued that Dewey did not sufficiently thematize the role that the genesis of problems must play in his own account of reconstruction, this is not because Dewey himself was unfamiliar with such work. Quite the contrary. Dewey was one of the great problematizers in the history of philosophy. This is what makes it so strange that his theory of experimental reconstruction says so little about the role of problematization. But this is also why his theory is so particularly inviting to the work of problematization. Joseph Margolis is therefore correct to claim both that "the absence of any explicit or sustained account of history (or, better, historicity) [is] a distinct limitation in Dewey's [pragmatism]" and that "pragmatism would be greatly strengthened by the addition of an account of historicity" (2002a, 114).

If we look for it, we can find in Dewey's own practice of philosophical inquiry a deep engagement with historical inquiry. Some of Dewey's most important texts are simply incomprehensible unless we read them as simultaneously philosophical and historical. I am thinking of quintessential Dewey texts such as *Reconstruction in Philosophy* and *The Quest for Certainty* as well as some of Dewey's most effective political writings, including *Individualism Old and New, Liberalism and Social Action,* and *Freedom and Culture.* In all of these books, Dewey is as much an intellectual historian as he is a critical philosopher. His arguments are often less of the "see how philosophically incoherent this view is" variety and more of the "look how these views were formulated as responses to cultural conditions that no longer apply" variety.

This aspect of Dewey's work has not gone unnoticed amongst commentators. Robert Westbrook helpfully describes some of Dewey's most important works as attempts to "exploit more fully the polemical possibilities of intellectual history" (1991, 347). Richard Rorty describes Dewey's mode of argumentation as a form of historical redescription that can be contrasted to philosophical demonstration, for example in his claim that "the most profitable ground maps Dewey provided were those to the history of Western philosophy" (1992, 295n16). Decades before Westbrook and Rorty, Max Fisch (1970) usefully surveyed the extensive breadth of Dewey's historical inquiries. Even earlier than that, three decades prior to Fisch, John Hermann Randall authored what still remains to this day the best account of Dewey's involvements in historical inquiry. Randall considered Dewey's point that philosophies always develop as a response to specific cultural problems and went on to show that this implies that "the history of that culture and its problems, and the historical criticism of its methods of inquiry and application, become of the very essence of any philosophy" (1939, 83).[22] Philosophical problem solving, in other words, must engage itself in historical inquiries concerning the genesis of the problems on which it works. Noteworthy in this regard is Randall's own work on a Dewey-inspired pragmatist historiography that explicitly conceptualizes history as a problematizing form of inquiry that sets the agenda for philosophy as a reconstructive inquiry: "History is thus fundamentally problematic: it is always setting problems. . . . Historical knowledge 'reveals' the genesis or origin of the problem, points to the active force that is generating a tension, to the points of tension themselves, thus locating the obstacles or 'deflecting forces,' and also to the instrument for dealing with the obstacles" (Randall 1937, 471; 1958, 99).[23] Randall's own work features valuable resources that pragmatists would be wise to reconsider today.[24]

All the commentary I have been citing helps us see that historical inquiry was for Dewey's pragmatism already very much internal to philosophical inquiry. This helps explain why time and time again Dewey used history to describe the crucial cultural conflicts to which he understood his philosophy as a reconstructive response. Past history functioned for Dewey as a mode of inquiry that helped furnish the present problems to which a philosophical mode of inquiry could then supply future solutions. In this sense, Dewey anticipated Foucault's (1975, 31) notion of a "history of the present" in describing historical inquiry as rooted in "the historic present" (1938a, 233).[25] This view of history's relation to the present was clearly affirmed by Dewey in his writings on the uses of history in education, where history is seen as "an organ for analysis of the warp and woof of the present social fabric, of making known the forces which have woven the pattern" (1916c, 217/MW9.225). It was also clearly reflected in Dewey's thinking on the relation between philosophy and history: "Philosophers are parts of history, caught in its movement; creators perhaps in some measure of its future, but also assuredly creatures of its past" (1928, 4/LW3.4). It follows from this view that genealogy (understood as the historical practice of problematizing the present) has a natural place alongside pragmatism (understood as the philosophical practice of reconstructing the present). By developing this connection between genealogy and pragmatism, genealogical pragmatists will be able to repair the difficulties within the pragmatist theory of inquiry described above. More importantly, genealogical pragmatists will also become better problem solvers—in the sense that they will become better solvers of better problems.

Foucault and Genealogical Problematization

Pragmatism and genealogy resonate on a philosophical level in so many ways that the general lack of attention to the possibilities for their integration comes as quite a surprise. Both philosophies quintessentially reject the familiar -isms of high-modern philosophy: dualism, representationalism, foundation-alism, subjectivism, and universalism. These familiar points of overlap enable pragmatists and genealogists to share a conception of philosophy's role as a critique of culture and all the attendant epistemic, ethical, and political modes contained therein. It turns out that genealogists are very much like pragmatists in offering a vision of philosophy as a contribution to transformational cultural critique. Foucault writes: "there is not a time for criticism and a time for transformation; there are not those who have to do criticism and those who have to transform" (1981, 457). These are rather the same times and the same tasks. With the pragmatists Foucault shares a sensibility for the need for critique as a means of transitioning the complex cultural spaces in which we find ourselves. Foucault elaborates this transitionalism as follows: "So many things can be changed, being as fragile as they are, tied more to contingencies than to necessities, more to what is arbitrary than to what is rationally established, more to complex but transitory historical contingences than to inevitable anthropological constants" (1981, 458).[26] Foucault's conception of critique is like the pragmatists' in that it clearly inhabits time and history.

But whereas the pragmatists practiced critique as a reconstructive problem-solving activity, Foucault practiced critique as an act of problematization. Adherents and expositors of both traditions have usually taken these different emphases as grounds for dismissing one another.[27] But on closer inspection, it turns out that these differing conceptions of critique are not at all incompatible. Indeed, both traditions stand to be positively enriched by being deployed alongside one another.

Foucault's final description of his genealogical enterprise in terms of the concept of "problematization" has proven perplexing for commentators.[28] We can make our way to a solid appreciation of Foucault's conception of problematization by briefly comparing three different forms of genealogy: Friedrich Nietzsche's, Bernard Williams's, and Foucault's. There are considerable differences separating Foucault's use of genealogy as a history of problematizations from Nietzsche's and Williams's more strictly normative uses of genealogy. Nietzsche and Williams used genealogy as a normatively determinative mode of inquiry that settles the question of the value of the practices inquired into. They, of course, use genealogy in two normatively different senses, insofar as Nietzsche's genealogy is an attempt to undermine modern moral practices and Williams's is an attempt to vindicate modern moral notions regarding the value of truth. Foucault's project is drastically different from both of these normative uses of genealogy, and much light is shed on Foucault's project by explicating this contrast.

One way of bringing the differences between normative and problematizing uses of genealogy into focus is to consider the well-known criticism that genealogy commits the genetic fallacy by conflating genesis with justification.[29] Genetic reasoning is, I believe, somewhat less fallacious than is commonly thought. The strong view that logical justification is fully distinct from historical evolution does not make sense on a pragmatist view of justification as a temporal process. Denying the pragmatist view of justification as a process requires a strong affirmation of some other synchronic account of justification. But despite any misgivings that we pragmatists, or anyone else, might have about the genetic fallacy, it is not difficult to discern ways in which the charge of the genetic fallacy has at least some purchase on the ambitious normative uses to which Nietzsche and Williams put genealogy. For it is not at all clear that the historical development of our practices can be as strictly determinative of the current justifiability of these practices as Nietzsche and Williams sometimes seem to claim. Surely genealogy in at least some instances has at least some bearing on normative issues of justification. However, the important question raised by the charge of the genetic fallacy concerns stronger claims that genealogy normatively bears on justification to such a degree that genealogy by itself can determine justifiability. Nietzsche and Williams explicitly employed genealogy in this strong sense. Nietzsche (1887) attempted to show that the history of a certain practice of morality can be used to denounce that moral practice and many of its central concepts. Williams (2002) attempted the similar project of showing how the history of certain of our practices connected to the concept of truth can result in a "vindicatory" gene-alogy that would defend our high valuation of truth against currently fashion-able criticisms. In both cases, genealogy was put to use for quite ambitious normative purposes. Although we should affirm the importance of history for philosophy, it is not quite clear that we can get this much out of history.

The genetic-fallacy criticism helps us focus attention on the possibility that genealogists such as Nietzsche and Williams have endorsed rather limited con-ceptions of the way in which development is relevant. Surely genesis does not strictly determine justification. But perhaps this is not because justification is itself atemporal, as many who charge genealogists with the genetic fallacy would hold. Perhaps, to seed a thought that I will return to harvest later, gene-sis does not determine justification because justification is temporal in a much broader fashion than certain genealogists have allowed. Perhaps justification must not only look backward into history but forward into the future as well. Justification, in this broader sense, shuttles back and forth between past and future. Although this broader sense of justification is not strictly incompatible with Nietzsche's and Williams's use of genealogy, it is hardly an explicit feature of their uses of genealogy.

Foucault was undoubtedly attentive to the problems facing any normatively ambitious use of genealogy. It may indeed have been his attentiveness to these matters that motivated him to redescribe his own historical researches late in his career under the banner of problematization. The point of genealogy prob-lematization for Foucault was not, as many of his most influential critics have wrongly argued, to use history to denounce or vindicate some of our most cen-tral modern practices.[30] The point was rather to use history to show the way in which certain practices have structured some of the core problematics that a given period of thought, most notably our own modernity, must face. Nietz-sche wanted to use genealogy as a global critique that would enable him to simply clear the board. Williams sought in genealogy a form of inquiry that would enable him to preserve much of the current setup. But Foucault thought genealogy might help us articulate certain problems on the board of which we were not formerly aware and that can only be addressed from some position upon the board. For Nietzsche and Williams, genealogy often remained a quest for origins that can be shown to be either base or best, whereas for Fou-cault genealogy concerned itself not with origins and beginnings so much as with the long and slow processes of emergence and descent.[31]

To explicate Foucault's view, which is far less understood than the more predictable uses of genealogy featured in Nietzsche and Williams, allow me to begin with a characterization of genealogy as problematization as a dual-aspect or two-part model of inquiry. The first aspect is clarifying inquiry into the emergence and descent of certain problems and their corollary conceptions of what might count as a solution. The second aspect concerns the way in which such inquiry functions to intensify the hybrid network of problems and solutions inquired into. Inquiry in the form of problematization is preceded by the problems that are the objects of its study (first aspect: articulation), but by studying their emergence, the problematizing form of inquiry is able to open these problems up to more rigorous forms of critical scrutiny (second aspect: intensification). By inquiring into the emergence of hybrid networks of problems and solutions, genealogy enables us to recognize our problems as contingent products rather than as necessary givens. By intensifying these hybrid networks, genealogy also enables us to adopt a more reflective relation to the problems in which we already find ourselves, whether consciously or not, enmeshed. In sum, problematization functions to open up problems in their emergence so as to make them available for critique. This dual-aspect description of genealogical problematization should be seen as a merely initial approximation of a very complex idea. With it in hand, I can now further explicate the idea by considering in turn Foucault's actual genealogies and then his methodological and metaphilosophical statements about genealogy.

Among Foucault's own histories, the concept of problematization is most clearly featured in his late writings on ancient ethical practices (1984a, 1984b). Here Foucault uses problematization neither to undermine nor to vindicate these practices but rather to show the way in which certain features of these practices were understood as the primary problems that these practices were made to address. A similar reading of problematization is also the best way to make sense of Foucault's (1975, 1976) famous genealogies of punishment and sexuality. These genealogies do not belie a strategy of undermining our modern notions of power and freedom as these are exemplified in our punitive and sexual practices. Rather these genealogies manifest an attempt to articulate ways in which these practices have themselves problematized certain assumptions about power and freedom constitutive of our historic present. Power as discipline and freedom as liberation are neither denounced nor vindicated by Foucault but rather are shown to be the most critical problematic on which we moderns find ourselves obsessively working.

Turning from these genealogies to Foucault's statements about them, the first thing to note is Foucault's claim that the concept of problematization was always at the center of his work: "The notion common to all the work that I have done since *History of Madness* [i.e., *Madness and Civilization*] is that of problematization, though it must be said that I never isolated this notion sufficiently" (1984c, 257). Although this self-description may have been subtly self-serving, it does clearly establish the great importance that the notion of problematization held for Foucault in his final years. In an interview with Paul Rabinow and Hubert Dreyfus, Foucault more precisely specified the way in which he saw his historical research functioning: "I would like to do the genealogy of problems, of *problématiques*. My point is not that everything is bad, but that everything is dangerous, which is not exactly the same as bad. If everything is dangerous, then we always have something to do" (1983, 256). Todd May glosses Foucault's view here with the term "fraught." It is not that certain of our practices are incoherent or inadequate, it is that they are fraught: "Instead of prohibitions there are dangers. Instead of obligations there are opportunities. Instead of allowances there are multiple ways these dangers and opportunities can be navigated" (2006, 103). Adam Takacs likewise notes that Foucault understood the term "problem" literally as "a structure of knowledge in which one cannot know for sure" such that problematization is "a practice of constant *opening* rather than a definitive march toward solutions" (2004, 880). It is clear that Foucault was more interested in posing challenging questions than in solving problems. His work functioned to open our practices up and to reveal ways in which they are fraught with tension, in short to articulate the problematicity inherent in our practices.

This view of genealogy as problematizations emerges throughout Foucault's reflections on his use of history in philosophy. Sometimes he would make only casual mention of this angle of his work: "What I have been trying to do this evening is not to solve a problem but to suggest a way to approach a problem" (1979, 311). But in many writings he was quite careful to establish this point in a more rigorous fashion: "My role is to raise questions in an effective, genuine way, and to raise them with the greatest possible rigor, with the maximum complexity and difficulty so that a solution doesn't spring from the head of some reformist intellectual or suddenly appear in the head of a party's political bureau" (1980a, 288). In another interview with Rabinow: "My attitude isn't a result of the form of critique that claims to be a methodical examination in order to reject all possible solutions except for the one valid one. It is more on the order of 'problematization'—which is to say, the development of a domain of acts, practices, and thoughts that seem to me to pose problems for politics" (1984e, 114). Last, consider this line from the essay on methodology published as the introduction to the second volume of *The History of Sexuality*: "The proper task of a history of thought is: to define the conditions in which human beings 'problematize' what they are, what they do, and the world in which they live" (1984b, 10).

Foucault's many methodological and metaphilosophical reflections on problematization make clear that the point of his genealogies was neither to denounce nor vindicate our extant practices, beliefs, and conceptions. The aim of his genealogies was rather to critically show the way in which certain of our practices, beliefs, and conceptions have become severely problematic sources of tension. To say that our practices are problematic is not to say that they are wrong. It is to insist that they constitute a fraught field on which we find that we must continue to work. Foucault was saying, for example, that we must concern ourselves with the problematic relations between modern disciplinary power and modern emancipatory freedom. Genealogy taken in this sense is an initiating, rather than a concluding, phase of thought. Genealogy brings into critical focus the problems to which further critical work must attempt to develop responses.

Interpreting Foucault's use of genealogy in this way helps explain why genealogy in Foucault's hands never approached anything like a global philosophy of history or even a global historical critique. Hans Sluga (2002, 2005) rightly points out that Foucault's genealogies were enormously more focused histories than what we find in Nietzsche's wildly speculative genealogies or, for that matter, in Williams's purely conjectural genealogy. Where Nietzsche and Williams were busy making claims on behalf of entire civilizations, Foucault patiently concerned himself with particular cultural practices as they developed in particular spaces in particular times. Of all three, Foucault is the only one who even approximates something that might be recognized by contemporary historians as history.[32] This serves to establish a further point of contrast between Foucault on the one hand and Nietzsche and Williams on the other in terms of the strength of their claims on behalf of genealogy. Nietzsche and Williams offered quite strong philosophical claims on the basis of their historical genealogies. They often took it that a genealogy could determine the normative value of at least some practices. Foucault's claims on behalf of genealogy were, by contrast, much more modest. Foucault is best understood as employing genealogy such that it is internal to, but certainly not sufficient for, the normative critique of our practices. Foucault held that genealogy must be a part of any project of normative critique, but he did not make the stronger claim that genealogy by itself constitutes such a critical project. On his view, genealogy is internal to justification just insofar as genealogy helps illuminate the incoherence of some of our practices. But Foucault would never have held that a philosopher can take incoherence in a practice as a demonstration of the worthlessness or wrongness of that practice (he recognized, as most philosophers fail to, that our lives are bursting with incoherence). What he more plausibly suggested is that genealogy is internal to the justification of practices only to the extent that genealogy reveals tensions that future thought must work on if it is not to lose a sense of the value of the practice in question.[33] This puts us in a good position to see that Foucault's modest use of genealogy as problematization is not open to the charge of confusing justification with genesis, for Foucault never insisted on a strict relation between historical genealogy and normative justification.

But does Foucault undermine the utility of a practice of genealogy in detaching genesis from justification? Because Foucault escapes the genetic fallacy by embracing a more modest conception of the role of genealogy than that featured in Nietzsche and Williams, we must ask whether or not Foucault's form of genealogy is robust enough for the project of critique in which all three thinkers were obviously interested. Genealogy in Foucault's sense is clearly relevant to normative critique, but is it necessary or even important for normative critique? If we must add something else to genealogical problematization in order to wield a usable critical apparatus (such as a theoretical account of truth that shows this concept to be a mere effect of power or a theoretical account of moral practice that situates normativity wholly within the exercise of reason), then is this something else doing *all* the normative work such that genealogy is not actually essential to critique even if it might sometimes be useful? If this were the case, then Foucault's importance as a critical thinker will have been much overrated.

I mentioned earlier that the genetic fallacy usefully focuses attention on the fact that genealogy taken by itself is probably not sufficient for normative critique. I suggested there that this might not be due to the familiar thought that justification is an atemporal project, a matter of the ahistorical logic of the heavens. Instead, I planted the seed of the thought that this might be due to a requirement for justification of a broader sense of temporality than that countenanced by genealogical inquiry. The kernel of this thought is that justification involves neither looking outside of time nor merely looking into the past but rather looking back at the past and forward to the future together. According to this view, genealogy is necessary for normative critique but is not by itself sufficient. On this view, genealogical problematization is at most one side of the project of critical inquiry, where the other side is forward-looking problem solving. Focusing on the limitations of genealogy in terms of this broader temporal conception of justification suggests that if genealogical problematization by itself does not comprise a complete critical apparatus, then we need not take this as implying that it is an unusable critical tool. That genealogy is less robust in Foucault than in Nietzsche and Williams may, then, not be a fatal flaw after all, and doubly so when we consider that genealogy as practiced by Nietzsche and Williams is always in danger of overcommitting itself and thereby committing the genetic fallacy. If genealogy in Foucault's sense can be integrated with another critical tool, something more forward looking and solution oriented, then genealogy could perhaps be shown to be an essential part of a workable critical apparatus. You can see where I am headed.

Such a conception of genealogy as just one aspect of a wider critical apparatus is, I think, a crucial but hitherto largely unnoticed feature of Foucault's overall critical project. Although it is clear that Foucault was more interested in using genealogy to pose problems than to develop solutions, there is nevertheless a way in which his histories specifically invite constructive, problem-solving responses. Viewing Foucault's critical apparatus in this way constitutes a useful reply to some of his most severe detractors, who saw in his work little more than dour denunciation. That critics have missed this point in Foucault is perhaps understandable given the dark tone of some of his major texts. But we can move beyond what Foucault *seemed* to be saying about his genealogies by focusing on what he actually *did* say about them. The view of Foucault's conception of genealogy that I am urging is borne out in some of his most important late works. It is clearly articulated in the late essay "What Is Enlightenment?" as well as in a late interview with Paul Rabinow in which Foucault responded at length to this very useful question: "What is a history of problematics?"

In response to Rabinow's question, Foucault described his work of problematization in terms of a "history of thought" that he distinguishes from "the analysis of systems of representation." Representation is "what inhabits a certain conduct and gives it its meaning." Thought is "what allows one to step back from this way of acting or reacting, to present it to oneself as an object of thought and to question it as to its meaning, its condition, and its goals." So while representations are ideas that are more or less received by the subject and deployed as givens without further consideration, thought is much closer to a picture of the mind as an active and selective phenomenon: "Thought is freedom in relation to what one does, the motion by which one detaches oneself from it, establishes it as an object, and reflects on it as a problem" (1984e, 117).

Foucault's description of thought as distinct from representation enables him to situate thought in relation to his incredibly useful notion of problematization: "For a domain of action, a behavior, to enter the field of thought, it is necessary for a certain number of factors to have made it uncertain, to have made it lose its familiarity, or to have provoked a number of difficulties around it" (1984e, 117). Though he did not intend it and probably did not realize it, Foucault is here developing almost a precise inversion of Dewey's model of inquiry as the transition from doubt to belief—what Foucault seemed to be interested in was the inverse but corollary process of the transition from belief to doubt. Problematization is, for Foucault, precisely this doubt-inducing work of provoking difficulties and rendering uncertainties. Problematization as such does not demonstrate that some practice is wrong or incoherent or bad. It only shows that some practice stands in need of further consideration and elaboration. Such elaboration may eventually take the form of replacing an outdated practice with a wholly new practice, or it may take the form of internal revisions to a problematic practice that enrich and sustain that practice for the foreseeable future.

As Foucault continues in the interview with Rabinow, he is very explicit that problematization does not so much aim at the elimination of certain practices as at the conversion of given solutions into problems provoking further thought: "This development of a given into a question, this transformation of a group of obstacles and difficulties into problems to which the diverse solutions will attempt to produce a response, this is what constitutes the point of problematization and the specific work of thought." Foucault writes that "when thought intervenes" into practices "it is an original or specific response—often taking many forms, sometimes even contradictory in its different aspects—to these difficulties, which are defined for it by a situation or a context, and which hold true as a possible question." Thought intervenes as a series of responses to problems. As such, problematization clearly invites solution. Foucault elaborates the idea in this way: "To one single set of difficulties, several responses can be made. And most of the time different responses actually are proposed. But what must be understood is what makes them simultaneously possible: it is the point in which their simultaneity is rooted." What is the common point of reference of the various responses that thought may pose to our difficulties? "The work of a history of thought would be to rediscover at the root of these diverse solutions the general form of problematization that has made them possible." The history of thought thus studies "the transformations of the difficulties and obstacles of a practice into a general problem for which one proposes diverse practical solutions" (1984e, 118).[34] Problematization thus turns practical difficulties into practical problems capable of receiving practical solutions.

Now, my claim is certainly not that Foucault himself sought to solve the problems his historical research posed. Rather, my claim is that Foucault quite clearly understood that his own mode of history as problematization invites a careful philosophical response that ultimately must seek to propose solutions to the problems effected by the historical analysis. Genealogical problematization does not credit or discredit current moral standards—it invites further work in which these standards will be normatively revised. Even if in his own work Foucault concentrated his attention on posing problems in such a way as to disallow superficial solutions, there is nothing in this practice that rules out the possibility of more sophisticated responses to the work of problematization. Another way of putting my point is to say quite simply that Foucault wrote problems in order to invite solutions. Foucault practiced problematization precisely for the reason he cited in response to Rabinow's important question: "why problematization?" "In order to provoke the difficult work of thought." I thus submit the following as a working definition of problematization, which I hope future employments of problematization can improve upon: inquiry that clarifies our understanding of the emergence of problems in such a way as to provide us with the means for exploring critical ways of responding to these problems.

That Foucault's work of problematization is plausibly characterized in this way is further evidenced in an important late essay where he problematized and responded to the concept of modernity. In "What Is Enlightenment?" Foucault begins with an interesting juxtaposition of Immanuel Kant and Charles Baudelaire. The result of Foucault's juxtaposition-cum-appropriation of these two quite different moderns is a conception of modernity as an "attitude" or "philosophical ethos" that consists in "a permanent critique of our historical era" (1984d, 312). Foucault locates this modern attitude in Kant's adoption of a critical relation to today and in Baudelaire's idea of a transfiguration of the present. The modern attitude, as Foucault mouths it through the figures of Kant and Baudelaire, consists in the critical transfiguration of the limits of our present situation.

Having located this critical and transfigural ethos in the work of Kant and Baudelaire, Foucault turns in the second half of his essay to his own careful elaboration of the modern attitude. After issuing a warning that such an attitude must not be employed for simplistic "for" and "against" polemics that certain other genealogists and inquirers of diverse orientation have not been so careful to avoid, Foucault turns to his own positive elaboration of how this philosophical ethos might take shape. Foucault carefully lays out three positive characteristics of his modern philosophical ethos. As the third characteristic is a response to objections that Foucault anticipates his readers will level at his ethos as defined by the other two characteristics, we can take the first two characteristics as elaborating the real kernel of Foucault's philosophical ethos. These two characteristics together suggest the interpretation of Foucault I have proposed above: Foucault as problematizer and as problem solver.

The first characteristic is focused in terms of a historical inquiry into our limits. Foucault describes "a historical investigation into the events that have led us to constitute ourselves and to recognize ourselves as subjects of what we are doing, thinking, saying" (1984d, 315). Foucault specifies this historical investigation in terms of a Kantian inquiry into the limits of ourselves. But whereas Kant aimed to understand our limits as universal and necessary, Foucault's histories will show them to be exceedingly constraining and at the same time particular and contingent. Foucault's historical investigations aim, in other words, to problematize the limits we understand as imposed upon us. Such investigation immediately leads to the second characteristic of Foucault's philosophical ethos: an "experimental" work that attempts "to grasp the points where change is possible and desirable, and to determine the precise form this change should take" (1984d, 316). Foucault describes this experimental work in terms of situated practical engagements with the limits of the present. The two characteristics of Foucault's modern ethos, then, turn out to be historical problematization and practical experimentation—genealogy and pragmatism.

Foucault is surprisingly clear in this essay about his leanings toward something like a genealogical pragmatism. He there summarizes his philosophical ethos as "a historico-practical test of the limits we may go beyond" (1984d, 316). This test or attitude is historical in that it problematizes the limits through which we have come to constitute ourselves, and it is practical in that it experimentally tests the reality of these limits in an effort to change them. What is historical problematization plus practical experimentation if not pragmatism plus genealogy? At the very end of the essay, Foucault reiterates this dual-aspect characterization of the modern philosophical ethos, which must be "at one and the same time the historical analysis of the limits imposed on us and an experiment with the possibility of going beyond them" (1984d, 319). This, I am urging, is precisely the same dual-aspect conception of philosophical activity as historical and practical made available by pragmatism. Genealogy will historically analyze the conditioning limits of the present, and pragmatism will experimentally test the possibilities for going beyond these limits.

Genealogical Pragmatism and Pragmatist Genealogy

Deep problematization invites sophisticated solutions, and lasting reconstruction requires profound problematics. Genealogy best prepares the way for pragmatism, and pragmatism is the best way to follow up on genealogy. An integrated conception of genealogical pragmatism thus follows quite naturally from the interpretations of genealogy and pragmatism I am offering. Here is a simplified—but not for that reason misleading—way of putting my larger point in this chapter: we should not turn to genealogists such as Foucault if the task before us is that of reconstruction, insofar as his work features scant resources for understanding how we should set about solving problems, and by the same reasoning we should not turn to pragmatists such as Dewey if the task before us is that of throwing our familiar ways of living into doubt, as his work really does not offer much help in understanding how we might work toward such problematization. An even quicker statement of my point: do not look to Foucault if you are trying to fix a problem, and do not look to Dewey if you are trying to problematize an existing solution, but look to both in order to together problematize and reconstruct. Having suggested how we might read both traditions of pragmatism and genealogy in order to attain such a conception of critical inquiry, I would like to conclude this chapter and this book by describing in just a little more detail what this two-part conception of critical inquiry involves.

One way of adding more detail is to frame my explication in light of the existing literature on Foucault and Dewey, a literature that is surprisingly small given the importance of both genealogy and pragmatism for so many aspects of twentieth-century thought. The most important engagement to date with questions concerning the relation between genealogy and pragmatism has been undertaken by John Stuhr (1997, 2003).[35] If we pay close attention to the way in which Stuhr stages the interaction between these two thinkers, his work provides a useful context for future work on Foucault and Dewey, including my work here. Stuhr's argument is not, or at least not usually, that pragmatism and genealogy happen to agree about some important philosophical topic. His argument is better described in terms of the view that pragmatism and genealogy offer compelling mutual challenges to each other, which enable each tradition to dialectically reinforce the other. Here is the most important aspect of Stuhr's genealogical pragmatism: "just as twentieth-century pragmatic theories of inquiry must be transformed by genealogical criticism, so too genealogical criticism must be transformed by attention to the facile gestures it has not rendered problematic or approached pragmatically" (2003, 150). The upshot of playing pragmatism and genealogy off of each other in this way might just be a new philosophical synthesis that stands on its own.

Stuhr's vision of a genealogical pragmatism constitutes a useful frame for thinking about the relations between these two traditions, but thus far his proposal remains more of a scaffolding than a fully worked-out construction. There are at least two ways in which future work might build out Stuhr's resourceful framing. First, one might look backward into the past in order to discern intellectual historical affinities between Dewey and Foucault, which would lend additional plausibility to the view that these two thinkers can complement one another in the present. Second, one might look forward to ways in which novel philosophical positions might be developed that blend the best of genealogy and pragmatism. Both kinds of work are essential for building out a genealogical pragmatism.

As for the first kind of historical work, there is now a small but growing body of research that explores intellectual-historical connections between pragmatism and genealogy. Of particular note is historian James Livingston's (2001, forthcoming) argument that pragmatism initiated a phase of modern thought that culminates, at least for now, in something quite close to genealogy. Also in this vein, Randall Auxier (2002) offers convincing evidence that suggests precise lines of intellectual influence that may have served to connect pragmatism to genealogy. Last, I (forthcoming-a) have argued that pragmatism and genealogy can be understood as offering highly compatible reflections on the status of modernity itself, reflections that moreover help us distinguish both genealogy and pragmatism from more influential but wrongheaded Weberian variants of modernity's interpretation.

The important intellectual historical affinities between pragmatism and genealogy discussed in these works can be complemented by the second more philosophical project of exploring the conceptual connections between these two traditions. For this sort of project, recent work by Paul Rabinow (2003, 2008) provides the most useful orientation. Rabinow's claims about Foucault and Dewey are focused on their descriptions of what might be called the work of thought. Rabinow describes Foucault thus: "the specific diacritic of thought is found . . . in the attempt to achieve a modal change from seeing a situation not only as 'a given' but as 'a question'" (2003, 18). And he describes Dewey in this way: "thinking was a temporal experiment . . . an action called forth and set into motion by a discordancy" such that the aim of thought is always "to rectify" a problematic situation produced by "a disruption" (2003, 16). On the basis of these depictions, both of which I find quite apt, Rabinow concludes that "Foucault's specification of what he means by problematization sounds unexpectedly quite similar to John Dewey's definition of thinking as problem solving" (2003, 48). Of course, there are important divergences between the two, which Rabinow is careful to note in saying that "the extent to which Foucault's practice could be assimilated to a reconstruction (in Dewey's sense) is therefore complicated" (2003, 18). Complicated, complex, and certainly worth considering.

Following the important leads laid down by Stuhr and Rabinow, I am proposing that we now work to bring pragmatism and genealogy closer together by both exploring their intellectual historical interconnections and developing their philosophical affinities. But I wish to be clear about the modality in which I am putting this proposal forward. For I do not find enticing the idea of *assimilating* genealogical problematization to pragmatist reconstruction.[36] What I find compelling rather is the idea of *integrating* the two phases of thought, which I have described as Foucaultian problematization and Deweyan reconstruction. An integration is compelling from the perspective of both traditions insofar as problematization and reconstruction cannot accomplish on their own the level of critical activity that is enabled by their integrated functioning. If we want to connect reconstruction and problematization in a way that advances both traditions of pragmatism and genealogy, then we should seek this connection in the form of philosophical and historical integration rather than in the form of thematic identification and assimilation just insofar as the latter sort of project could too easily connect both traditions without advancing them forward. So my claim is not that Foucault and Dewey were saying the same thing. I am rather claiming that what Foucault said and what Dewey said call for one another. Foucault is the call to Dewey and Dewey is the response to Foucault. At least that is how we should deploy them together today.

I take my approach in this respect to be in keeping with both Rabinow's project and Stuhr's proposal. For I take it that they would find congenial my proposal that we can largely leave to the side the erudite archival task of demonstrating the convergence of intellectual traditions once thought to be disparate. We ought not to attempt to reinforce pragmatism and genealogy by pointing to some unexpected theoretical convergence. We should instead attempt to fashion new forms of inquiry appropriate to the demands of our rapidly transforming contemporary conditions. In fashioning these new forms of inquiry, we can benefit from blending the theoretical, methodological, and conceptual armature featured in pragmatism and genealogy. This is not an attempt to assimilate pragmatism and genealogy to each other. It is an attempt to integrate them as part of the development of novel forms of inquiry. It is in this sense that both pragmatist genealogy and genealogical pragmatism are able to safely remain agnostic about the idea of assimilating pragmatism and genealogy. All we need for our inquiries are integrations of core concepts and theories featured in each tradition. I have provided above interpretations of genealogy and pragmatism that invite the sort of integration of Foucault and Dewey postulated by both Rabinow and Stuhr. These interpretations build out some of the precise elements of this integrated approach, which were available only in the background of the existing literature. These interpretations thus enable us to clearly recognize the importance and value of integrating genealogy and pragmatism into one fluid form of critical inquiry we could call genealogical pragmatism or pragmatist genealogy.

That this new form of critical inquiry yields a valuable approach to contemporary political and cultural criticism can be seen by noting its resonances with Michael Walzer's conception of "connected criticism" described above. Walzer summarizes his conception in terms of three critical tasks: "the critic exposes the false appearances of his own society; he gives expression to his people's deepest sense of how they ought to live; and he insists that there are other forms of falseness and other, equally legitimate, hopes and aspirations" (1998, 232).[37] Foucault provides us with an excellent model of the first task and Dewey of the second, and both of them continually insisted upon the sort of experimental attitude embodied in Walzer's third task. A theoretical apparatus formed by welding parts of Foucault and parts of Dewey together can thus constitute a full-scale critical theory of this sort. Such a full-scale critical theory has been envisioned along similar lines by Seyla Benhabib as a two-part engagement:

> First is the *explanatory-diagnostic* aspect through which the findings and methods of the social sciences are appropriated in such a way as to develop an empirically fruitful analysis of the crisis potential of the present. . . . The second dimension of critical theory is its *anticipatory-utopian* one; this constitutes the more properly normative aspect of critique. When explicating the dysfunctionalities of the present, a critical social theory should always do so in the name of a better future and a more humane society (1986, 226).[38]

My proposal is that genealogy can ably supply the diagnostic aspects and pragmatism the anticipatory aspects of such a philosophical practice of critical inquiry.

To conclude this argument on behalf of genealogical pragmatism, I would like to offer an overview of why both genealogists and pragmatists ought to find this new synthesized form of pragmatist genealogy enticing. In the first place, the very possibility of a fruitful integration of genealogy and pragmatism is made available by each tradition's elaboration of the work of thought in terms of the two-part activity of problematization and reconstruction, or articulating problems and solving problems. Both pragmatism and genealogy have attempted to develop this dual-aspect practice of intellectual inquiry in a way that distinguishes them from most other strands of modern philosophy— though there are of course prominent exceptions, including some of those whose work I have discussed in previous chapters. Although I think it undeniable that these two traditions find both problematization and reconstruction crucial, it is also undeniable that each tradition has thus far done a better job of emphasizing and developing only one of these aspects. My descriptions of genealogy and pragmatism above made it clear that genealogists such as Foucault have focused most of their energy on the problematizing work of historical inquiry, while pragmatists like Dewey have been largely interested in the reconstructive work of philosophical inquiry. Although both Foucault and Dewey understood the value of a historical-philosophical amalgam of these two projects, each in their own work revealed a decided preference, at least most of the time, for only one half of this enterprise. This has led to a persisting lacunae in both approaches, especially insofar as contemporary genealogists and pragmatists are, perhaps all too predictably, quite cautious about straying too far from the paths of their masters. Dewey described reconstruction as a response to a problematic situation but failed to spell out in sufficient detail how we come to recognize situations as problematic. We pragmatists can now affirm that problems do not appear out of nothing—problems have histories. Foucault described problematization as provoking the work of reconstructive thought but failed to engage in detailed reconstructive thought to the satisfaction of even his most charitable critics. We genealogists can now readily assert that problems stand in need of reconstructive responses—that is why we experience them as problematic. What these lacunae in the work of Dewey and Foucault suggest is that Deweyan pragmatism and Foucaultian genealogy stand to gain much by more fully engaging one another.

This process of mutual familiarization and engagement is a central challenge facing contemporary genealogists and pragmatists. Genealogists must learn to take on board the insights of pragmatists, and pragmatists must learn to absorb the strategies practiced by genealogists. Hence the importance, for both traditions, of what I am calling genealogical pragmatism or pragmatist genealogy.

Pragmatism without genealogy has nothing to do, no work to perform, no problem to solve. Genealogy without pragmatism will saddle us with insoluble problems, not get us further, and accomplish very little. It is only by bringing pragmatism and genealogy together that we can enact a truly impressive form of thought that might serve up a good deal of influence in the crucial cultural-critical debates to which pragmatists and genealogists understand themselves to be contributing. The integration of genealogy and pragmatism I have been sketching may indeed be our best available option for reactivating both traditions so as to transform them into effective forms of contemporary cultural criticism. To wield some degree of critical influence over the most salient concerns of our cultural configurations is a fair description of the intellectual aims of both Foucault and Dewey. Contemporary genealogists and pragmatists are well positioned to take this intellectual aim more seriously than is commonly advised in contemporary academic circles. Unfortunately, as things are now, even the most respected members of these circles enjoy, year by year, increasingly little influence in the crucial cultural-critical debates going on around them. Foucault and Dewey would have recognized this as a severe problem for our prevailing forms of intellectual practice. I suggest that the integrated practice of genealogical pragmatism can help us offer a reconstructive response to this most pressing problematic.

Concluding Remark

The proposal I have put forward for renewing pragmatism at the present moment is just one of many possible ways of furthering those contemporary critical inquiries that are developed under the auspices of a reconstructive sensibility. At the core of my proposal for a renewal of pragmatism is the thought that the time is now propitious for a reconsideration of the work of philosophy. We should now start envisioning our practices of critique and inquiry as processes whose forms are temporal and whose contents are historical. This is a transitionalist conception of philosophy. Reconstructive philosophy takes time when it involves itself in history. This is to our advantage. For a transitionalist philosophy is the only philosophy that can meliorate the historical-temporal streams in which we fragile humans ever flow forth. We bear the burden of our witherings as we are witness to our blossomings. We might allow ourselves not to neglect the transitions by which we become.

NOTES

1. Transitionalism, Meliorism, and Cultural Criticism

1. The best of this work includes Rorty (1989a, 1994a, 2002), West (1989), Stuhr (1997, 2003), and Green (1999, 2008). Other recent contributions to this vein include Shade (2001), McKenna (2001), Stout (2004), Saito (2005), Westbrook (2005), and Fishman and McCarthy (2007).

2. On the usual attribution of individualism to Emerson, see the summary exposition in a review by Harold Bloom (1984). In recent years, a number of scholars have raised problems with such an interpretation, including Kateb (1992, 98), Bercovitch (1993, 307–352), Sklansky (2002, 38–52), Lysaker (2003), Cavell (2003, 2004), Saito (2001, 2005), and Stout (2004, 19–41).

3. For more on democratic freedom as "personal" in James, see Koopman (2005).

4. Work on Rorty's meliorism is often quite circuitous, as instanced in Festenstein (2001), Marshall (2001), Peters (2001), and Talisse (2001); for a more fruitful treatment, see Voparil (2006).

5. See Rorty (2005, 40–41).

6. See Rorty (1982, 1986, 1995a, 1998a, 1998c).

7. That Emerson is best read as a cultural critic in this sense is widely affirmed. For an interpretation of my other pragmatists in these terms, see Cotkin (1990) on James, Ryan (1995) on Dewey, and in some respects Gross (2008) on Rorty. Broad interpretations of pragmatism in this cultural critical sense can be discerned in the work of other contemporary pragmatists besides Rorty, most obviously in West (1989) but also in McDermott (1976), Stuhr (1997), Hickman (2001), and Glaude (2007).

8. Draft copies indicate that Rorty began this piece while he was at Wellesley and continued working on it when he moved to Princeton. For further discussion of this piece, see Gross (2008, 162ff.). For generous permission to cite this unpublished draft, I kindly thank Mary Varney Rorty, who also informs me that this essay is scheduled for publication in a forthcoming edition of *Philosophy and the Mirror of Nature* with Princeton University Press.

9. Cf. Voparil (2006, 176). For reservations about Gross's interpretation, see Lewis-Krause (2009).

10. See Jacoby (1987), Posner (2002), and Etzioni and Bowditch (2006). See also recent exchanges over the meaning of public thought by Jacoby (2008), Drezner (2008), and Hitchens (2008), and the neat summary in the *Times* by Gewen (2008).

11. Cf. Rorty (1994b, 254).

12. For an early statement of just one aspect of this project in its philosophical perspective, where later iterations will involve ample historical and anthropological forays as well as much additional philosophical work, see Koopman (2007).

13. Rabinow continues to develop these notions in a direction that promisingly points toward both Foucauldian problematization and pragmatist reconstruction. See, for instance, Rabinow (forthcoming).

14. Among his major writings, Peirce's "Evolutionary Love" (1893) comes closest to a cultural criticism of the science-religion impasse; for a more positive evaluation of Peirce on religion, see Anderson (2004).

15. Cf. Misak (2000) and Talisse (2004, 2005).

16. Cf. Haslanger (2000) instructively combining aporematic metaphysics and feminist critique.

17. See, for example, Glaude (2007) and Green (2008).

2. Transitionalism in the Pragmatist Tradition

1. Cf. Gavin (1992, 87).

2. This idea permeates Dewey's works from early (1888) to late (1939b).

3. See also Brandom (2002, 32, 52, 210); the fullest account of historicist pragmatism in Brandom is offered in the context of a discussion of Hegel (2002, 210–234).

4. More recently, Melvin Rogers follows Glaude, and West before him, in discerning in Dewey's pragmatist philosophy "an understanding of humility that does not extinguish hope" (2008, xiii).

5. I would also insist that more valuable treatments of these issues can be found elsewhere, for example in Hoy (2009), on the phenomenology of temporality, and Turetzky (1998), on the philosophy of time.

6. A very incomplete selection of other contemporary classicopragmatist work emphasizing transitionalist themes would include Seigfried (1990), Shusterman (1997),

Colapietro (1998b), Eldridge (1998), Rosenthal (2000), McKenna (2001), Sullivan (2007), and Green (2008).

7. See Shook (2008) for a much more detailed pragmatist family tree.

3. Three Waves of Pragmatism

1. On these debates in political theory, see Bohman (1998) and Talisse (2005).

2. On these debates in history, see Toews (1987), Scott (1991), and Ankersmitt (1996); in anthropology, see the collection by Clifford and Marcus (1986).

3. It was Rorty (1979) who first convincingly drew out the pragmatist consequences of Sellars's critique of givenism, representationalism, and antifoundationalism. For a lucid summary of the continuing relevance of this critique for pragmatism, see Talisse and Aikin (2008, 40ff.).

4. See Dewey (1925).

5. See James (1885, 31; 1904b, 203; 1904c, 51; and especially 1909b and 1911); cf. Putnam (1990a, 242ff.; 1997, 175ff.).

6. James (1907, 103; 1908a, 29; 1908b, 121) reveal three such isolated passages.

7. On transcendentality in Peirce and Kant, see Pihlström (2003) and Apel (1967).

8. Cf. Putnam (1990a, 242).

9. This argument is summarized in Rorty (1977b). Note that although Donovan (1995) describes Rorty in similar terms, he does not tie his account into many of the broader themes in the intellectual history of pragmatism that I here discuss.

10. See Rorty (1998c) on Brandom (1994).

11. Rorty's best critics on these points are Hilary Putnam (1988), Richard Bernstein (1992a, 1992b), Barry Allen (2000a, 2000b), Richard Shusterman (2001), and Joseph Margolis (2002a, 2002b).

12. However, Rorty has on occasion endorsed the stronger view that all awareness is linguistic (1979, 182).

13. In addition to the penultimate section of chapter 6 below, see my earlier argument in Koopman (2004).

14. Cf. Margolis (1993, 1999a).

15. See Margolis (1998, 2007).

16. See Margolis (2002a, 2002b).

17. For a different view, see Pihlström (2003).

4. Knowledge as Transitioning

1. On connections to Dewey, see favorable remarks by Bourdieu (1992, 122). Recent path-clearing work that deserves attention includes contributions by Shusterman

(1999b), Margolis (1999b), other essays in Shusterman (1999a), and Colapietro (2004c); see also from a more sociological angle Emirbayer and Schneiderhan (forthcoming).

2. Cf. Bernard Williams (2000; 2002, 38ff.). See also on these matters quasi-pragmatist Michael Williams (1986, 223).

3. See more recently Rorty (1995b, 96ff.) and classically Rorty (1979, chap. 4), where the "crucial premise of this argument is that we understand knowledge when we understand the social justification of belief, and thus have no need to view it as accuracy of representation" (170).

4. Contrast Rorty's own claim to the contrary: "I tossed in Gadamer at the end of the book because I happened to be reading him when I was writing the final chapters" (2003, 228). But Raymond Geuss (2008) differently remembers Rorty's reading of Gadamer in those years as quite important to him. None of this should be taken as a denial of crucial differences between Rorty and Gadamer as discussed by Wachterhauser (2002).

5. On the hermeneutic turn in Heidegger and Gadamer, see Hoy (1993, 1997), Grondin (1999), and Madison (2003).

6. On the Habermas-Gadamer debate, see Jay (1982).

7. Cf. Gadamer (1960, 547); on this oft-misunderstood point see Madison (1997, 352ff.) and Grondin (1999, 128ff.).

8. Cf. Zagzebski (1996) and Sosa (2007).

9. Cf. Axtell (1997, 2006).

10. This criticism is offered on a local (but not global) scale by those working in the nascent program of "experimental philosophy," as in Weinberg, Nichols, and Stitch (2001) on Gettier cases. For a reflective take on experimental philosophy, see Appiah (2008); for a pragmatist take, see Koopman (forthcoming-f).

11. Cf. Peirce (1892b, 350), revising this view.

12. For work in this vein see, among others, Rosenthal (2000) and Colapietro (2004b, 2005) See also Johnson (2007) which richly develops a similar perspective that focuses on a pragmatist account of meaning without employing the vocabulary of semiotics. This work contains ample resources for the project I am proposing, but unfortunately it came to my attention too late to seriously incorporate into the perspective I develop here.

13. Cf. Putnam and Putnam (1989) and H. Putnam (1999).

14. See Jay (2005, 9–39) on premodern experience as experimental process versus modern experience as atemporal state.

5. Ethics as Perfecting

1. The best of this work is that of MacIntyre (1981) and Nussbaum (1986).

2. For a best recent attempt to save utilitarianism, see Brandt (1992).

3. Early statements of this general criticism were offered by Hegel (1821, §29R) and Mill (1861). For a best recent attempt to overcome this difficulty, see Korsgaard (1996).

4. Cf. Schneewind (1998, 487) and Arendt (1970, 17, 49).

5. Rorty here echoes James (1891) and Dewey (1930c).

6. Cf. Scheffler (1982) on hybrid theory.

7. Invaluable for an understanding of the similarities and differences between pragmatism and perfectionism is recent work by Saito (2005, 2001) and Goodman (2005b).

8. The passage in question is in Cavell (1998, 216), quoting Dewey (1938b, LW13.59), though it should be noted that in the context of the quoted passage, Dewey appears to be ironically attempting to diffuse the very criticism Cavell is mounting.

9. See my criticisms of the pragmatist conception of doubt developed in the final chapter below; references to the key arguments in the literature are cited there.

10. Encouraging in this regard is that Cavell has recently noted a potential connection between Emerson and Dewey (2003, 7–9), even if he continues to express suspicions (2005b, 93; 2005d, 158–162, 170–171).

11. Cf. Putnam (1990c), Kloppenberg (1996), and Gavin (2007).

12. Cf. Cavell (2005c, 120).

13. Cf. Cavell (1979).

14. Cavell's perfectionism, like my pragmatist perfectionism, differs on this point from other characterizations of perfectionism as narrowly teleological, such as those of Leibniz and Spinoza as described by Schneewind (1998) or, more recently, that developed by Hurka (1993).

15. There has been somewhat of a resurgence of pragmatist ethics recently. Important new veins of contribution have been struck by Rorty (1989a, 1994a), R. A. Putnam (1990, 1997b, 2006), and Pappas (1993, 1994, 1997a, 1997b, 1998, 2003, 2008); see also work by Alexander (1993), Welchman (1995), Honneth (1998a, 1998b), Schrader (1998), Lekan (2002), Fesmire (2003), and H. Putnam (2004a, 2004b).

16. Cf. Gouinlock (1978, 220; 1972, 295), Pappas (1994, 84; 2008, 45), Putnam (1990, 72–76), and Lekan (2002, 109–114).

17. Pappas here is running between the scientific focus of Welchman (1995) and the aesthetic focus of Fesmire (2003).

18. Cf. Dewey (1891, 1930c, 1932).

19. Cf. James (1890, II.565–566).

20. Exceptions that catch the right tone include Pappas (2008, 146ff.), Stuhr (1997, 178ff.), Suckiel (1996, 105ff.), and McDermott (1976, 99ff.).

21. Cf. Bird (1997, 262).

6. Politics as Progressing

1. Cf. Rawls (1971, 8; 2001, 13); on idealization in Rawls, see O'Neill (1989).

2. Cf. Rawls (1993, 45).

3. The most consistent statement of such a conception of politics is found in Oakeshott (1947). Hayek (1960) is far better in this respect, although he is properly not a "conservative"

so much as he is an "evolutionist liberal." For a fuller discussion of Hayek's relevance for but ultimate incoherence with pragmatism, see Koopman (forthcoming-c).

4. Cf. Rorty (2002a).

5. Cf. Williams (2006c) on Collingwood.

6. Cf. Williams (1999, 2002).

7. I consider Williams's views on these matters at greater length in Koopman (forthcoming-d); key texts for my explication include Williams (1992, 1999, 2000, 2002), and comparisons are made to Hampshire (1983) and Collingwood (1939).

8. Cf. Williams (2002, 226ff.).

9. See Williams (1989; 2002, 128ff.; 2000, 184ff.) visibly playing up disagreements with Rorty. See also Fricker (2000) drawing an interesting but mistaken contrast between "confidence" and "irony" when the proper terms of comparison are "confidence" and "hope."

10. Rorty (2002b) affirmed this convergence; for other comparisons, see Putnam (2004c), Allen (2003, 2008), and less instructively Sleat (2007).

11. Cf. Rorty (1989a, 1998b) and Williams (1985, 2002).

12. For helpful commentary, see Brown (2001, 2005) and Sluga (2005).

13. Cf. Rajchman (1985, 2000) and Walzer (1983).

14. For other recent pragmatist criticisms along these lines, see Pappas (2008, 251ff.), Vanderveen (2007), Brooks (forthcoming), and Ralston (forthcoming). For an argument describing how Jamesian pragmatism can be of potential use to deliberative democrats in addressing these problems, see Smith (2007).

15. Cf. Westbrook (2005) for a Deweyan view favorably disposed to Peircean deliberativism.

16. See also other critical essays in Macedo (1999) and Elster (1998) as well as an early piece by Jay (1992) anticipating many of these later concerns.

17. Cf. Young (1996; 2000, 36–51).

18. Talisse (2005, 132–140) offers a direct reply, which fails to address the central lesson of Young's discussion insofar as her argument is merely dismissed as "incomplete" (139) on this point.

19. I do not, however, find that such overemphasis on immediate, face-to-face democracy persists in Green's recent excellent book (2008).

20. Green (1999) and McKenna (2001) engage Young's city ideal in transitionalist terms emphasizing democratic transformation.

21. Cf. Pappas (2008, 231, 247ff.) and Green (2008; 1999, 9, 33ff.).

7. Critical Inquiry as Genealogical and Pragmatist

1. An argument for an integration of pragmatism and genealogy from the other perspective, namely that of genealogy, is a central subject of my next book, *Genealogy*

as Problematization, where I take up Foucault, Williams, Nietzsche, Deleuze, Hacking, Habermas, and of course James, Dewey, and Rorty.

2. Cf. Dewey (1933, 100/LW8.195).

3. See Dewey (1920, 1933, 1938a).

4. For one way of drawing these distinctions, see Dewey (1925).

5. Among the most important contributions to both sides of this debate are Royce (1891), Hook (1960), Weinstein (1982), Putnam (1990c), West (1993), Kloppenberg (1996), Cavell (1998), Saito (2003), Colapietro (2004a), Gavin (2007), and Glaude (2007).

6. Among the most influential statements of this critique are Royce (1891), Bourne (1917), Mumford (1926), Niebuhr (1932), Horkheimer (1947), Russell (1950), Mills (1964), and Diggins (1994); the current best line of reply to this criticism is given by Hickman (2007, 241–254; 2001, 65–82; 1990, 166–195).

7. For contrasting interpretations of the role that metaphysics should play in pragmatism, see the debate between Rorty (1977a, 1985) and Sleeper (1985).

8. Cf. Dewey (1929, LW4.144ff.), but for an example of persisting ambiguity, see Dewey (1905, 1906).

9. Cf. Dewey (1938a, LW12.109–112; 1933, 107–109/LW8.200–203).

10. See Dewey's generous acknowledgment of Peirce on the first page of his *Logic* (1938a, LW12.3) and the obvious influence of Peirce on the introductory remarks in *How We Think* (1933, 12/LW8.120).

11. Douglas Anderson (1995, 98) argues that along with surprise Peirce affirms socialization as productive of doubt. Even if so, my main point remains: Peirce offers little in the way of helping us understand how to orient ourselves toward inquiries that would produce doubt. His model of surprise-or-society conceptualizes doubt as being forced upon us: we might call this a banana-or-bludgeon model of doubt according to which doubt is either like slipping on a banana peel or like being beaten by a neighbor's bludgeon. I am urging that we model doubt as problematization such that doubt is more like the product of careful inquiry in which we aim to learn something new.

12. Cf. Brandom (1994, 176ff.; 2000d), Williams (1996, 2008), and for summary Axtell (2008) and Fricker (2008), the latter resonating especially well with my transitionalism in its call for expanding epistemology along the temporal dimension of knowledge, as also developed in Fricker (forthcoming).

13. On curiosity, see Blumenberg (1966, 229ff.) and Rabinow (1996, 15ff.).

14. As Kaag here explicates Cabot's original philosophic contributions, there appear to be generous doses of transitional themes in her work.

15. Habermas develops this point in the course of elaborating a neopragmatist political deliberativism (1992, 304–314, 379–384), which on many key points he traces back to Dewey (304, 316) and which he argues needs to be supplemented by parts of Nancy Fraser's work (1981), which could be regarded as in certain respects inspired by Foucault.

16. This perhaps offers a better way of situating Dewey's metaphysical-sounding claims that nature is constantly perched between stability and danger: "This mixture

gives poignancy to existence. If existence were either completely necessary or completely contingent, there would be neither comedy nor tragedy in life, nor need of the will to live" (1929, 194).

17. Cf. Habermas (1985); for his alternative account of problematization, see Habermas (1992, 379–384).

18. Cf. Fraser (1994, 122), Bernstein (1992a, 26–9), McCarthy (2004, 164), and especially Allen (2008).

19. Others before me have emphasized the importance of combining history and philosophy in order to put pragmatism to efficient work; see most notably Livingston (2001) and Green (2008).

20. Cf. Kloppenberg (1986) and Rorty (1989a).

21. For a discussion of some of the historiographical issues involved in such a pragmatist use of history, see Koopman (forthcoming-b), building on Dewey (1938a) and Randall (1958).

22. Dewey's (1939c) response to Randall's essay was very favorable.

23. Randall (1958, 95, 146) explicitly notes that historiography thus conceived may enable us to overcome a metaphysical givenism that refuses to take problems as historical.

24. For a valuable first step in this direction, see Colapietro (forthcoming).

25. Cf. Auxier (2002, 86ff.), drawing the link.

26. Cf. Foucault (1971b, 1984d).

27. For doubts about a connection between pragmatism and genealogy, see Rorty (1981), West (1989), and Diggins (1994); for a more complete literature survey, see Koopman (forthcoming-e).

28. Cf. Foucault (1983, 1984a, 1984e). The central aim of my previously mentioned forthcoming book *Genealogy as Problematization* is to make sense of Foucault's project in terms of what he called "problematization." Most of what follows in this section on Foucault is developed at much greater length there. Until such time as that work is published, I refer the reader to Koopman (2009), where these points are developed in greater detail, in the context of an argument contrasting Foucault to Nietzsche and Williams.

29. For a classic statement of the genetic fallacy, see Cohen and Nagel (1934). For important pragmatist responses to this critique, see Wiener (1946) and Lavine (1962). The best discussion of the genetic fallacy in (Nietzsche's) genealogy is by Alexander Nehamas (1985, 107ff.), but see also the discussion of Hume and Nietzsche by David Hoy (1986b, 32ff.). Paul Loeb (1995) argues that the genetic fallacy itself begs the question against Nietzsche's revaluation of values.

30. See Nancy Fraser (1981), Richard Rorty (1981), Michael Walzer (1983), Charles Taylor (1984), Jürgen Habermas (1985), Thomas McCarthy (1990), Alasdair MacIntyre (1990), and even Foucault's admiring biographer James Miller (1993).

31. Cf. Foucault (1971a).

32. This is not to say that historians have widely embraced Foucault's work, for they have not, as noted by Megill (1987) and as evidenced by the essays in Goldstein (1994).

For recent examples of useful historical-philosophical work in a Foucaultian vein, see Rabinow (1989), Hacking (1990, 2002), Rose (1999), and Davidson (2001).

33. Cf. Schaff (2004, 65ff.).

34. Note that this interview bears a striking resemblance to the discussion of problematization in the methodological "Introduction" to *The Use of Pleasure* (Foucault 1984a, 5–13).

35. In addition to work discussed below, other helpful counterweights to the prevailing negative assessment of the possibility of a genealogical pragmatism include Lentricchia (1988), Bernstein (1992a), Posnock (1992), and Colapietro (1998a). For a nearly complete survey of the literature on this subject, see Koopman (forthcoming-g).

36. Cf. Reynolds (2004).

37. Walzer unfortunately misinterprets Foucault and avoids Dewey in this book.

38. Benhabib unfortunately also misreads Foucault and neglects Dewey here.

BIBLIOGRAPHY

Addams, Jane. 1902. *Democracy and Social Ethics*. New York: Macmillan, 1902.
——. 1922. "v Reactions in Time of War." In *The Jane Addams Reader*, ed. Jean Bethke Elshtain. New York: Basic Books, 2002.
Aikin, Scott. 2009. "Pragmatism, Experience, and the Given." *Human Affairs* 19, no. 1, (2009): 19–27.
Alexander, Thomas. 1987. *John Dewey's Theory of Art, Experience, and Nature*. Albany: SUNY Press, 1987.
——. 1993. "Dewey and the Moral Imagination: Beyond Putman and Rorty Toward a Postmodern Ethics." *Transactions of the Charles S. Peirce Society* 29, no. 3 (Summer).
Allen, Amy. 2008. *The Politics of Our Selves*. New York: Columbia University Press, 2008.
Allen, Barry. 1993. *Truth in Philosophy*. Cambridge: Harvard University Press, 1993.
——. 2000a. "What Was Epistemology?" In Brandom 2000a.
——. 2000b. "Is It Pragmatism? Rorty and the American Tradition." In *A Pragmatist's Progress: Richard Rorty and American Intellectual History*, ed. John Pettegrew. Lanham, Md.: Rowman and Littlefield, 2000.
——. 2003. "Another New Nietzsche." *History and Theory* 42 (October): 363–377.
——. 2004. *Knowledge and Civilization*. Boulder, Colo.: Westview Press.
——. 2008. "A More Laudable Truthfulness." *Common Knowledge* 14, no. 2: 193–200.
Anderson, Douglas. 1995. *Strands of System*. West Lafayette, Ind.: Purdue University Press.

——. 2004. "Peirce's Common Sense Marriage of Religion and Science." In Misak 2004b.

Anderson, Elizabeth. 2006. "The Epistemology of Democracy." *Episteme: A Journal of Social Epistemology* 3, no. 1–2: 8–22.

Ankersmit, Frank R. 1996. "Can We Experience the Past?" In *History-Making*, ed. Rolf Torstendahl and Irmline Veit-Brause. Stockholm: Coronet.

Anscombe, G. E. M. 1958. "Modern Moral Philosophy." *Philosophy* 33 (January): 1–19.

Apel, Karl-Otto. 1967. *Charles S. Peirce: From Pragmatism to Pragmaticism.* Trans. John Michael Krois. Atlantic Highlands, N.J.: Humanities Press, 1995.

Appiah, Kwame Anthony. 2008. *Experiments in Ethics.* Cambridge: Harvard University Press.

Arendt, Hannah. 1970. *Lectures on Kant's Political Philosophy.* Ed. Ronald Beiner. Chicago: University of Chicago Press, 1992.

Auxier, Randall. 2002. "Foucault, Dewey, and the History of the Present." *Journal of Speculative Philosophy* 16, no. 2 (Summer): 75–102.

Axtell, Guy. 1997. "Recent Work on Virtue Epistemology." *American Philosophical Quarterly* 34, no. 1 (January): 1–26.

——. 2000. "Virtue Theory and the Fact/Value Problem." In *Knowledge, Belief, and Character: Readings in Virtue Epistemology*, ed. G. Axtell. Lanham, Md.: Rowman and Littlefield.

——. 2006. "The Present Dilemma in Philosophy." *Contemporary Pragmatism* 3, no. 1 (June): 15–36.

——. 2008. "Expanding Epistemology: A Responsibilist Approach." *Philosophical Papers* 37, no. 1 (March): 51–87.

Baldwin, James. 1955. *Notes of a Native Son.* Repr. Boston: Beacon, 1984.

——. 1963. *The Fire Next Time.* New York: Dell.

Barzun, Jacques. 1983. *A Stroll with William James.* New York: Harper and Row.

Benhabib, Seyla. 1986. *Critique, Norm, and Utopia.* New York: Columbia University Press.

Bentham, Jeremy. 1789. *The Principles of Morals and Legislation.* Repr. New York: Hafner, 1948.

Bercovitch, Sacvan. 1993. *The Rites of Assent: Transformations in the Symbolic Construction of America.* New York: Routledge.

Bernstein, Richard. 1966. *John Dewey.* Repr. Atascadero, Calif.: Ridgeview, 1981.

——. 1992a. *The New Constellation.* Cambridge: MIT Press.

——. 1992b. "The Resurgence of Pragmatism." *Social Research* 59, no. 4 (Winter): 813–840.

——. 2007. "The New Pragmatists." *Graduate Faculty Philosophy Journal* 28, no. 2 (Spring): 3–38.

Bird, Graham. 1997. "Moral Philosophy and the Development of Morality." In Putnam 1997a.

Bloom, Harold. 1984. "Mr. America." *The New York Review of Books* (November 22).

Blumenberg, Hans. 1966. *The Legitimacy of the Modern Age.* 2nd ed. Trans. Robert Wallace. Repr. Cambridge: MIT Press, 1983.

Bohman, James. 1998. "Survey Article: The Coming of Age of Deliberative Democracy." *Journal of Political Philosophy* 6, no. 4: 400–425.

——. 2007. *Democracy Across Borders: From Dêmos to Dêmoi.* Cambridge: MIT Press, 2007.

Bourdieu, Pierre. 1980. *The Logic of Practice.* Trans. Richard Nice. Stanford: Stanford University Press.

Bourdieu, Pierre. 1997. *Pascalian Meditations.* Trans. Richard Nice. Stanford: Stanford University Press.

Bourdieu, Pierre, and Loïc Wacquant. 1992. *An Invitation to Reflexive Sociology.* Chicago: University of Chicago Press.

Bourne, Randolph. 1913. "The Life of Irony." In Bourne 1977.

——. 1917. "Twilight of Idols." In Bourne 1977.

——. 1977. *The Radical Will.* Ed. Olaf Hansen. New York: Urizen.

Brandom, Robert. 1994. *Making It Explicit.* Cambridge: Harvard University Press.

——, ed. 2000a. *Rorty and His Critics.* Oxford: Blackwell.

——. 2000b. "Vocabularies of Pragmatism: Synthesizing Naturalism and Historicism." In Brandom 2000a.

——. 2000c. *Articulating Reasons: An Introduction to Inferentialism.* Cambridge: Harvard University Press.

——. 2000d. "Fighting Skepticism with Skepticism: Supervaluational Epistemology, Semantic Autonomy, and Natural Kind Skepticism." *Facta Philosophica* 2, no. 2: 163–178.

——. 2002. *Tales of the Mighty Dead.* Cambridge: Harvard University Press.

——. 2004. "The Pragmatist Enlightenment (and Its Problematic Semantics)." *European Journal of Philosophy* 12, no.1 (April): 1–16.

——. 2008. *Between Saying and Doing: Towards an Analytic Pragmatism.* Oxford: Oxford University Press, 2008. Available online at http://www.pitt.edu/~brandom/locke/index.html.

Brandt, Richard. 1992. *Morality, Utilitarianism, and Rights.* Cambridge: Cambridge University Press.

Brooks, Thom. Forthcoming. "A Critique of Pragmatism and Deliberative Democracy." *Transactions of the Charles S. Peirce Society.* Available online at http://papers.ssrn.com/sol3/papers.cfm?abstract_id=1107369.

Brown, Wendy. 2001. *Politics out of History.* Princeton: Princeton University Press.

——. 2005. *Edgework.* Princeton: Princeton University Press.

Cavell, Stanley. 1979. *The Claim of Reason.* Oxford: Oxford University Press.

——. 1986. "Hope Against Hope." In Cavell 2003.

——. 1990. *Conditions Handsome and Unhandsome: The Constitution of Emersonian Perfectionism.* Chicago: University of Chicago Press.

———. 1998. "What's the Use of Calling Emerson a Pragmatist?" In Cavell 2003.

———. 2003. *Emerson's Transcendental Etudes.* Ed. David Justin Hodge. Stanford: Stanford University Press.

———. 2004. *Cities of Words: Pedagogical Letters on a Register of the Moral Life.* Cambridge: Belknap.

———. 2005a. *Philosophy the Day After Tomorrow.* Cambridge: Belknap.

———. 2005b. "Henry James Returns to America and to Shakespeare." In Cavell 2005a.

———. 2005c. "Philosophy the Day After Tomorrow." In Cavell 2005a.

———. 2005d. "Responses." In Goodman 2005a.

Clifford, James, and George Marcus. 1986. *Writing Culture: The Poetics and Politics of Ethnography.* Oxford: Oxford University Press.

Cohen, Joshua. 1993. "Moral Pluralism and Political Consensus." In *The Idea of Democracy,* ed. Copp, Hampton, and Roemer. Cambridge: Cambridge University Press.

Cohen, Morris, and Ernest Nagel. 1934. *An Introduction to Logic and Scientific Method.* New York: Harcourt.

Colapietro, Vincent. 1998a. "American Evasions of Foucault." *Southern Journal of Philosophy* 36, no. 3 (Fall): 329–351.

———. 1998b. "Entangling Alliances and Critical Traditions: Reclaiming the Possibilities of Critique." *Journal of Speculative Philosophy* 12, no. 2: 114–133.

———. 2004a. "The Question of Voice and the Limits of Pragmatism: Emerson, Dewey, and Cavell." *Metaphilosophy* 35, no. 1/2 (January): 178–201.

———. 2004b. "The Routes of Significance: Reflections on Peirce's Theory of Interpretants." *Cognitio* 5, no. 1 (January): 11–27.

———. 2004c. "Doing—and Undoing—the Done Thing: Dewey and Bourdieu on Habituation, Agency, and Transformation." *Contemporary Pragmatism* 1, no. 2 (December): 65–93.

———. 2005. "Portrait of a Historicist: An Alternative Reading of Peircean Semiotic." In *Semiotics 2003,* ed. R. Williamson, L. Sbrocchi, and J. Deely. New York: Legas, 2005.

———. Forthcoming. "Historical Displacements and Situated Narratives: Recovering History by (Re)Reading Randall."

Collingwood, R. G. 1939. *An Autobiography.* Repr. Oxford: Oxford University Press, 1970.

Commager, Henry Steele. 1950. *The American Mind.* New Haven, Conn.: Yale University Press.

Cormier, Harvey. 2001. *The Truth Is What Works: William James, Pragmatism, and the Seed of Death.* Lanham, Md.: Rowman and Littlefield.

Cotkin, George. 1990. *William James: Public Philosopher.* Chicago: University of Illinois Press.

Curti, Merle. 1943. *The Growth of American Thought.* 3d edition. Repr. New York: Harper and Row, 1964.

Davidson, Arnold. 2001. *The Emergence of Sexuality: Historical Epistemology and the Formation of Concepts*. Cambridge: Harvard University Press.

Davidson, Donald. 1974. "On the Very Idea of a Conceptual Scheme." In *Inquiries Into Truth and Interpretation*, by D. Davidson. Repr. Oxford: Clarendon, 1985.

Dewey, John. 1969–1990. *The Complete Works of John Dewey* including *The Early Works* (EW1–5), *The Middle Works* (MW1–15), *and The Later Works* (LW1–17). Ed. Jo Ann Boydston et. al. Carbondale: Southern Illinois University. Dewey references are cited as follows: page numbers given for the earlier editions of the work before the slash and page numbers for the complete works edition after the slash; if only one page is cited, it is from the complete works.

——. 1888. "The Ethics of Democracy." In Dewey EW1.

——. 1891. "Moral Theory and Practice." In Dewey EW3.

——. 1903a. *Studies in Logical Theory*. In Dewey MW2.

——. 1903b. "Emerson: The Philosopher of Democracy." In Dewey MW3.

——. 1905. "The Postulate of Immediate Empiricism." In Dewey MW3.

——. 1906. "The Experimental Theory of Knowledge." In Dewey MW3.

——. 1915a. "The Logic of Judgments of Practice." In Dewey 1916a and Dewey MW10.

——. 1915b. "The Existence of the World as a Logical Problem." In Dewey 1916a and Dewey MW10.

——. 1916a. *Essays in Experimental Logic*. Repr. New York: Dover Press, 1958.

——. 1916b. "Introduction" to Dewey 1916a and in Dewey MW10.

——. 1916c. *Democracy and Education*. In Dewey MW9. Repr. New York: Free Press, 1966.

——. 1917. "The Need for a Recovery of Philosophy." In Dewey MW10.

——. 1919. "Syllabus of Eight Lectures on 'Problems of Philosophic Reconstruction.'" In Dewey MW11.

——. 1920. *Reconstruction in Philosophy*. Enlarged ed. In Dewey MW12. Repr. Boston: Beacon, 1948.

——. 1922. *Human Nature and Conduct*. In Dewey MW14.

——. 1925. *Experience and Nature*. In Dewey LW1. Repr. New York: Dover Press, 1958.

——. 1927. *The Public and Its Problems*. In Dewey LW2. Repr. New York: Swallow Press, 1954.

——. 1928. "Philosophy and Civilization." In Dewey LW3.

——. 1929. *The Quest for Certainty*. In Dewey LW4.

——. 1930a. *Individualism Old and New*. In Dewey LW5.

——. 1930b. "Qualitative Thought." In Dewey LW5.

——. 1930c. "Three Independent Factors in Morals." In Dewey LW5.

——. 1930d. *The Sources of a Science of Education*. In Dewey LW5.

——. 1933. *How We Think*. In Dewey LW8 and MW6.

——. 1934. *Art as Experience*. In Dewey LW10.

——. 1935. *Liberalism and Social Action*. Repr. New York: Capricon, 1963.

——. 1938a. *Logic: The Theory of Inquiry.* In Dewey LW12.

——. 1938b. *Experience and Education.* In Dewey LW13.

——. 1939a. *Freedom and Culture.* Repr. New York: Capricorn, 1963.

——. 1939b. "Creative Democracy—The Task Before Us." In Dewey LW14.

——. 1939c. "Experience, Knowledge, and Value: A Rejoinder." In Dewey LW14.

——. 1940. "Time and Individuality." In Dewey LW14.

——. 1945. "Addams." In Dewey LW15.

Dewey, John, and Arthur Bentley. 1949. *Knowing and the Known.* In Dewey LW16.

Dewey, John, and James Hayden Tufts. 1932. *Ethics.* In Dewey LW7.

Dickstein, Morris, ed. 1998. *The Revival of Pragmatism.* Durham, N.C.: Duke University Press.

Diggins, John Patrick. 1994. *The Promise of Pragmatism.* Chicago: University of Chicago Press.

Donovan, Rickard. 1995. "Rorty's Pragmatism and the Linguistic Turn." In *Pragmatism: From Progressivism to Postmodernism*, ed. Robert Hollinger and David Depew. Westport, Conn.: Praeger, 1995.

Drezner, Daniel W. 2008. "Public Intellectuals 2.0." Available online at http://daniel-drezner.com/blog/?p=3777.

Egginton, William, and Mike Sandbothe. 2004. *The Pragmatic Turn in Philosophy: Contemporary Engagements Between Analytic and Continental Thought.* Albany: SUNY Press.

Eldridge, Michael. 1998. *Transforming Experience: John Dewey's Cultural Instrumentalism.* Nashville: Vanderbilt University Press.

Elster, Jon, ed. 1998. *Deliberative Democracy.* Cambridge: Cambridge University Press, 1998.

Estlund, David. 2001. "Deliberation Down and Dirty: Must Political Expression Be Civil?" In *The Boundaries of Freedom of Expression and Order in American Democracy*, ed. Hensley. Kent, Ohio: Kent State University Press, 2001.

Emerson, Ralph Waldo. 1838. "An Address" (Harvard Divinity School Address). In Emerson 2000.

——. 1841. *Essays: First Series.* In Emerson 2000.

——. 1844. *Essays: Second Series.* In Emerson 2000.

——. 1868. "Quotation and Originality." In *Ralph Waldo Emerson: Essays and Lectures.* New York: Library of America, 1983.

——. 1960. *The Journals and Miscellaneous Notebooks of Ralph Waldo Emerson.* Ed. William H. Gilman et al. Cambridge: Harvard University Press.

——. 2000. *The Essential Writings of Ralph Waldo Emerson.* Ed. Brooks Atkinson. New York: Modern Library.

Emirbayer, Mustafa, and Erik Schneiderhan. Forthcoming. "Dewey and Bourdieu." In *Bourdieuian Theory and Historical Analysis*, ed. Philip Gorski.

Etzioni, Amitai, and Alyssa Bowditch, eds. 2006. *Public Intellectuals, An Endangered Species?* Lanham, Md.: Rowman and Littlefield.

Fesmire, Steve. 2003. *John Dewey and Moral Imagination: Pragmatism in Ethics.* Bloomington: Indiana University Press.

Festenstein, Matthew. 2001. "Pragmatism, Social Democracy, and Political Argument." In Festenstein and Thompson 2001.

Festenstein, Matthew, and Simon Thompson, eds. 2001. *Richard Rorty: Critical Dialogues.* New York: Polity.

Fisch, Max. 1970. "Dewey's Critical and Historical Studies." In *Guide to the Works of John Dewey,* ed. Jo Ann Boydston. Carbondale: Southern Illinois University Press.

Fish, Stanley. 1980. *Is There a Text in This Class?* Cambridge: Harvard University Press.

Fishman, Stephen M., and Lucille Parkinson McCarthy. 2007. *John Dewey and the Philosophy and Practice of Hope.* Urbana: University of Illinois Press.

Foucault, Michel. 1971a. "Nietzsche, Genealogy, History." In Foucault 1998.

——. 1971b. "Revolutionary Action: 'Until Now.'" In Foucault 1980b.

——. 1975. *Discipline and Punish: The Birth of the Prison.* Trans. Alan Sheridan. Vintage.

——. 1976. *The History of Sexuality, Volume 1: An Introduction.* Trans. Robert Hurley. Vintage.

——. 1977a. "Truth and Power." In Foucault 2000.

——. 1977b. "Powers and Strategies." In Foucault 1980c.

——. 1979. "'*Omnes et Singulatim*': Toward a Critique of Political Reason." In Foucault 2000.

——. 1980a. "Interview with Michel Foucault by D. Trombadori." In Foucault 2000.

——. 1980b. *Language, Counter-Memory, and Practice.* Ed. Donald Bouchard. Ithaca: Cornell University Press.

——. 1980c. *Power/Knowledge.* Ed. Colin Gordon. New York: Pantheon.

——. 1981. "So Is It Important to Think?" In Foucault 2000.

——. 1983. "On the Genealogy of Ethics: Overview of Work in Progress." Interview by Rabinow and Dreyfus. In Foucault 1997.

——. 1984a. *The Use of Pleasure: The History of Sexuality, Volume 2.* Trans. Robert Hurley. New York: Vintage.

——. 1984b. *The Care of the Self: The History of Sexuality, Volume 3.* Trans. Robert Hurley. New York: Vintage.

——. 1984c. "The Concern for Truth." In *Politics, Philosophy, Culture,* ed. Foucault and Kritzman. New York: Routledge.

——. 1984d. "What Is Enlightenment?" In Foucault 1997.

——. 1984e. "Polemics, Politics, and Problematizations." Interview by Paul Rabinow. In Foucault 1997.

——. 1984f. *The Foucault Reader.* Ed. Paul Rabinow. New York: Pantheon.

——. 1997. *Essential Works, Volume 1: Ethics, Subjectivity, and Truth*. Ed. Paul Rabinow. New York: New Press.

——. 1998. *Essential Works, Volume 2: Aesthetics, Method, and Epistemology*. Ed. Paul
Rabinow and James Faubion. New York: New Press.

——. 2000. *Essential Works, Volume 3: Power*. Ed. Paul Rabinow and James Faubion.
New York: New Press.

Foucault, Michel, and Gilles Deleuze. 1972. "Intellectuals and Power." In Foucault
1980b.

Fraser, Nancy. 1981. "Foucault on Modern Power: Empirical Insights and Normative
Confusions." In *Unruly Practices*. Minneapolis: University of Minnesota Press, 1989.

Fraser, Nancy, and Seyla Benhabib, eds. 2004. *Pragmatism, Critique, Judgment: Essays
for Richard J. Bernstein*. Cambridge: MIT Press.

Fraser, Nancy, and Linda Gordon. 1994. "A Genealogy of Dependency." In *Justice In-
terruptus*, ed. Fraser. New York: Routledge, 1997.

Fricker, Miranda. 2000. "Confidence and Irony." In *Morality, Reflection, and Ideology*,
ed. E. Harcourt. Oxford: Oxford University Press.

——. 2008. "Skepticism and the Genealogy of Knowledge: Situating Epistemology in
Time." *Philosophical Papers* 37, no. 1 (March): 27–50.

——. Forthcoming. "The Value of Knowledge and the Test of Time." In *Epistemology,
Royal Institute of Philosophy Series*. Cambridge: Cambridge University Press.

Gadamer, Hans-Georg. 1960. *Truth and Method*. Trans. Joel Weinsheimer and Donald
G. Marshall. New York: Continuum, 1989.

Gavin, William. 1992. *William James and the Reinstatement of the Vague*. Philadel-
phia: Temple University Press.

——. 2007. "'Problem' vs. 'Trouble': James, Kafka, Dostoevsky, and 'The Will to Believe.'" *William James Studies* 2, no. 1.

Geuss, Raymond. 2008. "Richard Rorty at Princeton: Personal Recollections." *Arion*
15, no. 3 (Winter): 85–100.

Gewen, Barry. 2008. "Who Is a Public Intellectual?" *New York Times* (June 11, 2008).
Available online at http://papercuts.blogs.nytimes.com/2008/06/11/who-is-a-public
-intellectual/index.html.

Glaude, Eddie. 2007. *In a Shade of Blue: Pragmatism and the Politics of Black America*.
Chicago: University of Chicago Press.

Goldstein, Jan, ed. 1994. *Foucault and the Writing of History*. Oxford: Blackwell.

Goodman, Russell. 2005a. *Contending with Stanley Cavell*. Oxford: Oxford University
Press.

——. 2005b. "Cavell and American Philosophy." In Goodman 2005a.

Gouinlock, James. 1972. *John Dewey's Philosophy of Value*. New York: Humanities
Press.

——. 1978. "Dewey's Theory of Moral Deliberation." *Ethics* 88, no. 3 (April).

——. 1993a. *Rediscovering the Moral Life*. Amherst, Mass.: Prometheus Books.

———. 1993b. "Dewey and Contemporary Moral Philosophy." In *Philosophy and the Reconstruction of Culture*, ed. John Stuhr. Albany: SUNY Press.

———. 1995. "What Is the Legacy of Instrumentalism? Rorty's Interpretation of Dewey." In Saatkamp 1995.

Green, Judith. 1999. *Deep Democracy: Community, Diversity, and Transformation.* Lanham, Md.: Rowman and Littlefield.

———. 2008. *Pragmatism and Social Hope: Deepening Democracy in Global Contexts.* New York: Columbia University Press.

Grondin, Jean. 1999. *The Philosophy of Gadamer.* Trans. Kathryn Plant. Chesham: Acumen.

Gross, Neil. 2008. *Richard Rorty: The Making of an American Philosopher.* Chicago: University of Chicago Press.

Haack, Susan. 1993. *Evidence and Inquiry: Towards Reconstruction in Epistemology.* Oxford: Blackwell.

———. 1996. "Reflections of a Critical Common-Sensist." *Transactions of the Charles S. Peirce Society* 32, no. 3 (Summer): 359–373.

Habermas, Jürgen. 1985. *The Philosophical Discourse of Modernity.* Trans. Frederick Lawrence. Cambridge: MIT Press.

———. 1992. *Between Facts and Norms.* Trans. William Rehg. Cambridge: MIT Press.

Hacking, Ian. 1990. *The Taming of Chance.* Cambridge: Cambridge University Press.

———. 2002. *Mad Travelers.* Cambridge: Harvard University Press.

Hahn, Lewis, ed. 1997. *The Philosophy of Hans-Georg Gadamer.* Chicago: Open Court.

Hampshire, Stuart. 1983. *Morality and Conflict.* Oxford: Basil Blackwell.

Haslanger, Sally. 2000. "Feminism in Metaphysics: Negotiating the Natural." In *The Cambridge Companion to Feminism in Philosophy*, ed. Miranda Fricker and Jennifer Hornsby. Cambridge: Cambridge University.

Hawthorn, Geoffrey. 2005. Introduction to Williams 2005a.

Hayek, F. A. 1960. *The Constitution of Liberty.* Chicago: University of Chicago Press.

Hegel, G. W. F. 1821. *The Philosophy of Right.* Trans. Alan White. Focus Publishing, 2002.

Helm, Bertrand. 1985. *Time and Reality in American Philosophy.* Amherst: University of Massachusetts Press.

Hickman, Larry. 1990. *John Dewey's Pragmatic Technology.* Bloomington: Indiana University Press.

———. 2001. *Philosophical Tools for Technological Culture.* Bloomington: Indiana University Press.

———. 2007. *Pragmatism as Post-Postmodernism.* New York: Fordham University Press, 2007.

Hildebrand, David. 2003. *Beyond Realism and Anti-Realism: John Dewey and the Neopragmatists.* Nashville: Vanderbilt University.

Hitchens, Christopher. 2008. "The Plight of the Public Intellectual." *Foreign Policy* 166 (May–June).

Hollinger, David. 1980. "The Problem of Pragmatism in American History." In Hollinger 1985.

——. 1981. "William James and the Culture of Inquiry." In Hollinger 1985.

——. 1985. *In the American Province: Studies in the History and Historiography of Ideas*. Baltimore, Md.: Johns Hopkins University Press.

Honneth, Axel. 1998a. "Democracy as Reflexive Cooperation: John Dewey and the Theory of Democracy Today." *Political Theory* 26, no. 6 (December): 763–783.

——. 1998b. "Between Proceduralism and Teleology: An Unresolved Conflict in Dewey's Moral Theory." *Transactions of the Charles S. Peirce Society* 34, no. 3 (Summer): 689–710.

Hook, Sidney. 1960. "Pragmatism and the Tragic Sense of Life." In *Sidney Hook on Pragmatism, Democracy, and Freedom*, ed. S. Hook, R. Talisse, and R. Tempio. Amherst, Mass.: Prometheus, 2002.

Horkheimer, Max. 1947. *The Eclipse of Reason*. Repr. New York: Seabury Press, 1974.

Hoy, David, ed. 1986a. *Foucault: A Critical Reader*. Oxford: Blackwell.

——. 1986b. "Nietzsche, Hume, and the Genealogical Method." In *Nietzsche as Affirmative Thinker*, ed. Y. Yovel. Dordrecht: Martinus Nijhoff, 1986.

——. 1993. "Heidegger and the Hermeneutic Turn." In *The Cambridge Companion to Heidegger*, ed. C. Guignon. Cambridge: Cambridge University Press.

——. 1997. "Post-Cartesian Interpretation: Hans-Georg Gadamer and Donald Davidson." In Hahn 1997.

——. 2009. *The Time of Our Lives: A Critical History of the Phenomenology of Temporality*. Cambridge: MIT Press.

Hurka, Thomas. 1993. *Perfectionism*. Oxford: Oxford University Press.

Jacoby, Russell. 1987. *The Last Intellectuals: American Culture in the Age of Academe*. New York: Basic Books.

——. 2008. "Big Brains, Small Impact." *The Chronicle Review* 54, no. 18 (January 11): B5. Available online at http://chronicle.com/free/v54/i18/18b00501.htm.

James, William. 1885. "The Function of Cognition." In James 1975.

——. 1890. *The Principles of Psychology*. Repr. New York: Dover, 1950.

——. 1891. "The Moral Philosopher and the Moral Life." In James 1977.

——. 1899a. *Talks to Teachers on Psychology; and to Students on Some of Life's Ideals*. Repr. New York: W. W. Norton, 1958.

——. 1899b. "What Makes a Life Significant?" In James 1977.

——. 1899c. "On A Certain Blindness in Human Beings." In James 1977.

——. 1903b. "Address at the Emerson Centenary in Concord." In *The James Family*, by F. O. Matthiessen. New York: Knopf, 1947.

——. 1904a. "Does 'Consciousness' Exist?" In James 1977.

——. 1904b. "A World of Pure Experience." In James 1977.

——. 1904c. "Humanism and Truth." In James 1909a.

——. 1905. "The Thing and Its Relations." In James 1977.

——. 1906. "The Absolute and the Strenuous Life." In James 1909a.

——. 1907. *Pragmatism*. In James 1975.

——. 1908a. "Professor Hébert on Pragmatism." In James 1975.

——. 1908b. "The Existence of Julius Caesar (Truth Versus Truthfulness)." In James 1975.

——. 1909a. *The Meaning of Truth*. In James 1975.

——. 1909b. *A Pluralistic Universe*. In James 1977.

——. 1910. "The Moral Equivalent of War." In James 1977.

——. 1911. *Some Problems of Philosophy*. Ed. F. H. Burkhardt, F. Bowers, and I. K. Skrupskelis. Cambridge: Harvard University Press, 1979.

——. 1920. *The Letters of William James*. Ed. Henry James. Boston: Atlantic Monthly.

——. 1975. *Pragmatism and the Meaning of Truth*. Ed. Frederick Burkhardt. Cambridge: Harvard University Press.

——. 1977. *William James: A Comprehensive Edition*. Ed. John J. McDermott. Chicago: University of Chicago Press, 1977.

Jay, Martin. 1982. "Should Intellectual History Take a Linguistic Turn? Reflections on the Habermas-Gadamer Debate." In *Modern European Intellectual History*, ed. D. LaCapra and S. Kaplan. Ithaca: Cornell University Press, 1982.

——. 1992. "The Debate Over Performative Contradiction: Habermas Versus the Poststructuralists." In *Force Fields*, by Martin Jay. New York: Routledge.

——. 2005. *Songs of Experience*. Berkeley: University of California Press.

Johnson, Mark. 2007. *The Meaning of the Body: Aesthetics of Human Understanding*. Chicago: University of Chicago Press.

Kaag, John. 2008. "Women and Forgotten Movements in American Philosophy: The Work of Ella Lyman Cabot and Mary Parker Follett." *Transactions of the Charles S. Peirce Society* 44, no. 1 (Winter): 134–157.

Kadlec, Alison. 2007. *Dewey's Critical Pragmatism*. Lanham, Md.: Lexington Books.

Kant, Immanuel. 1781. *Critique of Pure Reason*. Trans. Norman Kemp Smith. New York: St. Martin's Press, 1965.

——. 1784. "Idea for a Universal History from a Cosmopolitan Point of View." In Kant 1970.

——. 1785. *Groundwork for the Metaphysics of Morals*. Trans. Mary Gregor. Cambridge: Cambridge University Press, 1998.

——. 1795. "Perpetual Peace: A Philosophical Sketch." In Kant 1970.

——. 1970. *Kant's Political Writings*. Ed. Hans Reiss. Cambridge: Cambridge University Press.

Kateb, George. 1992. *The Inner Ocean: Individualism and Democratic Culture*. Ithaca: Cornell University Press, 1992.

Kloppenberg, James. 1986. *Uncertain Victory: Social Democracy and Progressivism in European and American Thought: 1870–1920*. Oxford: Oxford University Press, 1986.

——. 1996. "Pragmatism: An Old Name for Some New Ways of Thinking?" *The Journal of American History* 83, no. 1 (June): 100–138.

Koopman, Colin. 2004. "The Authority of Consensus: Richard Rorty's Liberalism." *Theory at Buffalo* 9 (December). Available online at http://wings.buffalo.edu/ theory/archive/pdfs/Koopman.pdf.

——. 2005. "William James's Politics of Personal Freedom." *Journal of Speculative Philosophy* 19, no. 2 (Summer): 175–186.

——. 2006. "Pragmatism as a Philosophy of Hope: Emerson, James, Dewey, and Rorty." *The Journal of Speculative Philosophy* 20, no. 2 (Summer): 106–116.

——. 2007. "Rorty's Moral Philosophy for Liberal Democratic Culture." *Contemporary Pragmatism* 4, no. 2 (December): 45–64.

——. 2009. "Two Uses of Genealogy: Michel Foucault and Bernard Williams." In *Foucault's Legacy*, ed. Carlos Prado, 90–108. New York: Continuum Books.

——. Forthcoming-a. "Weber, Dewey, and Foucault on the Problems of Modernity." In *Dewey and Continental Philosophy*, ed. Paul Fairfield.

——. Forthcoming-b. "Historicism in Pragmatism: Lessons in Historiography, Philosophy, and Politics." *Metaphilosophy*.

——. Forthcoming-c. "Morals and Markets: Liberal Democracy Through Dewey and Hayek." *Journal of Speculative Philosophy*.

——. Forthcoming-d. "Bernard Williams on Philosophy's Need for History."

——. Forthcoming-e. "Pragmatism and Genealogy: An Overview of the Literature." Available online at http://papers.ssrn.com/sol3/papers.cfm?abstract_id=1011513.

——. Forthcoming-f. "Pragmatist Resources for Experimental Philosophy: Notes on Appiah's *Experiments in Ethics*."

Korsgaard, Christine. 1996. *Creating the Kingdom of Ends*. Cambridge: Cambridge University Press, 1996.

Lavine, Thelma Z. 1962. "Reflections on the Genetic Fallacy." *Social Research* 29, no. 3 (Fall): 321–337.

Lekan, Todd. 2002. *Making Morality: Pragmatist Reconstruction in Ethical Theory*. Nashville: Vanderbilt University Press.

Lentricchia, Frank. 1988. *Ariel and the Police*. Madison: University of Wisconsin Press.

Levin, Jonathan. 1999. *The Poetics of Transition: Emerson, Pragmatism, and American Literary Modernism*. Durham, N.C.: Duke University Press.

Lewis-Krause, Gideon. 2009. "Head of the Class: Neil Gross's *Richard Rorty*." *N1BR* 1 (January 13). Available online at http://www.nplusonemag.com/head-class-neil -gross-richard-rorty.

Lippmann, Walter. 1913. *A Preface to Politics*. Repr. Ann Arbor: University of Michigan Press, 1969.

Livingston, James. 1994. *Pragmatism and the Political Economy of Cultural Revolution, 1850–1940*. Repr. Chapel Hill: University of North Carolina Press, 1997.

——. 2001. *Pragmatism, Feminism, and Democracy: Rethinking the Politics of American History*. New York: Routledge.

———. Forthcoming. "Pragmatism, Nihilism, and Democracy: What Is Called Thinking at the End of Modernity?" In *One Hundred Years of Pragmatism: William James's Revolutionary Philosophy*, ed. John Stuhr. Bloomington: Indiana University Press.

Loeb, Paul S. 1995. "Is There a Genetic Fallacy in Nietzsche's Genealogy of Morals?" *International Studies in Philosophy* 27, no. 3: 125–141.

Lysaker, John T. 2003. "Relentless Unfolding: Emerson's Individual." *The Journal of Speculative Philosophy* 17, no. 3.

Macedo, Stephen, ed. 1999. *Deliberative Politics*. Oxford: Oxford University Press.

MacIntyre, Alasdair. 1981. *After Virtue*. 3rd ed. Notre Dame, Ind.: University of Notre Dame Press.

———. 1990. *Three Rival Versions of Moral Enquiry*. Notre Dame, Ind.: University of Notre Dame Press.

Madison, Gary B. 1997. "Hermeneutics' Claim to Universality." In Hahn 1997.

———. 2003. "The Interpretive Turn in Phenomenology: A Philosophical History." *Symposium* 8, no. 2 (Summer).

Margolis, Joseph. 1986. *Pragmatism Without Foundations*. Oxford: Blackwell.

———. 1993. *The Flux of History and the Flux of Science*. Berkeley: University of California Press.

———. 1998. "Peirce's Fallibilism." *Transactions of the Charles S. Peirce Society* 34, no. 3 (Winter).

———. 1999a. "Replies in Search of Self Discovery." In *Interpretation, Relativism, and the Metaphysics of Culture: Themes in the Philosophy of Joseph Margolis*, ed. Michael Krausz and Richard Shusterman. Amherst: Humanity Books.

———. 1999b. "Pierre Bourdieu: *Habitus* and the Logic of Practice." In Shusterman 1999a.

———. 2002a. *Reinventing Pragmatism: American Philosophy at the End of the Twentieth Century*. Ithaca: Cornell University Press.

———. 2002b. "Dewey's and Rorty's Opposed Pragmatisms." In *Transactions of the Charles S. Peirce Society* 38, nos. 1–2 (Winter–Spring).

———. 2004. "Pluralism, Relativism, and Historicism." In *A Companion to Pragmatism*, ed. Margolis and Shook. Oxford: Blackwell.

———. 2007. "Rethinking Peirce's Fallibilism." *Transactions of the Charles S. Peirce Society* 43, no. 2 (Spring).

———. Forthcoming. "Pragmatism and the Prospect of a Rapprochement Within Eurocentric Philosophy." *Cognitio*.

Marshall, James D. 2001. "On What We May Hope: Rorty on Dewey and Foucault." In Peters and Ghiraldelli 2001.

Matthiessen, F. O. 1947. *The James Family*. Repr. New York: Vintage, 1980.

May, Todd. 2006. *The Philosophy of Foucault*. Chesham: Acumen.

McCarthy, Thomas. 1990. "The Critique of Impure Reason: Foucault and the Frankfurt School." *Political Theory* 18, no. 3 (August): 437–469.

——. 2004. "Political Philosophy and Racial Injustice: From Normative to Critical Theory." In Fraser and Benhabib 2004.

McDermott, John. 1965. "An American Angle of Vision." In McDermott 2007.

——. 1968. "To Be Human Is to Humanize—A Radically Empirical Aesthetic." In McDermott 1976.

——. 1976. *The Culture of Experience: Philosophical Essays in the American Grain.* Prospect Heights, Ill.: Waveland Press.

——. 1977. "Person, Process, and the Risk of Belief." Introduction to *The Writings of William James*, ed. John McDermott. Chicago: University of Chicago Press.

——. 2007. *The Drama of Possibility: Experience as Philosophy.* New York: Fordham University Press.

McDowell, John. 1994. *Mind and World.* Cambridge: Harvard University Press.

——. 2000. "Toward Rehabilitating Objectivity." In Brandom 2000a.

McKenna, Erin. 2001. *The Task of Utopia: A Pragmatist and Feminist Perspective.* Lanham, Md.: Rowman and Littlefield.

Mead, George Herbert. 1932. *The Philosophy of the Present.* Repr. LaSalle, Ill.: Open Court Press, 1959.

Megill, Allan. 1987. "The Reception of Foucault by Historians." *Journal of the History of Ideas* 48, no. 1 (January–March): 117–141.

Melville. Herman. 1957 [1852]. *Pierre; or, The Ambiguities.* New York: Grove.

Mill, John Stuart. 1859. *On Liberty and Other Essays.* Ed. John Gray. Oxford: Oxford World Classics, 1998.

——. 1861. *Utilitarianism.* Repr. Indianapolis, Ind.: Hackett, 1979.

Miller, Hugh T. 2005. "Residues of Foundationalism in Classic Pragmatism." *Administration and Society* 37, no. 3 (July): 360–374.

Miller, James. 1993. *The Passion of Michel Foucault.* New York: Anchor Books.

Mills, C. Wright. 1964. *Sociology and Pragmatism.* New York: Oxford University Press.

Misak, Cheryl. 2000. *Truth, Politics, Morality: Pragmatism and Deliberation.* New York: Routledge.

——. 2004a. "Making Disagreement Matter: Pragmatism and Deliberative Democracy." In *Journal of Speculative Philosophy* 18, no. 1 (February).

——, ed. 2004b. *The Cambridge Companion to Peirce.* Cambridge: Cambridge University Press.

——. 2004c. "C. S. Peirce on Vital Matters." In Misak 2004b.

——, ed. 2007. *New Pragmatists.* Oxford: Oxford University Press.

Mounce, H. O. 1997. *The Two Pragmatisms.* New York: Routledge.

Mumford, Lewis. 1926. *The Golden Day.* Repr. Westport, Conn.: Greenwood, 1983.

Nagel, Thomas. 1979. *Mortal Questions.* Cambridge: Cambridge University Press.

——. 1991. *Equality and Partiality.* New York: Oxford University Press.

Nehamas, Alexander. 1985. *Nietzsche: Life as Literature.* Cambridge: Harvard University Press.

Niebuhr, Reinhold. 1932. *Moral Man and Immoral Society*. New York: Scribner's.

Nietzsche, Friedrich. 1887. *On the Genealogy of Morality*. Trans. Carol Diethe. Cambridge: Cambridge University Press, 1994.

Nussbaum, Martha. 1986. *The Fragility of Goodness*. Cambridge: Cambridge University Press.

Oakeshott, Michael. 1947. "Rationalism in Politics." In *Rationalism in Politics and Other Essays*, by M. Oakeshott. Indianapolis: Liberty Fund, 1991.

O'Neill, Onora. 1989. *Constructions of Reason*. Cambridge: Cambridge University Press.

Pappas, Gregory. 1993. "Dewey and Feminism: The Affective and Relationships in Dewey's Ethics." *Hypatia* 8, no. 2 (Spring).

——. 1994. "William James' Virtuous Believer." *Transactions of the Charles S. Peirce Society* 30, no. 1 (Winter).

——. 1997a. "Dewey's Moral Theory: Experience as Method." *Transactions of the Charles S. Peirce Society* 33, no. 3 (Summer): 520–556.

——. 1997b. "To Be or to Do: John Dewey and the Great Divide in Ethics." *History of Philosophy Quarterly* 14, no. 4 (October).

——. 1998. "Dewey's Ethics: Morality as Experience." In *Reading Dewey: Interpretations for a Postmodern Generation*, ed. Larry Hickman. Bloomington: Indiana University Press.

——. 2003. "New Directions and Uses in the Reconstruction of Dewey's Ethics." In *In Dewey's Wake*, ed. William Gavin. Albany: SUNY Press.

——. 2008. *John Dewey's Ethics: Democracy as Experience*. Bloomington: Indiana University Press.

Peirce, Charles S. 1868a. "Questions Concerning Certain Faculties Claimed for Man." In Peirce 1992.

——. 1868b. "Some Consequences of Four Incapacities." In Peirce 1992.

——. 1877. "The Fixation of Belief." In Peirce 1992.

——. 1891. "The Architecture of Theories." In Peirce 1992.

——. 1892a. "The Law of Mind." In Peirce 1992.

——. 1892b. "Man's Glassy Essence." In Peirce 1992.

——. 1893. "Evolutionary Love." In Peirce 1992.

——. 1897. "A Fragment." In *Collected Papers of Charles Sanders Peirce*, ed. C. S. Peirce and Paul Weiss. Cambridge: Harvard University Press, 1931–1958.

——. 1903. "Harvard Lectures on Pragmatism." In Peirce 1998.

——. 1905a. "Issues of Pragmaticism." In Peirce 1998.

——. 1905b. "The Basis of Pragmaticism in Phaneroscopy." In Peirce 1998.

——. 1992. *The Essential Peirce, Volume 1, 1867–1893*. Ed. N. Houser et al. Bloomington: Indiana University Press.

——. 1998. *The Essential Peirce, Volume 2, 1893–1913*. Ed. N. Houser et al. Bloomington: Indiana University Press.

Perry, Ralph Barton. 1935. *The Thought and Character of William James.* Repr. Nashville: Vanderbilt University, 1996.

Peters, Michael. 2001. "Achieving America: Postmodernism and Rorty's Critique of the Cultural Left." In Peters and Ghiraldelli 2001.

Peters, Michael, and Paulo Ghiraldelli, eds. 2001. *Richard Rorty: Education, Philosophy, and Politics.* Lanham, Md.: Rowman and Littlefield.

Pihlström, Sami. 2003. *Naturalizing the Transcendental: A Pragmatic View.* Amherst, Mass.: Humanity Books.

Poirier, Richard. 1987. *The Renewal of Literature: Emersonian Reflections.* New York: Random House.

——. 1992. *Poetry and Pragmatism.* Cambridge: Harvard University Press.

——. 1998. "Why Do Pragmatists Want to Be Like Poets?" In Dickstein 1998.

Posner, Richard. 2002. *Public Intellectuals: A Study of Decline.* Cambridge: Harvard University Press.

Posnock, Ross. 1992. "The Politics of Nonidentity: A Genealogy." In *boundary 2* 19, no. 1 (Spring).

Pritchard, Duncan. 2007. "Recent Work on Epistemic Value." *American Philosophical Quarterly* 44, no. 2: 85–110.

Putnam, Hilary. 1988. "Realism with a Human Face." In Putnam 1990b.

——. 1990a. "James's Theory of Perception." In Putnam 1990b.

——. 1990b. *Realism with a Human Face.* Cambridge: Harvard University Press.

——. 1990c. "A Reconsideration of Deweyan Democracy." In *Renewing Philosophy*, by Hilary Putnam. Cambridge: Harvard University Press, 1992.

——. 1992. *Pragmatism: An Open Question.* Oxford: Blackwell.

——. 1997. "James's Theory of Truth." in R. A. Putnam 1997a.

——. 1999. *The Threefold Cord: Mind, Body, and World.* New York: Columbia University Press.

——. 2004a. *The Collapse of the Fact/Value Dichotomy and Other Essays.* Cambridge: Harvard University Press.

——. 2004b. "Philosophy as Reconstructive Activity: William James on Moral Philosophy." In Egginton and Sandbothe 2004.

——. 2004c. *Ethics Without Ontology.* Cambridge: Harvard University Press.

Putnam, Hilary, and Ruth Anna Putnam. 1989. "William James's Ideas." In H. Putnam 1990b.

Putnam, Ruth Anna. 1990. "The Moral Life of a Pragmatist." In *Identity, Character, and Morality*, ed. O. Flanagan and A. O. Rorty. Cambridge: MIT Press.

——. 1997a. *The Cambridge Companion to William James.* Cambridge: Cambridge University Press.

——. 1997b. "Some of Life's Ideals." In Putnam 1997a.

——. 2006. "William James and Moral Objectivity." In *William James Studies* 1, no. 1 (June).

Quine, Willard Van Orman. 1951. "Two Dogmas of Empiricism." In *From a Logical Point of View*, 2nd ed. Cambridge: Harvard University Press, 1980.

——. 1963. "Carnap and Logical Truth." In *The Philosophy of Rudolf Carnap*, ed. Paul Schilpp. LaSalle, Ill.: Open Court Press.

Rabinow, Paul. 1989. *French Modern: Norms and Forms of the Social Environment.* Chicago: University of Chicago Press.

——. 1996. "Science as a Practice: Ethos, Logos, Pathos." In *Essays on the Anthropology of Reason*, by Paul Rabinow. Princeton: Princeton University Press.

——. 2003. *Anthropos Today: Reflections on Modern Equipment.* Princeton: Princeton University Press.

——. 2008. *Marking Time: On the Anthropology of the Contemporary.* Princeton: Princeton University Press.

——. Forthcoming. "Untimely and Inconsiderate Observations: Toward an Anthropology of Concepts, Practices, and Venues." Presented at the Foucault Across the Disciplines Conference, University of California at Santa Cruz, March 1, 2008.

Rajchman, John. 1985. *Michel Foucault: The Freedom of Philosophy.* New York: Columbia University Press.

——. 2000. *The Deleuze Connections.* Cambridge: MIT Press.

Ralston, Shane J. Forthcoming. "Dewey's Theory of Moral (and Political) Deliberation." Available online at http://papers.ssrn.com/sol3/papers.cfm?abstract_id=1147721.

Randall, John Herman. 1935. "Historical Naturalism." Prologue to Randall 1958.

——. 1937. "On Understanding the History of Philosophy." *The Journal of Philosophy* 36, no. 17 (August 17): 460–474.

——. 1939. "Dewey's Interpretation of the History of Philosophy." In *The Philosophy of John Dewey: The Library of Living Philosophers*, by P. A. Schilpp. New York: Tudor.

——. 1958. *Nature and Historical Experience.* New York: Columbia University Press.

Rawls, John. 1971. *A Theory of Justice.* Cambridge: Belknap.

——. 1993. *Political Liberalism.* New York: Columbia University Press.

——. 1999. *The Law of Peoples.* Cambridge: Harvard University Press.

——. 2001. *Justice as Fairness: A Restatement.* Ed. Erin Kelly. Cambridge: Belknap.

——. 2007. *Lectures on the History of Political Philosophy.* Ed. Samuel Freeman. Cambridge: Belknap.

Reynolds, Joan. 2004. "Pragmatic Humanism in Foucault's Later Work." *Canadian Journal of Political Science* 37: 951–977.

Richardson, Robert D. 2006. *William James.* New York: Houghton Mifflin.

Rogers, Melvin. 2009. *The Undiscovered Dewey: Religion, Morality, and the Ethos of Democracy.* New York: Columbia University Press.

Rorty, Richard. N.d. "The Philosopher as Expert." Unpublished manuscript in the Richard Rorty Papers, Stanford University, Stanford, Calif.

——. 1977a. "Dewey's Metaphysics." In Rorty 1982.

———. 1977b. "Ten Years After." In *The Linguistic Turn*, ed. Richard Rorty. Chicago: University of Chicago Press, 1992.

———. 1979. *Philosophy and the Mirror of Nature*. Princeton: Princeton University Press.

———. 1980. "Pragmatism, Relativism, and Irrationalism." In Rorty 1982.

———. 1981. "Method, Social Science, and Social Hope." In Rorty 1982.

———. 1982. *Consequences of Pragmatism*. Minneapolis: University of Minnesota.

———. 1985. "Comments on Sleeper and Edel." In *Transactions of the Charles S. Peirce Society* 21, no. 1 (Winter): 40–48.

———. 1986. "Pragmatism, Davidson, and Truth." In Rorty 1991a.

———. 1988. "The Priority of Democracy to Philosophy." In Rorty 1991a.

———. 1989a. *Contingency, Irony, and Solidarity*. Cambridge: Cambridge University Press.

———. 1989b. "Education as Socialization and as Individuation." In Rorty 1999.

———. 1991a. *Objectivity, Relativism, and Truth: Philosophical Papers 1*. Cambridge: Cambridge University Press.

———. 1992. "Dewey Between Hegel and Darwin." In Rorty 1998a.

———. 1993. "Wittgenstein, Heidegger, and the Reification of Language." In *The Cambridge Companion to Heidegger*, ed. Charles Guignon. Cambridge: Cambridge University Press.

———. 1994a. "Hope in Place of Knowledge: A Version of Pragmatism." In Rorty 1999.

———. 1994b. "The Unpatriotic Academy." In Rorty 1999.

———. 1994c. "Feminism and Pragmatism." In Rorty 1998a.

———. 1995a. "Is Truth a Goal of Inquiry? Donald Davidson Versus Crispin Wright." In Rorty 1998a.

———. 1995b. "Replies." In Saatkamp 1995.

———. 1998a. *Truth and Progress: Philosophical Papers 3*. Cambridge: Cambridge University Press.

———. 1998b. *Achieving Our Country: Leftist Thought in Twentieth-Century America*. Cambridge: Harvard University Press.

———. 1998c. "Afterword: Pragmatism, Pluralism, and Postmodernism." In Rorty 1999.

———. 1998d. "The Very Idea of Human Answerability to the World: John McDowell's Version of Empiricism." In Rorty 1998a.

———. 1998e. "Failed Prophecies, Glorious Hopes." In Rorty 1999.

———. 1999. *Philosophy and Social Hope*. New York: Penguin.

———. 2000a. "Universality and Truth" and "Responses." In Brandom 2000a.

———. 2000b. "Being That Can Be Understood Is Language." In *Gadamer's Repercussions: Reconsidering Philosophical Hermeneutics*, ed. Bruce Krajewski. Berkeley, University of California Press.

———. 2001. "Response to Richard Shusterman." In Festenstein and Thompson 2001.

———. 2002a. "Hope and the Future." In *Peace Review* 14, no. 2 (Spring).

———. 2002b. "To the Sunlit Uplands." *London Review of Books* 24, no. 21 (October 31).

———. 2003. "A Conversation with Richard Rorty: An Interview by C. G. Prado." *Symposium* 7, no. 2 (Fall): 227–231.

———. 2004a. "Trapped Between Kant and Dewey: The Current Situation of Moral Philosophy." In *New Essays on the History of Autonomy: A Collection Honoring J .B. Schneewind*, ed. Natalie Brender. Cambridge: Cambridge University Press.

———. 2004b. "Philosophy as a Transitional Genre." In Fraser and Benhabib 2004.

———. 2007a. *Philosophy as Cultural Politics: Philosophical Papers 4*. Cambridge: Cambridge University Press.

———. 2007b. "Wittgenstein and the Linguistic Turn." In Rorty 2007a.

Rorty, Richard, and Pascal Engel. 2005. *What's the Use of Truth?* Ed. Patrick Savidan. New York: Columbia University Press.

Rose, Nikolas. 1999. *Powers of Freedom: Reframing Political Thought*. New York: Cambridge University Press.

Rosen, Stanley. 1989. *The Ancients and the Moderns: Rethinking Modernity*. New Haven, Conn.: Yale University Press.

Rosenthal, Sandra B. 2000. *Time, Continuity, and Indeterminacy: A Pragmatic Engagement with Contemporary Perspectives*. Albany: SUNY Press.

Royce, Josiah. 1891. "Review of Dewey's *Outlines of a Critical Theory of Ethics*." *International Journal of Ethics* 1.

Russell, Bertrand. 1908. "William James's Conception of Truth." In *Philosophical Essays*. London: George Allen and Unwin, 1966.

———. 1946. *History of Western Philosophy*. London: George Allen and Unwin.

———. 1950. *An Inquiry Into Meaning and Truth*. Repr. New York: Routledge, 1992.

Ryan, Alan. 1995. *John Dewey and the High Tide of American Liberalism*. New York: Norton.

Saatkamp, Herman, ed. 1995. *Rorty and Pragmatism: The Philosopher Responds to His Critics*. Nashville: Vanderbilt University.

Saito, Naoko. 2001. "Reconstructing Deweyan Pragmatism in Dialogue with Emerson and Cavell." *Transactions of the Charles S. Peirce Society* 37, no. 3 (Summer).

———. 2003. "Transcending the Tragic with Dewey and Emerson: Beyond the Morse-Boisvert Debate." *Transactions of the Charles S. Peirce Society* 39, no. 2 (Spring): 275–292.

———. 2005. *The Gleam of Light: Dewey, Emerson, and the Pursuit of Perfection*. New York: Fordham University Press.

Santayana, George. 1925. "Dewey's Naturalistic Metaphysics." *The Journal of Philosophy* 22, no. 25 (December): 673–688.

Schaff, Kory. 2004. "Agency and Institutional Rationality: Foucault's Critique of Normativity." *Philosophy and Social Criticism* 30, no. 1 (January): 51–71.

Scheffler, Samuel. 1982. *The Rejection of Consequentialism*. Oxford: Oxford University Press.

——. 1992. *Human Morality*. New York: Oxford University Press.

——. 1994. "The Appeal of Political Liberalism." In *Boundaries and Allegiances*, by Samuel Scheffler. Oxford: Oxford University Press, 2001.

Schneewind, J. B. 1998. *The Invention of Autonomy: A History of Modern Moral Philosophy*. Cambridge: Cambridge University Press.

Schrader, David. 1998. "Simonizing James: Taking Demand Seriously." *Transactions of the Charles S. Peirce Society* 34, no. 4 (Fall).

Scott, Joan Wallach. 1991. "The Evidence of Experience." *Critical Inquiry* 17, no. 4 (Summer): 773–797.

Seigfried, Charlene Haddock. 1990. *William James's Radical Reconstruction of Philosophy*. Albany: SUNY Press.

——. 2001. "Pragmatist Metaphysics? Why Terminology Matters." *Transactions of the Charles S. Peirce Society* 37, no. 1 (Winter): 13–22.

Sellars, Wilfrid. 1956. *Empiricism and the Philosophy of Mind*. Ed. Robert Brandom. Repr. Cambridge: Harvard University Press, 1997.

——. 1968. *Science and Metaphysics*. Repr. Atascadero: Ridgeview, 1993.

Sen, Amartya. 1981. "Rights and Agency." *Philosophy and Public Affairs* 11, no. 1 (Winter).

——. 2006. "What Do We Want from a Theory of Justice?" *The Journal of Philosophy* 102, no. 5 (May): 215–238.

Shade, Patrick. 2001. *Habits of Hope: A Pragmatic Theory*. Nashville: Vanderbilt University Press.

Shook, John. 2000. *Dewey's Theory of Knowledge and Reality*. Nashville: Vanderbilt University Press.

——. 2008. "Where Do Pragmatists Come From?" *The Pragmatist Cybrary*. Available online at http://www.pragmatism.org/genealogy/genealogy.htm.

Shusterman, Richard. 1997. *Practicing Philosophy: Pragmatism and the Philosophical Life*. New York: Routledge.

——. 1999a. *Bourdieu: A Critical Reader*. Oxford: Blackwell.

——. 1999b. "Bourdieu and Anglo-American Philosophy" In Shusterman 1999a.

——. 2001. "Reason and Aesthetics Between Modernity and Postmodernity: Habermas and Rorty." In Festenstein and Thompson 2001.

Sklansky, Jeffrey. 2002. *The Soul's Economy: Market Society and Selfhood in American Thought, 1820–1920*. Chapel Hill: University of North Carolina Press.

Sleat, Matthew. 2007. "On the Relationship Between Truth and Liberal Politics." *Inquiry* 50, no. 3 (June): 288–305.

Sleeper, Ralph. 1985. "Rorty's Pragmatism: Afloat in Neurath's Boat, but Why Adrift?" *Transactions of the Charles S. Peirce Society* 21, no. 1 (Winter): 9–20.

——. 1986. *The Necessity of Pragmatism: John Dewey's Conception of Philosophy*. New Haven, Conn.: Yale University Press.

Sluga, Hans. 2002. "Foucault Rethinks the Genealogy of Morals." In *Weltanschauungen des Wiener Fin de Siècle*, ed. Gertraud Diem-Wille et al. Frankfurt: Peter Lang.

——. 2005. "Foucault's Encounter with Heidegger and Nietzsche." In *The Cambridge Companion to Foucault*, 2nd ed., ed. Gary Gutting. Cambridge: Cambridge University Press.

Smith, Andrew F. 2007. "Communication and Conviction: A Jamesian Contribution to Deliberative Democracy." *Journal of Speculative Philosophy* 21, no. 4: 259–274.

Smith, John. 1974. "The Value of Community: Dewey and Royce." In Smith 1992.

——. 1980. "Receptivity, Change, and Relevance: Some Hallmarks of Philosophy in America." In Smith 1992.

——. 1992. *America's Philosophical Vision*. Chicago: University of Chicago Press.

Sosa, Ernest. 2007. *A Virtue Epistemology*. Oxford: Oxford University Press.

Stout, Jeffrey. 2004. *Democracy and Tradition*. Princeton: Princeton University Press.

Stuhr, John. 1997. *Genealogical Pragmatism*. Albany: SUNY Press.

——. 2002. "Power/Inquiry: Criticism and the Logic of Pragmatism." In Stuhr 2003.

——. 2003. *Pragmatism, Postmodernism, and the Future of Philosophy*. New York: Routledge.

Suckiel, Ellen Kappy. 1996. *Heaven's Champion: William James's Philosophy of Religion*. Notre Dame, Ind.: Notre Dame University Press.

Sullivan, Michael. 2007. *Legal Pragmatism: Community, Rights, and Democracy*. Bloomington: Indiana University Press.

Takacs, Adam. 2004. "Between Theory and History: On the Interdisciplinary Practice in Michel Foucault's Work." *MLN* 119: 869–884.

Talisse, Robert. 2001. "A Pragmatist Critique of Richard Rorty's Hopeless Politics." *The Southern Journal of Philosophy* 39, no. 4.

——. 2005. *Democracy After Liberalism: Pragmatism and Deliberative Politics*. New York: Routledge.

——. 2007a. *A Pragmatist Philosophy of Democracy*. New York: Routledge.

——. 2007b. "From Pragmatism to Perfectionism." *Philosophy and Social Criticism* 33, no. 3: 387–406.

Talisse, Robert, and Scott Aikin. 2008. *Pragmatism: A Guide for the Perplexed*. New York: Continuum.

Taylor, Charles. 1984. "Foucault on Freedom and Truth." In Hoy 1986a.

——. 1989. *Sources of the Self: The Making of Modern Identity*. Cambridge: Harvard University Press.

Thayer, H. S. 1952. *The Logic of Pragmatism: An Examination of Dewey's Logic*. New York: Humanities.

——. 1968. *Meaning and Action: A Critical History of Pragmatism*. Repr. Indianapolis, Ind.: Hackett, 1981.

Toews, John. 1987. "Intellectual History After the Linguistic Turn: The Autonomy of Meaning and the Irreducibility of Experience." *The American Historical Review* 92, no. 4 (October): 879–907.

Turetzky, Philip. 1998. *Time*. New York: Routledge.

Vanderveen, Zach. 2007. "Pragmatic and Democratic Legitimacy: Beyond Minimalist Accounts of Deliberation." *Journal of Speculative Philosophy* 21, no. 4: 243–258.

Voparil, Christopher. 2006. *Richard Rorty: Politics and Vision*. Lanham, Md.: Rowman and Littlefield.

Wachterhauser, Bruce. 2002. "Getting It Right: Relativism, Realism, and Truth." In *The Cambridge Companion to Gadamer*, ed. Robert Dorstal. Cambridge: Cambridge University Press.

Walzer, Michael. 1983. "The Politics of Michel Foucault." In Hoy 1986a.

——. 1998. *The Company of Critics*. 2nd ed. New York: Basic Books, 2002.

——. 1999. "Deliberation and What Else?" In Macedo 1999.

Weinberg, Jonathan, Shaun Nichols, and Stephen Stich. 2001. "Normativity and Epistemic Intuitions." *Philosophical Topics* 29: 429–460.

Weinstein, Michael. 1982. *The Wilderness and the City: American Classical Philosophy as a Moral Quest*. Amherst: University of Massachusetts Press.

Welchman, Jennifer. 1995. *Dewey's Ethical Thought*. Ithaca: Cornell University Press.

West, Cornel. 1989. *The American Evasion of Philosophy: A Genealogy of Pragmatism*. Madison: University of Wisconsin Press.

——. 1990. "The Limits of Neopragmatism." In *The Cornel West Reader*. New York: Basic Civitas, 1999.

——. 1993. *Keeping Faith*. New York: Routledge.

——. 2004. *Democracy Matters*. New York: Penguin.

Westbrook, Robert. 1991. *John Dewey and American Democracy*. Ithaca: Cornell University Press.

——. 2005. *Democratic Hope: Pragmatism and the Politics of Truth*. Ithaca: Cornell University Press.

White, Morton. 1947. *Social Thought in America: The Revolt Against Formalism*. Boston: Beacon.

Whitman, Walt. 1867. *Democratic Vistas*. In *Leaves of Grass and Selected Prose*, ed. Sculley Bradley Whitman. New York: Holt, Rinehart, and Winston, 1949.

Wiener, Philip. 1946. "Logical Significance of the History of Thought." *Journal of the History of Ideas* 7, no. 3 (June): 366–373.

——. 1949. *Evolution and the Founders of Pragmatism*. New York: Harper.

Williams, Bernard. 1976. "Persons, Character, and Morality." In *Moral Luck, Philosophical Papers 1973–1980*, by Bernard Williams. Cambridge: Cambridge University Press, 1981.

——. 1980. "Political Philosophy and the Analytical Tradition." In Williams 2006b.

——. 1985. *Ethics and the Limits of Philosophy*. Cambridge: Harvard University Press.

——. 1992. "Pluralism, Community, and Left Wittgensteinianism." In Williams 2005a.

——. 1996. "Tolerance, a Political or Moral Question?" In Williams 2005a.

——. 1999. "In the Beginning Was the Deed." In Williams 2005a.

——. 2000. "Philosophy as a Humanistic Discipline." In Williams 2006b.

——. 2002. *Truth and Truthfulness: An Essay in Genealogy.* Princeton: Princeton University Press.

——. 2005a. *In the Beginning Was the Deed: Realism and Moralism in Political Argument.* Ed. Geoffrey Hawthorn. Princeton: Princeton University Press, 2005.

——. 2005b. "The Liberalism of Fear." In Williams 2005a.

——. 2005c. "Realism and Moralism in Political Theory." In Williams 2005a.

——. 2006a. *The Sense of the Past.* Princeton: Princeton University Press.

——. 2006b. *Philosophy as a Humanistic Discipline.* Princeton: Princeton University Press.

——. 2006c. "An Essay on Collingwood." In Williams 2006a.

Williams, Michael. 1986. "Do We (Epistemologists) Need a Theory of Truth?" *Philosophical Topics* 14: 223–241.

——. 1996. *Unnatural Doubts.* Princeton: Princeton University Press.

——. 2008. "Responsibility and Reliability." *Philosophical Papers* 37, no. 1: 1–26.

Young, Iris Marion. 1990. *Justice and the Politics of Difference.* Princeton: Princeton University Press.

——. 1996. "Communication and the Other: Beyond Deliberative Democracy." In *Democracy and Difference*, ed. S. Benhabib. Princeton: Princeton University Press.

——. 2000. *Inclusion and Democracy.* Oxford: Oxford University Press.

——. 2001. "Activist Challenges to Deliberative Democracy." *Political Theory* 29, no. 5: 670–690.

Zagzebski, Linda. 1996. *Virtues of the Mind.* Cambridge: Cambridge University Press.

Žižek, Slavoj. 1989. The Sublime Object of Ideology. New York: Verso.

——. 2006. *The Parallax View.* Cambridge: MIT Press.

INDEX